SHIFTING GEARS IN INNOVATION POLICY

SHIFTING GEARS IN INNOVATION POLICY

STRATEGIES FROM ASIA

Edited by Yong Suk Lee, Takeo Hoshi, and Gi-Wook Shin

Stanford | Walter H. Shorenstein
Asia-Pacific Research Center
Freeman Spogli Institute

THE WALTER H. SHORENSTEIN ASIA-PACIFIC RESEARCH CENTER (Shorenstein APARC) addresses critical issues affecting the countries of Asia, their regional and global affairs, and U.S.-Asia relations. As Stanford University's hub for the interdisciplinary study of contemporary Asia, we produce policy-relevant research, provide education and training to students, scholars, and practitioners, and strengthen dialogue and cooperation between counterparts in the Asia-Pacific and the United States.

The Walter H. Shorenstein Asia-Pacific Research Center
Freeman Spogli Institute for International Studies
Stanford University
Encina Hall
Stanford, CA 94305-6055
http://aparc.fsi.stanford.edu

Shifting Gears in Innovation Policy: Strategies from Asia
may be ordered from:
Brookings Institution Press
https://www.brookings.edu/bipress/
books@brookings.edu

Walter H. Shorenstein Asia-Pacific Research Center, 2020.

Library of Congress Control Number: 2020947822

First printing, 2020

ISBN 978-1-931368-55-1

Contents

Tables and Figures

Tables

Figures

Abbreviations

A*STAR	Agency for Science, Technology and Research
API	application programming interface
ARTC	Automotive Research and Testing Center
ASEAN	Association of Southeast Asian Nations
ASIC	application-specific integrated circuit
B2C	business-to-consumer
BIRDC	Bicycle R&D Center
C2C	consumer-to-consumer
CMC	Computer Maintenance Corporation
DLT	distributed ledger technology
DOE	Department of Electronics
DOS	Department of Statistics
DRAM	dynamic random-access memory
DSO	Defence Science Organisation
ECIL	Electronics Corporation of India Limited
EDB	Economic Development Board
ESVF	Early Stage Venture Fund
FEC	Future Economy Council
FOB	Free on Board
FTRC	Footwear Technology Research Center
GDP	gross domestic product
GRI	government research institution
GVC	global value chain

HGF	high-growth firm
HHI	Herfindahl-Hirschman Index
HRS	household responsibility system
HSIP	Hsinchu Science-Based Industrial Park
IC	integrated circuit
ICO	initial crypto-token offering/initial coin offering
ICT	information and communication technology
IDB	Industrial Development Bureau
IIPL	Infocomm Investments Pte Ltd
IIT	Indian Institute of Technology
IMDA	Infocomm Media Development Authority
IPO	initial public offering
ISIC	International Standard Industrial Classification
IT	information technology
ITRI	Industrial Technology Research Institute
KEONICS	Karnataka State Electronics Development Corporation
LE	large enterprise
MAS	Monetary Authority of Singapore
METI	Ministry of Economy, Trade, and Industry
MEXT	Ministry of Education, Culture, Sports, Science, and Technology
MIRDC	Metal Industries Research and Development Center
MNC	multinational corporation
NASSCOM	National Association of Software and Services Companies
NCI	Network Concentration Index
NRF	National Research Foundation
NTP	Networked Trade Platform
NTU	Nanyang Technological University
NUS	National University of Singapore
OECD	Organisation for Economic Co-operation and Development
OEM	original equipment manufacturing
OICQ	Open ICQ, predecessor to Tencent QQ
P2P	peer-to-peer
PIDC	Plastic Industry Development Center
PMC	Precision Machinery Research and Development Center
PRC	People's Republic of China

PRI	public research institute
R&D	research and development
RIE	research, innovation, and enterprise
SEEDS	Startup Enterprise Development Scheme
SEZ	special economic zone
SME	small- and medium-sized enterprise
SOE	state-owned enterprise
TCS	Tata Consultancy Services
TIFR	Tata Institute for Fundamental Research
TIS	Technology Incubation Scheme
TPS	Toyota Production System
TSMC	Taiwan Semiconductor Manufacturing Corporation
TSR	Tokyo Shoko Research
TVE	town-village enterprise
UNESCO	United Nations Educational, Scientific and Cultural Organization
USPTO	U.S. Patent and Trade Office
VC	venture capital

Preface

This volume is based on papers presented at a conference held at Stanford University in October 2017. The event was part of the Shorenstein Asia-Pacific Research Center's ongoing Asia-Pacific Innovation Project, which aims to produce academic and policy research that will help promote innovation and entrepreneurship in Asia. The project's research has examined the impact of public education and financial policies pursued by Asian countries to promote innovation and entrepreneurship. We have also explored how demographic changes, especially aging populations, affect the labor force and productivity, and the ways in which population aging and technology can influence each other.

At the October 2017 conference and in this book, we focus on national and regional innovation systems and policies. In particular, we ask a number of interrelated questions: How do institutions and policies affect the incentives for innovation and entrepreneurship? Are Asia's innovation systems similar to or different from those of other countries, especially Silicon Valley, that they try to emulate? If so, what has worked and what has not? Going forward, are there promising strategies to promote innovation? In addressing these questions, we have compared the policies and practices of Japan, Korea, China, Taiwan, India, and Singapore.

My colleague Yong S. Lee led this part of the project. I am very grateful to James Chen of D&C, China, for his generous support of the conference. Shorenstein APARC's Kristen Lee provided administrative support for the event and George Krompacky assisted in editing and publishing this volume.

Gi-Wook Shin
Director, Shorenstein Asia-Pacific Research Center

Contributors

TAKEO HOSHI is a professor of economics at the University of Tokyo. His research area includes corporate finance, banking, monetary policy, and the Japanese economy. Hoshi is also co-chairman of the Academic Board of the Center for Industrial Development and Environmental Governance (Tsinghua University). His past positions include Henri and Tomoye Takahashi Senior Fellow at the Freeman Spogli Institute for International Studies at Stanford University and Pacific Economic Cooperation Professor in International Economic Relations at the University of California, San Diego. His awards include the 2015 Japanese Bankers Academic Research Promotion Foundation Award, 2011 Reischauer International Education Award of Japan Society of San Diego and Tijuana, 2006 Enjoji Jiro Memorial Prize of Nihon Keizai Shimbun, and the 2005 Japan Economic Association-Nakahara Prize. His book *Corporate Financing and Governance in Japan: The Road to the Future* (MIT Press, 2001), co-authored with Anil Kashyap, received the Nikkei Award for the Best Economics Books. He co-authored *The Japanese Economy* (MIT Press, 2020) with Takatoshi Ito. His book on the political economy of the Abe administration, co-edited with Phillip Lipscy, will be published by Cambridge University Press in 2021. Hoshi received his PhD in economics from the Massachusetts Institute of Technology.

MICHELLE F. HSIEH is an associate research fellow in the Institute of Sociology, Academia Sinica, Taipei, Taiwan. She received her PhD in sociology from McGill University and was a Shorenstein Postdoctoral Fellow at the Shorenstein Asia-Pacific Research Center at Stanford University. Her research interests include economic sociology, sociology of development, comparative political economy, and East Asian societies. Her prior and current research explores the variations and consequences of industrial upgrading among the East Asian latecomers. Her other ongoing research investigates the origins of the East Asian developmental state and the connection between technology development and Cold War geopolitics.

WONJOON KIM is the head of the Graduate School of Innovation and Entrepreneurship and a professor at the School of Business and Technology Management in the Korea Advanced Institute of Science and Technology (KAIST). He is also the director of the KAIST Center for Innovation Strategy and Policy. Currently, he serves as the president of the Asia Innovation and Entrepreneurship Association (AIEA), the Organizing Committee Chair for the AIEA-NBER Conference, and as a vice president of the Korean Federation of Science and Technology Societies. His research focuses on the strategic management of innovation of firms, industry, and governments centering on emerging innovation paradigms, including the changing nature of innovation, artificial intelligence and industrial and social change, the convergence of technology and industry, mobility innovation, big data, as well as the changing nature of the entrepreneurship process.

DAVID KUO CHUEN LEE is a professor at the Singapore University of Social Sciences and the Shanghai University of Finance and Economics. He is also an adjunct professor at the National University of Singapore. His other appointments include chairman of the Global Fintech Institute, vice president of the Economic Society of Singapore, and council member of the British Blockchain Association. As a Fulbright Scholar at Stanford University in 2015, he started researching, mentoring, and investing in inclusive blockchain projects. He devotes his time to learning and sharing his knowledge on inclusive financial technology (fintech), and publishing books and articles on artificial intelligence, blockchain, quantum computing, and other emerging technologies. He has twenty years of experience as the CEO and independent director of companies involved in fintech, manufacturing, fund management, and real estate development. He holds editorial positions at the *Journal of FinTech* and *Journal of the British Blockchain Association*, among others. His latest publications include *The Handbook of Digital Currency*, the *Handbooks of Blockchain, Inclusive FinTech, AI and Quantum Computing*, and *Artificial Intelligence, Data and Blockchain in a Digital Economy* (Elsevier and World Scientific). He is also a consultant to the United Nations Development Programme and the Asian Development Bank on blockchain, fintech, and Central Bank Digital Currency.

INJEONG LEE received her master's degree in business and technology management from the Korea Advanced Institute of Science and Technology in 2015. She is currently a senior research associate at the Korea Development Institute and participates in research projects on innovation economics and technological change. Her contributions to the field fall in the areas of examining regional innovation systems from the perspective of the triple helix model and scrutinizing the relationships among innovative actors; finding global trends in the research and development of new technologies such as big data and artificial intelligence; and determining the economic and social effects of technological change.

YEON W. LEE is an adjunct professor at Seoul Business School, aSSIST, in Korea. She received her PhD in international studies with a concentration in business strategy and competitiveness from Seoul National University. Her research interests include innovation, (digital) value creation, the (digital) ecosystem, and the shared value perspective on business. Lee's work is focused on comparing the growth of Asian firms and economies, particularly the newly emerging media and entertainment industries and information technology/electronics industries. She has completed numerous consulting projects for both private companies and governments relating to her research on the global value chain, creative industries, international competitiveness, and creating shared value. Currently she is conducting research on the digital transformation of South Korean finance, healthcare, and pharmaceutical industries.

YONG SUK LEE is the SK Center Fellow at the Freeman Spogli Institute for International Studies and the deputy director of the Korea Program at the Walter H. Shorenstein Asia-Pacific Research Center at Stanford University. Lee's research is in the fields of labor economics, technology and entrepreneurship, and urban economics. His current research examines digital technology and labor, focusing on how new technologies will affect labor and how societies react to new technologies. In relation to technology and labor, Lee's research also examines various aspects of entrepreneurship, e.g., entrepreneurship and economic growth, entrepreneurship education, and factors that promote productive entrepreneurship. Prior to joining Stanford, Lee was an assistant professor of economics at Williams College in Massachusetts. He received his PhD in economics from Brown University, an MPP from Duke University, and BA and MA in architecture from Seoul National University.

DINSHA MISTREE is a research fellow and lecturer in the Rule of Law Program at Stanford Law School and a visiting fellow at the Hoover Institution. His research focuses on institutions and economic development, with a special focus on India. Mistree earned a PhD in politics from Princeton University as well as a BS and an MS in political science from the Massachusetts Institute of Technology.

HWY-CHANG MOON received his PhD from the University of Washington. He is professor emeritus at the Graduate School of International Studies at Seoul National University, where he also served as dean, and chairperson of the Institute for Policy and Strategy on National Competitiveness. Moon is also a consultant to the United Nations Conference on Trade and Development (UNCTAD) and an honorary ambassador of foreign investment promotion for South Korea. He has taught as a full-time or invited professor at the University of Washington, University of the Pacific, State University of New York at Stony Brook, Helsinki School of Economics, Keio University, Hitotsubashi University, Stanford University, and Beijing Normal University. His area of expertise includes topics such as international competitiveness, cross-cultural management, and Korean (and Asian) business and economy. Moon has conducted many consulting/research projects for multinational companies like Samsung Electronics Co., international organizations such as UNCTAD, and governments (e.g., Korea, Malaysia, Dubai, Azerbaijan, China's Guangdong Province, and India). He has participated in interviews and debates in international newspapers and media, such as the *New York Times*, NHK World TV, and Reuters. He has published numerous articles and books, including *The Strategy for Korea's Economic Success* (Oxford University Press, 2016) and *The Art of Strategy: Sun Tzu, Michael Porter, and Beyond* (Cambridge University Press, 2018).

TOSHIHIRO OKUBO is a professor of international economics in the Faculty of Economics, Keio University (Tokyo, Japan). His research interests are international trade, economic geography, environmental economics, and industrial cluster policies. In particular, he has conducted several studies on international trade and economic geography with firm heterogeneity and on firm heterogeneity and environmental policies. He received a PhD from the Graduate Institute (Geneva) and the University of Geneva, and received an MA from the University of Michigan. He has more than sixty papers in refereed academic journals such as the *Journal of International Economics, European Economic Review, Journal of Economic Geography, Journal of Economic History, Journal of Environmental Economics and Management,* and *Journal of the Association of Environmental and*

Resource Economists. He is a member of several committees and councils of the Japanese government.

GI-WOOK SHIN is the director of the Walter H. Shorenstein Asia-Pacific Research Center; the William J. Perry Professor of Contemporary Korea; the founding director of the Korea Program; a senior fellow of the Freeman Spogli Institute for International Studies; and a professor of sociology, all at Stanford University. His research concentrates on social movements, nationalism, development, and international relations, with focus on Korea and broader Asia. Shin is the author/editor of over twenty books and numerous articles, including *Policy and Social Innovation for a Post-Industrial Korea: Beyond the Miracle; Superficial Korea* (in Korean); *Divergent Memories: Opinion Leaders and the Asia-Pacific War; Global Talent: Skilled Labor as Social Capital in Korea; One Alliance, Two Lenses: U.S.-Korea Relations in a New Era,* and *Ethnic Nationalism in Korea.* He is currently working on a book on global talent flows, in which he examines the growing importance of transnational human and social capital and assesses the strategies and policies of talent development and recruitment in the Asia-Pacific region. Before coming to Stanford, Shin taught at the University of Iowa and the University of California, Los Angeles. He holds a BA from Yonsei University in Korea and an MA and PhD from the University of Washington.

EDISON TSE is an associate professor in the Department of Management Science and Engineering at Stanford University. He is also the director of the Asia Center of Management Science and Engineering, which has a charter to conduct research on the growth of the emerging economy in Asia, with a special focus on China, Korea, and India. In 1973, he received the prestigious Donald Eckman Award from the American Automatic Control Council in recognition of his outstanding contributions in the field of automatic control. In 2003, he received the Golden Nugget Award from General Motors R&D and Planning. In 2008, he received the Dean's Award for Industry Education Innovation from the School of Engineering, Stanford University. He has served as an associate editor of *IEEE Transactions of Automatic Control,* and a co-editor of the *Journal of Economic Dynamics and Control,* which he co-founded. Since 2003, he has dedicated his research efforts to dynamic entrepreneurial strategy and the transformation of the Chinese production economy to an innovation economy. His book on this theory, *Yuan Chuangxin* (Source innovation), was published in China in 2012. A second edition of this book, with new chapters incorporating some experiences of practicing the theory in China, was published in 2016 by China CITIC Press as *Chongxin Dingyi Chuangxin* (Redefine innovation). He is now working on the extension of this theory to developing countries. His main thesis is that innovation is culturally dependent. Successful innovation in a developing country must be synergistic with its culture, its political, social, and economic environment. Tse received his BS, MS, and PhD in electrical engineering from the Massachusetts Institute of Technology.

POH KAM WONG is a professor at the National University of Singapore (NUS) Business School. He received two BSs, an MS, and a PhD from the Massachusetts Institute of Technology. He has published extensively in leading international refereed journals on entrepreneurship and innovation, including *Organization Science*, *Strategic Entrepreneurship Journal*, *Journal of Management*, *Journal of Business Venturing*, and *Research Policy*. He has also consulted widely for international agencies including the World Bank, OECD, and Asian Devleopment Bank, various government agencies in Singapore, and many private corporations in Asia. He was a Fulbright Visiting Scholar at UC Berkeley, a visiting scholar at Stanford University and Oxford University, and a Pacific Leadership Fellow at UC San Diego. Besides his academic position, he has held a concurrent role as the director of the NUS Entrepreneurship Centre. An active angel investor, he is an advisor to two venture capital funds in Singapore. He received the Public Administration Medal (Silver) Award from the Singapore Government in 2013 for his contribution to entrepreneurship education in Singapore, and the "Entrepreneur for the World" Award (Educator Category) from the World Entrepreneurship Forum in 2015. He has been a board member of the Competition and Consumer Commission of Singapore since 2017.

SHIFTING GEARS IN INNOVATION POLICY

CHAPTER 1

Shifting Gears from Industrial to Innovation Policy
An Overview

Yong Suk Lee, Takeo Hoshi, and Gi-Wook Shin

More than ten years ago, in response to wide interest in the state of Asia's technology sector, Stanford University's Shorenstein Asia-Pacific Research Center convened scholars to conduct a collaborative study of information technology (IT) in Asia. The culmination of this effort was the book *Making IT: The Rise of Asia in High Tech*, edited by Henry S. Rowen, Marguerite Gong Hancock, and William F. Miller (Stanford University Press, 2006). The book discusses the then expanding influence of Japan, Taiwan, Singapore, South Korea, China, and India in the IT sector, and the progress they had made up to the early 2000s.

The domestic and international context has changed considerably since then. Manufacturing, which once drove the economic growth of these countries, has started to lose momentum in some industries. Aging has considerably changed the demographic structure of the labor force. An elderly population above 65 now comprises more than one-quarter of Japan's population, and a rapidly increasing share of South Korea's. The international attitude toward the export-led growth model, which the East Asian economies pursued successfully for several decades, had turned less favorable even before the risk of trade wars heightened in 2018, when the United States and China started to raise tariffs on each other's products. In short, the catch-up phase of economic growth has ended or is ending for high-growth economies in East Asia.

The rapid growth of these economies was achieved by importing new technologies from advanced economies, using them more effectively, and expanding exports. Abundant labor forces that were young, well educated, and relatively cheap helped this strategy. Now that many East Asian economies have successfully caught up to the technological frontier, they need to come up with their own innovations in order to continue growing. Indeed, governments in Asia have recently put forward various policies related to innovation. Related programs and goals include Mass Innovation and Entrepreneurship in China, Innovation Japan under "Abenomics," and the Creative Economy in South Korea.

Recognizing the importance of innovation and entrepreneurship for future economic growth in Asia, in 2018 the Shorenstein Asia-Pacific Research Center again convened scholars to assess their status and the policies some countries are using in pursuit of these goals. This book, the first in a series that examines innovation and entrepreneurship in Asia, focuses on national and regional innovation systems and policies. The definition of innovation used here is intentionally broad to incorporate a wide variety of perspectives as well as the different institutional settings of the countries discussed. Some chapters focus on patents, which is a rather narrow measurement of innovation. Others consider broader issues concerning entrepreneurship and innovation, such as changing mindsets to foster creativity and risk-taking.

A common line of inquiry seen across many chapters is how institutions and policies affect the incentives for innovation and entrepreneurship. Are Asia's innovation systems different from those of other regions? If so, what has worked and what has not? How can we tell? Are there any strategies aimed at promoting innovation that appear promising? These are among the questions asked in this volume.

This study focuses on six Asian countries: China, India, Japan, Singapore, South Korea, and Taiwan. These countries have successfully achieved high levels of growth in many industrial sectors, a large share of which are already at or near the technological frontier. At this stage, relying on past strategies will not guarantee new growth, especially when both the domestic and global contexts are changing. These six countries are at a critical juncture and will likely need to seek out new strategies for economic growth through innovation and entrepreneurship. In this overview, we will examine the specifics of each country, followed by comparative analyses. Before we discuss the key findings and suggestions put forward in each chapter, however, let us first elaborate on this turning point for economic growth in Asia and the heightened importance of innovation and entrepreneurship for future growth.

Nothing Short of a Miracle

One of the most dramatic events in economic history has been the rapid rise of income and living standards in East Asia. Japan after World War II, South Korea in the later decades of the twentieth century, and most recently China in the twenty-first century have all sustained high levels of economic growth, ranging from 6 percent to 10 percent per year, over decades. Similar patterns of economic growth may be seen across the region, from Singapore, Hong Kong, and Taiwan to Malaysia, Indonesia, Thailand, and Vietnam. Once devastated and poor cities of Asia are now gleaming with high-rises and connected with the fastest broadband wireless networks in the world. Studies of average wireless connection speeds across the world find those in Singapore and South Korea among the fastest. The people of Asia are now among the longest living and healthiest. According to the World Health Organization, average life expectancy in Japan, Singapore, and South Korea is among the longest in the world. Such accomplishments have been primarily achieved through catch-up economic growth, fueled by rapid learning and emulation of technologies and industrial production (Birdsall et al. 1993). Countries in the region were good at adopting the best practices of more developed countries. This strategy was particularly successful in East Asia in part due to a well-educated labor force, effective industrial policy, and export promotion. Catch-up growth, however, has already run its course for many East Asian countries. Income levels in Japan and South Korea rose rapidly and then closed in on the most developed countries in the world. China, the largest high-growth performer, is showing signs of a slowdown, with annual growth rates steadily declining since 2010.

In order to continue growing past this point, these countries need to have indigenous innovation and technological progress; they can no longer just rely on foreign technologies. For many East Asian economies, however, indigenous innovation was not an important factor of the catch-up phase. For example, Kim and Lau (1994) and Young (1995) show that the miracle growth of the then "newly industrialized" East Asian countries—such as Hong Kong, Singapore, South Korea, and Taiwan—was driven more by factor accumulation than by total factor productivity growth, in a setup that Paul Krugman calls an "input-driven economy." These countries were good at working long hours, copying products and technologies, and putting capital to work in increasingly productive sectors, but less so at innovating and creating breakthroughs. The findings of these statistical studies also fit casual observations. There have been many innovative companies in Asia—think of Sony or Samsung, for example—but compared with Apple, Microsoft, or Google, their innovations seem incremental.

Just when the catch-up phase of economic growth was coming to an end in many East Asian countries, several factors supporting that growth started to disappear. On the global stage, East Asian countries had benefited from stable (and somewhat undervalued) foreign exchange rates and a reduction in barriers to trade after World War II. At home, they benefited from young and well-educated workforces. Both of these conditions started to change as early as the 1970s, and the changes have intensified in the twenty-first century.

Evolving Global and Domestic Contexts

International trade has played an important role in the growth of many Asian economies since World War II. Global trade was expanding during this period and many Asian countries promoted exports as a means to expand beyond their domestic markets. The relatively open North American and European economies and their consumers embraced the lower-priced yet high-quality goods that were being produced in Asia.

The postwar international currency regime that came to be known as the Bretton Woods system also helped the export-led growth strategies of Asian economies by providing them with stable and somewhat undervalued currencies. Although the Bretton Woods system formally ended in the 1970s and the currencies of advanced economies started to float, many Asian countries were able to retain fixed exchange rates against the U.S. dollar by imposing capital controls and accumulating U.S. dollar securities as foreign reserves. Dooley, Folkerts-Landau, and Garber (2004) call this regime "Bretton Woods II." It allowed these countries to continue export-led growth strategies.

Export-led strategies, however, could not be sustained past the catch-up phase of growth. For one, successful growth made East Asian economies such as Japan too big to continue relying primarily on external demand. Perhaps more important, an export-led growth strategy has a problem of distancing the process of resource allocation from market forces, as Rajan (2010) points out. The cost of ignoring market signals (other than those in export markets) may be small when an economy is catching up with more advanced economies, as it is relatively clear which industries and export products to promote. As the economy matures, however, the role of well-functioning markets in distinguishing efficient production arrangements from inefficient ones becomes essential. The same problem applies to industrial policy, which we discuss in the next section. The problem gets especially severe for nontradable services that are not exported.

Meanwhile, a recent rise in antiglobalization sentiment, especially in the United States, could directly limit Asian exports. As of this writing, a tariff war between the United States and China, the two largest economies in the world, had started to brew and was likely to have ramifications for many countries. Moreover, with the United States drawing back from many of its roles as a global superpower, other countries, notably Russia and China, have become more assertive in international economic affairs. In this changing geopolitical landscape, traditional alliances have become weaker, and such changes could have considerable impact on international economic transactions.

Though the West, especially the United States, remains an important market for Asia, its importance has declined, and Asian firms are increasingly looking into opportunities within Asia, as well as other parts of the world. Asia itself has become more important for the global economy, and consequentially the economy of each country within Asia. China's economy continues to grow and is expected to take over as the largest economy in the world. Meanwhile, China's regional leadership can be seen in initiatives such as the Asia Infrastructure Investment Bank and One Belt, One Road, and the nation is increasingly engaging the international community.

Asian economies are also facing the challenges of a stark demographic change, amid rapidly aging populations and low birth rates. The drastic decline of Japan's population, ongoing for several years, is the first of its kind not caused by war or disease in the modern world. Korea's labor force started to shrink in 2018 as well. China's huge population will start to age soon, even as a large share remains poor.

Many Asian countries are facing the challenges outlined above, with various responses. Japan was the first to achieve rapid economic growth and the first to face these challenges. Japan's catch-up phase of economic growth ended by the end of the 1980s (or probably earlier, as Hoshi and Kashyap [2011] have pointed out). After years of stagnant growth, Japan is seemingly back on track to a more vibrant economy. Unemployment is low, economic growth has been picking up, and Japanese investment has increased globally. Whether this growth recovery trend will continue remains to be seen.

Many South Korean firms have been successful over the past decades, establishing themselves as leaders in their fields. However, South Korea's reliance on a small number of large conglomerates has put its economy in a precarious situation. The value added by the four largest conglomerates amounted to nearly 10 percent of the nation's gross domestic product in 2015. Some industries, such as shipping, have faltered, and there are increasing signs that even the nation's prized manufacturing sector is strained. In 2018, one of the largest automobile manufacturing plants operated by General Motors in the country shut down, sending shockwaves in the local economy and furthering a rise in unemployment. The economic conditions in South

Korea seem particularly susceptible to the country's political situation, especially in relation to developments in North Korea. Political ideology strongly influences economic policies, and economic policies—especially those connected to the support of large business—swing from left to right and back again following presidential elections.

East Asia's traditional economic hubs—including Singapore, Hong Kong, and Taiwan— remain vibrant. Singapore's economic and political stability continues to render it one of the most business-friendly countries in the world. Hong Kong is a key global financial hub, though this remains to be seen in light of recent conflict with Beijing, and Taiwan continues to be a leading manufacturer of high-tech products. India, under relatively new leadership, is actively reaching out to East Asia for collaborative economic partnerships. Both South Asia and Southeast Asia, with large and young labor forces, possess the potential to drive the region's future economic growth.

North Korea remains a big unknown; how its relations with South Korea, the United States, and the international community will pan out remains to be seen. Southeast Asia is a diverse region with Buddhists, Christians, Hindus, and Muslims all living close together. Whether it will be able to maintain harmony without falling into the factional conflicts and terrorism that inhibit the Middle East will be a critical test for the region's ability to sustain economic growth.

Today Asia is at a juncture. According to the October 2018 edition of the International Monetary Fund's *World Economic Outlook*, East Asia (Mongolia, South Korea, Japan, and China, including Hong Kong, Macao, and Taiwan) alone has a greater real economic output than North America. East Asia's share of global gross domestic product, based on purchasing power, was 25.78 percent in 2018; North America's was 18.54 percent. East Asian countries are at the technological frontier. South Asia and Southeast Asia, meanwhile, possess enormous economic potential due to their sheer size and natural resources. Furthermore, the countries of Asia are becoming more connected by both trade and diplomacy. It is at this juncture that we examine and reassess Asia's innovation.

From Industrial Policy to Innovation Policy

Asian governments have long emphasized innovation as part of their economic policies. However, most focus on the high-tech sector, and the major policy tools used to promote it are the traditional ones originating in industrial policy. Governments have typically identified promising high-tech industries and then tried to promote them. Through direct subsidies, tax breaks, and preferential financing, domestic firms were encouraged to import essential technologies from more advanced economies, improve them, and succeed in global markets.

As we outlined above, the catch-up phase of economic growth is over or ending for many East Asian countries. They can no longer merely emulate the technologies of more advanced countries; they need to come up with indigenous innovations. Traditional policies targeting specific industries will not be effective, either, because it is very difficult for policymakers (or anyone in general) to predict which industries will be the successful ones.

Asian governments now seem to understand the importance of specifically indigenous innovation. Recent administrations in China, Japan, and South Korea have all put forward innovation and entrepreneurship as their primary economic policy goals. It is less clear if they appreciate the necessity of breaking away from traditional industrial policies that pick promising industries and divert resources to them. The literature that examines the determinants of East Asian economic growth has focused on industrial policy as well. For instance, Lin and Chang (2009) agree that industrial policy was critical for East Asia's growth, but debate whether East Asia's industrial policies conformed to or defied comparative advantage. If the focus was on innovation, it was often confined to the industrial policies supporting the IT sector, as observed in the 2006 book *Making IT*. To be successful, the Asian model of innovation and entrepreneurship (if such a thing emerges) has to diverge from the Asian model of development of the past.

This book, we believe, is the first to critically examine this point and reassess what type of innovation policy Asia should pursue. Recognizing the limitations of past industrial policies, Choi, Lee, and Shin (2018) underscore the importance of social innovation surrounding immigration, education, and business policy for postindustrial growth, but their focus is on South Korea. Here, we address the larger Asia-Pacific and focus on national innovation strategies and regional cluster policies that can promote entrepreneurship and innovation. We neither blindly advocate for replicating Silicon Valley nor for a government-driven industrial-focused innovation policy. We will be neutral as to the importance of large corporations versus start-ups for innovation in Asia. The main contribution of this book is in this critical approach to seeking out a fresh direction for innovation and entrepreneurship in the context of Asia today and the near future. With this background, we now turn to the key findings of the individual chapters in this volume.

National Innovation Policies

In chapter 2, Edison Tse discusses how disruptive innovation can be initiated through platforms that link different economic agents in China. Tse explains how China's rapid economic growth can be traced to the two disruptive innovations (in contrast to "incremental" innovations) it underwent in the past 36 years. The first began in 1978 with China's reform and opening-up policy, and the second started in 2005 with China's internet wave. Today, as China and other Asian countries seek a new round of disruptive innovation that can sustain and spur growth, a general aversion toward entrepreneurship, especially among the educated, remains a key challenge. Ostensibly safe and stable jobs are still often preferred over the risky path taken by entrepreneurs and inventors. Such occupational preferences are rooted in long-established institutions and cultural norms, and also in people's perceptions of entrepreneurship. Tse presents a novel viewpoint that what is most crucial to disruptive innovation in China is the transformation of mindsets. However, he underscores the difficulty of such a transformation: "It cannot be achieved through rational argument, because mindsets are usually based on myths, dogma, ideologies, and past experiences. It can only be achieved gradually after people have positive experiences with the change." He also argues that government can effectively initiate the process. Echoing Deng Xiaoping's gradual modification of Chinese attitudes toward capitalism, beginning in 1978, today the Chinese government intends to change attitudes toward entrepreneurship, and announced "Mass Innovation and Entrepreneurship" as a new engine for Chinese economic growth in September 2014. This broad set of government-supported guidelines resulted in the setup of more than 2,000 incubators and accelerators from 2014 to 2016. Indeed, a top-down method of changing mindsets seems to be working in China, and the successes of companies like Alibaba, Tencent, and Baidu are motivating young people to become entrepreneurial.

Based on this and other recent government initiatives, Tse believes that China is ready to implement a three-pronged strategy to spur disruptive innovation: (1) creatively imitate IT-related disruptive innovations that have been successful in the United States, (2) transform traditional businesses by adapting new technology and business model innovations to ease the pains introduced by rapid economic development, and (3) creatively imitate China's first disruptive innovation in developing countries in support of the Belt and Road vision.

There is no one perfect way to foster national innovation, however, and the successful recipe for one country will likely differ from that needed in another. In chapter 3, Dinsha Mistree discusses India's national innovation policy in relation to its software industry and examines the government's role in creating a successful cluster of firms. Observers often describe the recent success of some Indian industries as a result of the adoption of a laissez-faire policy approach. The Indian government used to promote state-owned enterprises and a few large private-sector businesses through heavy-handed industrial policies. Then, in the 1980s, the government started to liberalize industries, and some, such as the software industry, flourished. However, Mistree points out that policy toward the software industry after liberalization was *not* laissez-faire. Instead, the Indian government, at the federal and state levels, adopted a broad set of measures fostering an innovation-friendly environment for its growing software industry. This was in sharp contrast to traditional industrial policy, which tries to identify promising industries and pick winners among them. Policies for the software industry included investment in technical education, development of telecommunications infrastructure, and creation of technology parks. Although Mistree does not directly assess the effectiveness of government policies in creating an innovation-conducive environment—we cannot predict the outcome if technology parks had *not* been created, for example—he presents a careful case study of India's software industry. Economic liberalization in India did not mean a shift from social planning to a laissez-faire market. The Indian government maintained an active industrial policy even after industrialization, but it promoted the entire software industry rather than targeting a few winners, and it was successful. Many would point out Japanese industrial policies were often like this, especially after the 1970s. It is worth noting that industrial policy, but with an emphasis on promoting foundations, may still play an important role in developing innovative sectors as it did for the Indian software industry.

While the first two chapters examine innovation strategies in the two most populous economies in the world, chapter 4, by Poh Kam Wong, assesses Singapore's innovation and entrepreneurship ecosystem. Wong, one of the contributors to *Making IT*, focuses on the changes in Singapore since the early 2000s. One of the most important points, which resonates in many other countries in Asia, is that government initiatives to promote entrepreneurship and innovation have increased start-ups in the internet, mobile, and IT services sectors, but not in "deep technology" sectors. Wong's deep-tech sectors are those that may incur high fixed research and development (R&D) costs but have the potential for greater payoffs in the future (e.g., biomedical, clean tech/energy, and advanced engineering). In fact, these are sectors where government investment in R&D can be best put to use. Long-term projects that lack immediate payoffs can have difficulty attracting adequate market financing. Many of the most impactful innovations in the world, such as the internet or GPS technology, were initially funded by the U.S. government for many years before becoming commercialized. However, government policies promoting innovation and entrepreneurship often seek out immediate accomplishments at the cost of more fundamental long-term objectives.

Wong highlights that, despite the increase in the number of start-ups, the pace of innovation has been slow in Singapore. He stresses the importance of promoting indigenous private innovation. Government-linked corporations compose a relatively large part of Singapore's economy but they are slow to innovate or to invest in innovative capabilities. Singapore's unique context as a small city-state with a high reliance on foreign investment and trade can offer insight into other small developing economies, and Wong presents some useful policy advice in this regard. He emphasizes the need to (1) promote technology entrepreneurship, not simply IT service-oriented entrepreneurship; (2) balance the promotion of innovative capability between incumbent firms and start-ups; (3) develop international connections to draw talent and capital, and enter larger markets; and (4) support universities to serve as local incubators.

Overall, these initial three chapters indicate that governments still play an important role for innovation and entrepreneurship in Asia. However, the findings suggest that future national innovation policies need to differ from industrial policies of the past. If the latter involved direct administrative guidance by picking industries and national champions, innovation policies going forward should focus less on the specifics and more on promoting and establishing an ecosystem and environment that can help foster innovative firms, people, and ideas. Disruptive innovation is about finding new values, and because it is impossible to reliably predict the next "big thing" in advance, the best the government can do is to educate people and to create an environment conducive to entrepreneurship and innovation.

Networks and Regional Clusters

Taking a network approach to understanding innovation and entrepreneurship, Michelle Hsieh (chapter 5) shows how innovation occurs through collaborative learning and technology diffusion, using the case of Taiwan's small- and medium-sized enterprises, which complement one another and tap into external economies. In what she calls "the less-celebrated model," these initiatives tend to be invisible and decentralized in the sense that they deploy relatively flattened resources and low budgets. This is contrary to common policy practices that focus on inducing innovation by increasing investment in R&D subsidies to selected firms (as in Japan), or policies that induce entrepreneurship by increasing the number of firms in targeted clusters or government subsidies to a growing number of start-ups (as in Singapore). In the less-celebrated model, building capability is a matter of bridging different production networks to induce technological advancement along the entire supply chain, and sustaining clusters. Therefore, what makes a cluster tick is not the size of the firms in it, but the specific ways in which the network of firms and public research institutes are linked in a decentralized system. Each actor is connected in multiple ways to tap into external economies so as to pursue collaborative learning; this kind of flexible and dynamic ecosystem enables some clusters to remain resilient, territorially rooted, and globally connected in the face of globalization.

Governments around the world have created regional clusters to promote industries and R&D. As Toshihiro Okubo illustrates in chapter 6, Japan has a long tradition of regional cluster policies. However, Okubo sees problems with the assessment of these policies. In an extensive survey of the empirical research on the efficacy of Japan's regional cluster policies, Okubo finds that these policies did successfully increase the number of firms and industrial clusters, but the resulting firms were neither highly productive nor innovative. In particular, Japan's industrial clusters were the least likely to be successful. Promoting a certain industry by encouraging firms within the same industry to locate closer together actually attracted less productive firms. These types of regional cluster policies are quite expensive from the taxpayer's point of view. However, governments, preoccupied with designing, implementing, and administrating such policies, often placed a low priority on careful evaluation of their causal effects. Okubo notes that government officials in Japan are now realizing the importance of rigorous econometric analysis of innovation and cluster policies, and academics have recently been involved in using microdata and advanced econometrics to measure the impact of cluster policies on productivity and firm location. Governments in Asia have generally been hesitant to collect data and assess the policies they implement. Japan's willingness to invest in examining the efficacy of policies is a change in the right direction. Okubo suggests that rather than a top-down fully funded approach to regional cluster policies, Japan should implement a matched scheme where the government matches 50 percent of the funds. Such schemes provide better incentives for firms to become productive and innovative and have been found to be effective in other countries.

The efficacy of regional innovation clusters depends not only on the performance of each constituent but also on how the actors interact with one another. Chapter 7, by Injeong Lee and Wonjoon Kim, examines the connections among three key actors—universities, industries, and government research institutions—and their roles in two representative innovation clusters of South Korea and Germany (i.e., Daedeok Innopolis and Silicon Saxony). Their comparative analysis of patent applications, utilizing social network theories, provides several interesting insights. Silicon Saxony's economic contribution to Germany's national economy is substantially larger than Daedeok Innopolis's contribution to Korea's. However, the quantity of interactions among organizations in producing patents is larger in the Korean example, and interactions are not concentrated in as small a number of organizations as they are in Germany. Universities and government research institutions play a more central role in South Korea, whereas industrial firms play the central role in Germany. Concentrated collaboration led by a smaller number of firms seems to be related to better overall economic performance, rather than diffused collaboration among a large number of actors within the cluster. In other words, there seems to be a quality-quantity trade-off. Lee and Kim argue that, when promoting joint R&D activities among entities within a cluster via subsidies or other policies, governments should incentivize entities to strengthen and deepen their collaboration rather than promote the overall quantity of R&D collaborations. Another related problem the authors point out, especially relevant for South Korea, is the government's emphasis on measuring the number of patent applications as an output of universities and government research institutions. Counting numbers is an easy way to measure an organization's performance, but simply linking government funding to the number of patent applications distorts incentives and results in ineffective technological knowledge creation.

Looking Ahead

Governments of many countries have been trying to nurture innovation but have often failed. In chapter 8 David Lee Kuo Chuen points out the problems of top-down national innovation strategies, especially pertinent to many developing countries, and finds a more promising approach in decentralized innovation policies and distributed innovation models. Usually, proponents of government-led innovation argue that a top-down approach is necessary because developing countries lack human capital and organizational capacity in the private sector. Lee turns this argument around and points to a lack of human capital and organizational capacity in the central government as the key problem. Although it is hard to prove which view is right—both may be, in fact—this is a novel point worth pondering. Another key argument from this chapter is that recent technological development itself, especially blockchain technology, can help solve the problem of technological progress in developing countries by allowing innovation to progress in a decentralized and distributed fashion. This is a reasonable conjecture, although no country is there yet, as Lee's case studies of China and Singapore show. Asian countries have been active in utilizing blockchains and cryptocurrency. Inherent to blockchain technology are small start-ups working separately but directly exchanging ideas with one another. However, even with such a decentralized technology, the government can still often play a role. Whether central governments can help small start-ups utilizing decentralized technology to thrive will be critical in how Asia operates on this new technological frontier.

The final chapter, by Hwy-Chang Moon and Yeon W. Lee, posits an interesting question: What drives innovation in Asia—large businesses or small businesses and start-ups? Should governments work to create an environment more amenable to one versus the other? A prevailing notion, especially related to places like Silicon Valley, is that start-ups are the drivers of innovation. However, Moon and Lee argue that this is not necessarily so, and suggest that governments and the media have unjustly criticized the growth of large enterprises without providing accurate evidence of their contributive economic role, especially with regard to innovation. They argue, using case studies of small, medium, and large enterprises, that there is little relationship between firm size and the health of the national economy. Indeed, even in Silicon Valley, it seems that behemoths like Google, Apple, and Facebook are driving the region's economic growth, rather than the nimble and small start-ups. Silicon Valley is an ecosystem where the large innovators and small innovators feed off one another. The giant tech firms produce innovation but also acquire small companies. At the same time, employees at these large businesses eventually become entrepreneurs and investors who further foster the innovation and entrepreneurship of start-ups.

Moon and Lee emphasize that enterprises of all sizes—small, medium, and large—contribute, albeit differently, to economic growth, and that innovation policy should emphasize the cooperation and harmony among them rather than trying to implement a one-sided policy that favors one over the others. The Asian economies that Moon and Lee survey have developed despite significant differences in their political institutions and histories. As the authors ultimately emphasize, they have all succeeded in maintaining growth and competitiveness by being a part of the global economy. This point seems quite relevant going forward. Industries and international and domestic contexts have evolved since East Asia's hyper-growth years. However, what remains the same is that Asian countries should continue to be active members of the global economic system for their innovation and entrepreneurship policies to be successful going forward.

Currently, there is a big push for innovation and entrepreneurship in Asia. A universal lesson in effective management is to not micromanage. This is something that will be especially relevant for successful innovation policy in Asia. While each government's active encouragement of innovation is welcomed, the lessons from this book are that innovation is unlike industrial growth, and rather than defining narrow policy goals or trying to pick winners, innovation policy should focus on a fostering environment. There is evidence that Asia's current wave of innovation policies have increased the quantity of start-ups and knowledge sets. We believe the suggestions outlined in the following chapters—changing mindsets, promoting technical education, embracing investment in deep technologies that may require higher initial costs and long-term investment, embracing new cutting-edge technologies like blockchain, implementing matching funds for start-ups, encouraging a holistic approach to collaboration involving the global value chain—will further help Asian countries to generate more disruptive and impactful innovation that can sustain economic growth and distributed wealth to their citizens.

References

Birdsall, Nancy M., Jose Edgardo L. Campos, Chang-Shik Kim, W. Max
    Corden, Lawrence MacDonald [editor], Howard Pack, John Page,
    Richard Sabor, and Joseph E. Stiglitz. 1993. *The East Asian Miracle:
    Economic Growth and Public Policy: Main Report (English)*. A World
    Bank policy research report. New York: Oxford University Press.
Choi, Joon Nak, Yong Suk Lee, and Gi-Wook Shin, eds. 2018. *Strategic,
    Policy, and Social Innovation for a Post-Industrial Korea: Beyond the
    Miracle*. New York: Routledge.
Dooley, Michael P., David Folkerts-Landau, and Peter Garber. 2004. "The
    Revived Bretton Woods System." *International Journal of Finance and
    Economics* 9, no. 4: 307–13.
Hoshi, Takeo, and Anil Kashyap. 2011. *Why Did Japan Stop Growing?*
    Report prepared for Nippon Institute for Research Advancement
    (NIRA), Tokyo, Japan.
Kim, Jong-Il, and Lawrence J. Lau. 1994. "The Sources of Economic
    Growth of the East Asian Newly Industrialized Countries." *Journal of
    the Japanese and International Economies* 8, no. 3: 235–71.
Lin, Justin, and Ha-joon Chang. 2009. "Should Industrial Policy in
    Developing Countries Conform to Comparative Advantage or Defy
    it? A Debate Between Justin Lin and Ha-joon Chang." *Development
    Policy Review* 27, no. 5: 483–502.
Rajan, Raghuram G. 2010. *Fault Lines: How Hidden Fractures Still
    Threaten the World Economy*. Princeton, NJ: Princeton University
    Press.
Young, Alwyn. 1995. "The Tyranny of Numbers: Confronting the
    Statistical Realities of the East Asian Growth Experience." *Quarterly
    Journal of Economics* 110, no. 3: 641–80.

CHAPTER 2

Is China Ready for the Next Disruptive Innovation?

Edison Tse

In 1976 the first personal computer, the Altair 8800, was introduced to the U.S. market. The exciting vision for this product was a computer that everyone could own. This triggered a movement by young engineers, hardware industries, and software industries that disrupted the U.S. computer industry. In the beginning, many start-up companies embraced the movement, not from a rational basis, but from an emotional one. The failures of their early attempts provided lessons to later entrepreneurs who would find a path to developing an ecosystem that was able to realize the value proposition projected by the vision of personal computing. In the field of business administration, this phenomenon is termed disruptive innovation triggered by advanced technology (Christensen 1997, 2003; Johnson, Christensen, and Kagermann 2008). We saw similar disruptive innovation in the United States, triggered by the internet and wireless technologies. In 1978, there was a movement that disrupted the worldwide economy: China's reform and opening-up (*gaige kaifang*). In many respects, this was very similar to the disruption triggered by technologies like personal computing, the internet, and wireless connectivity: it contributed to global economic growth, changed the pecking order, and changed how people lived. The only difference is that China's reform and opening-up was not triggered by new technology, but by the desire to move the Chinese people out of poverty.

There are extensive studies on why China was able to grow so quickly after reform and opening-up (Sachs and Woo 1997; Kanbur and Zhang 2009; Lin, Cai, and Li 1996). These studies can be broadly grouped into two categories. One category correlates the growth path with factor inputs and determines the major factors that shaped China's economic growth. Unsurprisingly, these studies find that human capital growth, foreign trade, foreign capital investment, and productivity growth were the major factors contributing to China's growth in the period 1978–95 (Hu and Khan 1997; Wang and Yao 2003; Chen, Chang, and Zhang 1995). The second category analyzes how the implementation of reform and opening-up led to the improvement of micromanagement, allowance of private enterprises, planned resource allocation, and the adoption of a market economy, resulting in human capital growth, foreign trade, foreign capital investment, and productivity growth (Headey, Kanbur, and Zhang 2009; Sachs and Woo 1997; Lin, Cai, and Li 1996; Qian and Xu 1993; Lau, Qian, and Roland 2000; Zhu 2010). Many of these analyses were based on established economic schools of thought. From an *ex post* point of view, they give a logical explanation of China's growth from 1978 to 1995. But from an *ex ante* point of view, these analyses may not be very helpful in projecting China's possible future growth, as China may undergo another transformation in the future.

It is an irony that the implementation of the world's greatest miracle in economic growth was not based on a detailed plan supported by profound economic analysis, but rather on Deng Xiaoping's vision of raising the Chinese people from poverty. Through small-scale experimentation, he found what worked and then scaled up (Qian and Xu 1993; Headey, Kanbur, and Zhang 2009). Later on, he developed policies to adjust allocation and the market economy. This is very much the approach of a high-tech entrepreneur, not of a policymaker: to rely on experimentation to find the entry point to the market and later adapt to market adjustments to maintain expansion and growth. This is like a combination of the experimentalist and the convergence schools of economic thought (Sachs and Woo 1997; Headey, Kanbur, and Zhang 2009). In a sense, Deng was an institutional entrepreneur who induced an institutional change (Eisenstadt 1980; DiMaggio 1988). A complementary approach to analyzing China's 1978 success would be from an entrepreneurial point of view of disruptive innovation. The focus of this approach is to analyze, from an *ex ante* point of view, whether a disruptive innovation will take place that will induce new economic growth. In this chapter, I shall develop a theoretical framework that links innovation with economic growth. Using this framework, I shall explain China's rapid economic growth from 1978 to 2016. During this period, China built up unique innovation clusters and Chinese firms built up core assets, abilities, and company cultures. Based on these and recent government initiatives, I shall assess if China is ready for the next disruptive innovation, and the possible paths that different firms can take to find new growth.

Innovation and Economic Growth

I distinguish two types of innovation: scientific and commercial. Scientific innovation is any new discovery or invention based on science. Commercial innovation is any new activity that can create value. Since "value" is subjective, so commercial innovation must specify the groups it is creating value for (Tse 2012, 2016). I also distinguish two types of commercial innovation: incremental and disruptive. When a product is accepted by a group of customers, its value becomes objective to this group. Firms can focus on increasing value for this group of customers by improving the product, reducing cost, improving the efficiency of the supply chain, or improving its distribution channel. I refer to all these activities as incremental innovation. Incremental innovation will increase a firm's competitiveness in a free market economy. As more firms engage to compete in incremental innovation, marginal incremental investment will increase and marginal incremental return will decrease, leading to diminishing returns. When an industry starts to emerge, the value proposition of its product is starting to be recognized and customers will desire to derive more value from the product. This offers opportunities for firms to benefit by engaging in incremental innovation. As more firms enter to compete by incremental innovation, the whole industry will grow but then will gradually become stagnant.

New possibilities can trigger the introduction of new value propositions. These new value propositions are intended to improve our way of life. However, for intended values to be realized, supporting infrastructure may be required. I use the phrase *disruptive innovation* to describe the activities that lead to the creation of such infrastructure. Take the automobile as an example. When the first car was introduced, it provided little practical value as roads were not paved and there were no gas stations. The intended value of the car as a convenient mode of transportation could only be realized when paved roads, neighborhood repair stations, roadside gas stations, fast-food restaurants, motels, and many other supporting products and services that made automobile travel convenient became available. I refer to all those products and services—that contributed to the realization of the intended value of the automobile as a convenient mode of transportation—as its supporting infrastructure. This infrastructure is a value net consisting of many value chains: car value chain, road value chain, gas station value chain, etc. The people that desire to use the car as a means of convenient transportation and all the economic agents, including car producers and those providing supporting infrastructure, form an ecosystem in which the car is indeed a convenient mode of transportation. The creation of this ecosystem was triggered by the vision that the car would one day become a more convenient mode of transportation than the horse-drawn carriage. The government took the first step by paving roads, and oil companies saw the opportunity to build roadside gas stations, which would in turn increase car sales. With more people owning cars, entrepreneurs saw new business opportunities to open repair stations, fast-food restaurants, motels, and other pieces of the automobile-supporting infrastructure. As more cars were sold and more people knew more about cars, they desired to have related products and services to derive more value from owning a car. This provided business opportunities for economic agents to provide more and better products and services to increase the value of a car, which would attract more people to buy cars, thus creating positive network effects across car owners, car producers, and supporting economic agents. Once this happened, the system seemed to take on a life of its own and therefore is called an *ecosystem*. People's unending desire to derive more value and economic agents' incremental innovation activities to satisfy that desire resulted in the exponential growth of the car ecosystem.

Scientific innovation provides a new possibility. One can apply this new possibility to incremental innovation or trigger a disruptive innovation. From the perspective of commercial innovation, an activity's innovativeness is not measured by the activity's novelty or originality, but by the total value that the activity brings to society. A fast follower or imitator that implements a disruptive innovation to create new and high total value is more innovative than an inventor that applies the invention in a way that adds incrementally to existing value.

An incremental innovation is initiated by a firm in response to people's desire to derive more value from an accepted product or service, and its success hinges on the firm's core assets and its ability to satisfy its customers' desires. A disruptive innovation is triggered by a new possibility. This new possibility may come from an exciting new technology, a global trend, a change in government vision and intention, or any macrolevel change. Based on the new possibility, a government, a region, a group of firms in an industry, or a single firm can initiate a vision to create a new value proposition that could benefit many people and trigger a disruptive innovation. If the initiation is at the firm or industry level, then it will cause a structural change in the market or the industry. If the initiation is at the government or regional level, it will induce institutional change to support the disruption. To implement a disruptive innovation, the initiator establishes a platform that links two groups of economic agents together: one group will benefit from the value proposition, and the other group will provide products or services to realize the value proposition. As more agents in the first group benefit from the value proposition, market demand for the value proposition will increase. This will draw in more agents into the second group. The desire of the agents in the first group to derive more value will provide incremental innovation opportunities for the agents in the second group to act independently and use their creativity to improve products and services to satisfy the desire of agents in the first group. The desire of agents in the first group to derive more value, and the incremental innovation of agents in the second group, will increase network effects between the two groups. The platform initiator, by focusing on balancing the benefits of all agents in the ecosystem, will further strengthen the network effects that will lead to faster exponential growth of the ecosystem. I envision the dynamic formation of the new ecosystem using a two-sided market model, illustrated in figure 2.1 (Armstrong 2005; Rochet and Tirole 2003; Roson 2005; Sun and Tse 2007a, 2007b).

FIGURE 2.1 Disruptive innovation model: Two-sided markets

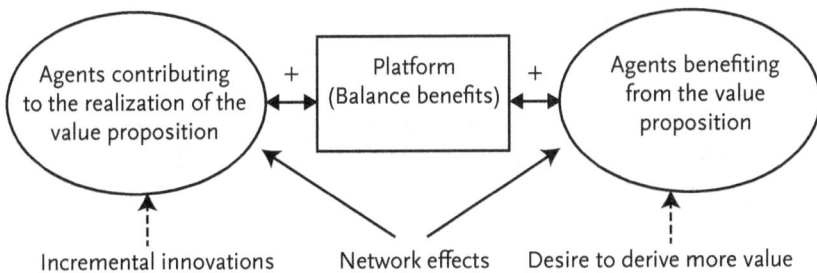

SOURCE: Author.

Implementing a disruptive innovation is very different from implementing an incremental innovation. Since it is not possible to know *a priori* the structure of the ecosystem that a disruptive innovation will create, the initiator cannot implement a disruptive innovation by following a carefully analyzed plan. Instead, the initiator needs to experiment and find out what will work on a small scale before scaling up to be compatible with the environment. It is important to note that disruptive innovation needs grassroots support to promote the new value proposition. And again, disruptive innovation is promoting a new value proposition. If this new value is different from or goes against the old accepted value, the biggest obstacle in implementing a disruptive innovation will come from the people who hold the old mindset. Many of them may feel that accepting this new value proposition might hurt their current situation. They will try their best to put up resistance to prevent this from happening. Therefore, the success of disruptive innovation hinges on the ability of its initiator to gradually change this mindset to reduce resistance and leverage core assets to mobilize appropriate economic agents to participate and collectively create value for all agents within the ecosystem to fulfill the vision. Thus, the dynamic formation of an ecosystem to support a disruptive innovation is path dependent. History, culture, and the political, economic, and social environment will shape the dynamic formation of such an ecosystem. Economic agents will stay with the ecosystem as long as they can derive net benefit from it, and thus the total economic activities in an ecosystem are directly proportional to the total members in the ecosystem and the total net benefit they receive. A disruptive innovation's coverage is the region(s) where the platform initiator and the ecosystem members are located. If the coverage includes many countries, then the disruptive innovation will impact economic growth in those countries. If the coverage is mainly within a single country, then the disruptive innovation will mainly impact economic growth in that country.

All successful commercial innovation will induce economic growth. Successful incremental innovation will increase the value of an existing value chain, and the customers in the market can quickly recognize the increased value. This will increase the economic activities of production and distribution of this increased value to the customers. Thus, successful incremental innovation will impact the economic growth in the regions in which the firm, its value chain, and its market are located. The induced economic growth will follow a logarithmic growth curve: it rises sharply in the beginning, but as time goes on gains decrease and become more difficult to achieve. A disruptive innovation requires building a new ecosystem consisting of many value chains to realize the value proposition. The initiator of disruptive innovation establishes a platform to create incremental innovation opportunities for all its members in the ecosystem; its success will impact the economic growth of its coverage regions. It takes time to change mindsets and to find appropriate incentives to draw in enough members before the network effect between the two groups in the ecosystem becomes tangible; the induced economic growth curve will follow an S-shaped curve. At the beginning, growth is negligible, until enough members are built up to have an effective network effect. Then rapid exponential growth takes place, as the positive network effects between the two groups ramp up. But when the network effects slow down, growth will plateau.

If all firms in a region engage in only incremental innovation to improve value in existing value chains, the region's economy will eventually stagnate. One way for a region to revive its growth is to initiate a new disruptive innovation or help local firms do so. Another way is to engage in incremental innovation that supports an ongoing disruptive innovation in another region. When firms in Silicon Valley initiated the disruptive innovation of personal computing, many firms in Taiwan supported this disruption and revived that state's growth. Whether a region will have a new growth trend can be assessed by analyzing whether it is ready and able to initiate the next disruptive innovation or to support an ongoing disruptive innovation. This assessment can be based on an analysis of global trends, government vision, core assets, business environment, firms' assets and abilities, problems facing the firms, business cultures, and people's mindsets. In the next two sections, I shall apply such an analysis to examine two consecutive disruptive innovations in China: the first was the government-initiated reform and opening-up (*gaige kaifang*) of 1978; the second disruption, the so-called China internet wave, began in 1998 and was initiated by Chinese internet firms. I will analyze the major difficulties the initiators faced and how they took steps to overcome them, leading to the successful implementation of these disruptions. I will then examine what kind of assets, abilities, business culture, mindsets, and supporting innovation clusters were developed during these two disruptions and assess whether China is ready for the next disruptive innovation.

China's First Disruptive Innovation: Reform and Opening-Up

The first disruptive innovation in China was initiated by Deng Xiaoping at the country level in 1978 with the reform and opening-up policy. It is important to understand the historical background and difficulties that Deng faced in initiating this policy. In 1966, Mao Zedong set the Cultural Revolution in motion, with the goal to preserve "true" Communist ideology in China and to impose Maoist thought as the dominant ideology within the Party. Many leaders, including Deng, were purged because they were pro–economic development, which Mao considered a threat that would lead to the restoration of capitalism and end Communist ideology in China. The Cultural Revolution would not come to an end until Mao's death in September 1976. During the movement's ten years, Mao's cult of personality grew immensely, China's economy suffered, and Maoist ideology and anti-capitalism became deeply rooted in the minds of the people. After Mao's death, Hua Guofeng became the chairman of China's Communist Party and brought Deng back to active duty in the Party. Even though Mao was dead, most Chinese still worshiped him. To stabilize the situation, Hua announced in October 1976 that nothing Chairman Mao had said should be criticized. Later, in February 1977, an editorial based on this appeared in the *People's Daily*. The so-called two-whatevers (*liangge fanshi*)—shorthand for, "We are determined to follow whatever decisions Chairman Mao made, and we will unswervingly follow whatever instructions Chairman Mao gave"—became an ideological guideline. When Deng returned to duty in 1977, his priority was to turn around China's economy. The two-whatevers were his first big obstacle. If they were not overturned, economic development would be unacceptable, as Mao had opposed it. Deng, instead of trying to discredit Mao, put forward that Mao's core thought was to seek truth from facts (*shishi qiushi*), and that the two-whatevers were wrong because the concept was not in accord with seeking fact-based truths. His argument gained the support of a majority of Party leaders, leading to the complete dismissal of the two-whatevers in March 1978. The 3rd Plenary Session of the 11th Central Committee of the Communist Party of China (December 1978) marked the beginning of reform and opening-up; it would trigger the first disruptive innovation in China and was a clear indication that Deng had assumed the reins of power.

Deng's vision was to take Chinese people out of poverty. China was poor and its domestic consumer market was limited. To increase economic activity, it needed to reach out to foreign markets in the United States, Europe, and Japan, and likewise needed to attract foreign investors. China's planned economy had resulted in extensive economic inefficiency, so economic reform to increase production efficiency was necessary. The second major obstacle Deng faced was a deep-rooted anti-capitalism. A planned economy was considered the right model for a socialist state; some early successful attempts by local groups to improve production efficiency that violated the planned economy model were heavily criticized by local Party leaders, and early attempts to bring in foreign capital were also subjected to criticism. To change this mindset, Deng announced the idea of socialism with Chinese characteristics—socialism did not mean people have to be poor, and a market economy could exist in a socialist state. To stress that capital was merely a means to improve the people's standard of living, Deng made his famous statement about the color of a cat: whether it is white or black, if it can catch a mouse, it is a good cat. If capital could improve living standards, it was good capital, and could be used. He used the same argument for a market economy. In December 1978, Deng made a speech that advocated the emancipation of thought (*jiefang sixiang*), the seeking of truth through facts (*shishi qiushi*), and the need for everyone to unite to look to the future (*jietun yizhi xiangqian kan*).

Deng had set the stage to create a disruptive innovation with a two-sided market model, as illustrated in figure 2.2. Deng's guidance to seek the truth from facts, and its acceptance by all Party leaders, helped him avoid falling into extensive debate with many still holding an anti-capitalist mindset. He encouraged small-scale experimentation with disruptive innovation at the local level; if such experiments were successful, they were rolled out at the national level with policy support.

FIGURE 2.2 Reform and opening-up: China's first disruptive innovation, 1978

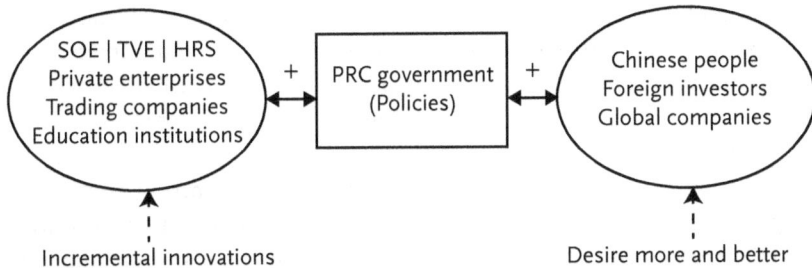

SOURCE: Author.
NOTE: HRS = household responsibility system; PRC = People's Republic of China; SOE = state-owned enterprise; TVE = town-village enterprise.

One famous example of this local-level experimentation was the household responsibility system (HRS), which was first secretly implemented by a poor village in Anhui despite the risk of being branded as counterrevolutionary. The system, which transferred responsibility for profit and loss from the state to local leaders, was very successful and gained Deng's support. Leaders from other villages were invited to visit and learn and then went on to implement similar systems, adjusted to fit local environments (Lin 1987). This system later evolved and was adopted in other economic sectors. In 1979, the Ministry of Communications in Guangdong and a few merchants in Hong Kong developed a small piece of industrial property in Shenzhen (at that time just a small village). This opened up a direct link to Hong Kong's cargo harbor, and some Hong Kong investors were soon motivated to open factories in the area. This gave the Guangdong leadership the idea of setting up a special economic zone (SEZ) to experiment with foreign direct investment and market liberalization. China's first SEZ was formally set up in Shenzhen in August 1980 (Chen and de'Medici 2009). At first, it was criticized by some Party leaders as pro-capitalist, but Deng supported the Shenzhen experiment and it eventually proved successful. In 1984, Deng announced publicly that the experience in Shenzhen had proved that the policy of establishing SEZs was a correct one. Many other Chinese SEZs were later set up with policy support in order to attract foreign capital. Some local regions that did not get SEZ approval offered similar incentive packages to attract foreign capital and companies. Another example is Wenzhou's experiment in reforming town-village enterprises (TVEs) and legalizing private firms. After observing its success, many TVEs and small and medium state-owned enterprises (SOEs) were privatized by the late 1990s (Zhu 2010).

By encouraging an emancipation of the mind, and not objecting to practices merely on the grounds that they resembled those of capitalist nations, Deng mobilized a grassroots movement of entrepreneurs throughout the country to act independently, to learn and use their creativity to develop systems, and to improve production efficiency and management. Local success was creatively imitated throughout the nation. Resource and infrastructure development businesses were mainly controlled by SOEs, which provided a base to boost domestic economic activities. With the opening-up policy, foreign investors were encouraged to invest and set up factories in China to engage in original equipment manufacturing (OEM) production and in supplying low-cost products to the world market. As the Chinese economy picked up, privately owned consumer product companies sprouted up to fill growing domestic demand. Reform and opening-up initiated a disruptive innovation in China in December 1978, but the resulting growth of China's gross domestic product (GDP) did not manifest until 1984. Since then, and once the network effects of the platform in figure 2.2 became apparent, the economy grew rapidly, as shown by the tremendous rise in China's GDP in figure 2.3.

From 1980 to 2005, economic growth in China was driven by government implementation of policies supporting the rollout of successful local experiments (e.g., HRS, SEZs, TVE reform, and privatization of SOEs) and aimed at balancing the benefits of all agents through, for example, dual-track pricing (Lau, Qian, and Roland 2000), and providing incremental innovation opportunities through increased productivity (Lin, Cai, and Li 1996), increased human capital (Wang and Yao 2003), and improved management (Lin, Cai, and Li 1996). The government also engaged in foreign trade by joining the World Trade Organization, which increased the network effect of the first disruptive innovation. The coverage of this disruption was global: it benefited China, foreign investors, multinational companies, and consumers in developed countries. During this period, industrial parks supporting incremental innovation in product and parts production sprang up in different cities in China, forming the first innovation clusters in the country.

FIGURE 2.3 China's gross domestic product, 1980–2015 (current prices, US$ billions)

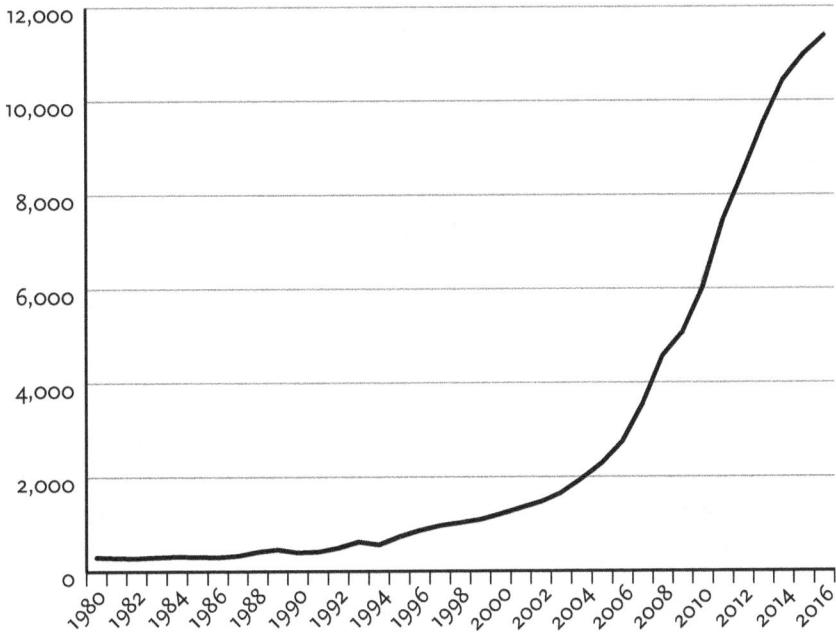

SOURCE: World Bank.

China's Second Disruptive Innovation:
The Internet Wave (1998)

The first disruptive innovation in China resulted in a growing domestic consumer market. China became an OEM production center for many global companies, and many young engineers were exposed to technological development in developed countries and acquired knowledge of high technology. Before 1998, cross-region creative imitation was practiced in China, as the success of one Chinese region was copied by another; after 2000, the focus shifted to imitating the United States. From 1995 to 1998, many U.S. internet startups related to messaging, e-commerce, and search successfully issued initial public offerings (IPOs) only a few years after being founded and prior to being profitable. Yahoo! was founded in 1994 and issued an IPO in 1996; Amazon.com was founded in 1994 and issued an IPO in 1997; and eBay issued an IPO in 1998, just three years after being founded in 1995. Many investors were eager to put their money into any internet-related start-up. This excessive speculation, from roughly 1997 to 2000, created the so-called internet bubble, with many internet start-ups receiving venture financing without much consideration of their chance of success. Many young Chinese engineers with backgrounds in technology creatively imitated successful U.S. internet business-to-consumer (B2C) businesses starting around 1998: Sina (1998) imitated Yahoo, Tencent's QQ (1998) imitated AOL Instant Messenger, Alibaba (1999) imitated eBay and Amazon, Baidu (2000) imitated Google, Ctrip (2003) imitated Expedia, and so on. These very same U.S. companies likewise entered the Chinese market but all lost out to their Chinese counterparts. In emerging economies, there are institutional voids that prevent buyers from efficiently connecting to sellers. Understanding these voids and learning how to work with them in specific markets is necessary in order to succeed (Khanna and Palepu 2010). In a consumer market, the notion of what is considered valuable might differ depending on the local social, political, cultural, and business environment, including the readiness of the local infrastructure. Moreover, the realization of such value is unique to the local environment; the ability of a firm to execute and deliver such value to the local markets is the key to success. I shall use the cases of Alibaba and Tencent to illustrate this point.

Alibaba started in 1999 as a business-to-business (B2B) portal that connected Chinese manufacturers with overseas buyers. With the Chinese consumer market rapidly growing, Alibaba started Taobao as a B2C and consumer-to-consumer (C2C) e-commerce platform in 2003. Both eBay and Amazon had attempted to enter the Chinese market through the acquisition of (at the time) the largest local C2C and B2C platforms in China but failed and withdrew from the Chinese market. The major reason for their failure was their inability to deal with the institutional void in China. At that time, China lacked a nationwide credit system; even though China UnionPay began issuing credit cards in 2002, only individuals with a high net worth were issued credit cards. Any e-commerce platform that relied on credit cards for online payments thus had limited access to consumers. Moreover, because of China's weak consumer protection laws, many consumers were reluctant to buy online. Alibaba launched Alipay in 2005 to provide secure transactions on the Taobao platform, despite the lack of a nationwide credit system and weak consumer protection laws. In the beginning, Alipay resembled an escrow service with no transaction fees. When a buyer bought something on Taobao, he made a payment to Alipay. When the payment was received, Taobao notified the seller to ship the item. After the buyer notified Alipay that he had received and was satisfied with the item, Alipay paid the seller in full. If the buyer complained and appealed for a return, he could ship the item back for free and get a full refund from Alipay. This built up merchant and customer trust in the Taobao platform, which created a strong network effect that led to the rapid growth of the platform. The time between when the funds were received by Alipay and then either released to the seller or refunded to the buyer was around seven days. As the volume of transactions grew, this escrow money also began generating good interest income. Alipay started as an online payment service exclusive to the Taobao platform and evolved into the world's largest online and mobile payment system by 2014. Increasingly, merchants worldwide are using Alipay to sell directly to consumers in China, and it currently supports transactions in fourteen major foreign currencies.

In 2013, Alipay launched a financial platform called Yu'ebao through which Alipay users deposited extra (*yu'e*) funds, other than for purchases. These were invested in a money market fund managed by the Tian Hong Fund Management Firm. While traditional money market funds required a minimum subscription amount of CN¥1,000, Yu'ebao's requirement was ¥.01. Yu'ebao's annual fee was 0.38 percent, compared to the traditional 0.43 percent. On top of that, dividends were distributed daily, and redemption of funds was very flexible. This attracted many Taobao and Tmall customers (Tmall is Alibaba's second e-commerce platform, selling brand-name items to consumers) to put their savings into Yu'ebao because they could earn more than from the bank. Flexible redemption meant they could freely use the money to pay for a purchase. Yu'ebao's annualized return was around 3.9 percent in 2017. Yu'ebao's fund size grew extremely rapidly, and by the end of the first quarter of 2017, had reached US$170 billion, about 30 percent of China's total money market fund size. Over the years, Alibaba collected large amounts of transaction data from Taobao, Tmall, Alipay, and Yu'ebao, and applied analytics to develop its propriety credit system of customers and small merchants. This gave Alibaba a competitive position to enter the internet personal and small business loan market.

In the United States, instant messaging gained popularity in the late 1990s, with AOL Instant Messenger as the leader in 1997. In late 1999, Tencent entered the market with OICQ, by integrating its instant messaging software for Chinese internet users with services such as paging, chatting, and file sharing. At that time there were numerous instant messaging application software products appearing in China, including AOL Instant Messenger. All these competing products stored users' contact information on their local personal computers (PCs), but OICQ did something different: it stored all users' contact information on its own server. Most internet users in China in those days did not have their own PCs and had to frequent internet cafes to surf the web. OICQ's centralized contact management system enabled users to remain in contact with their friends regardless of which PC they were on. This advantage was crucial to the success of OICQ. Very soon, OICQ became ubiquitous among web servers in internet cafes. This created a positive network effect between the users and the internet cafes, and soon an OICQ (renamed QQ in 2000) account became the de facto online identity for Chinese internet users. In June 2000 QQ recorded 10 million users, with no revenue.

At that time in China, it was impossible for internet service providers to collect fees for their services because they effectively lacked legal protection—the cost of engaging a legal service to collect payment was much too high. In December 2000, China Mobile offered data application services through third-party providers like Tencent. China Mobile, acting as a fee collection agency for service providers, would collect service fees from customers as part of their monthly phone bill. Tencent introduced Mobile QQ IM (instant messaging) and other wireless value-added services. Through China Mobile's payment system, these services resulted in US$1.5 million net profit for Tencent by the end of 2001. In March 2002, QQ boasted more than 100 million users. Inspired by the China Mobile payment system, Tencent introduced its virtual currency system, Q coins, in May 2002. Users can purchase Q coins by charging their mobile phone bills, through online banking payment systems, and through gift cards sold at convenience stores. Q coins can then be used to purchase QQ-related products and services online. QQ's popularity has resulted in Q coins becoming broadly accepted by online stores and gaming sites. Leveraging its massive user base, Tencent developed a set of microtransaction businesses. QQ Avatar Show is a good example of one. Each QQ user was provided with a virtual avatar, a cartoon figure wearing only underwear. Users could use Q coins to purchase virtual clothing, accessories, and even background settings from the QQ Show Shop to decorate their avatar figures, which appeared in IM conversation boxes, chatrooms, and QQ bulletin boards. QQ Avatar Show took off among a massive user base who would not want their virtual selves online in underwear. The Avatar Show quickly evolved into a virtual lifestyle as fashion-prone users were keen on trying out different virtual goods on their avatars, goods that typically cost between ¥0.50 and ¥1. Tencent further developed entertainment-oriented services (including games) and products that brought as many real-life elements as possible into the virtual social world. Microtransactions and entertainment services provided Tencent with a sustainable revenue stream. Instead of imitating U.S. internet business models, where revenue was derived mainly from advertising, Tencent developed a unique business model based on microtransactions.

By December 31, 2010, there were 648 million active QQ user accounts. QQ introduced a smartphone chat application, WeChat, in 2011 and by 2017 there were over 900 million active users. WeChat incorporated WeChat Pay, which allows users to make mobile payments and send money between contacts and make payments to vendors through debit or credit cards. In 2017, WeChat Pay had over 600 million active users worldwide.

In both these cases, the success of Chinese creative imitators hinged on their ability to execute and deliver internet services value in China's unique cultural, social, and business environment. In the process, each developed skills to overcome the institutional void and develop a new ecosystem that each leveraged to pivot into new, related businesses that had positive network effects with the original business. Alibaba pivoted from e-commerce to a payment system, and then to financial services. Tencent pivoted from instant messaging to microtransactions, social networking, and mobile payment services. Even though they began as imitators, each created unique ecosystems to transform themselves and establish new identities as major players in multi-related sectors. In all B2C business where the local social, political, cultural, and business environments (including readiness of infrastructure) play an important role in finding the right way to execute and deliver value to local markets, local firms have a competitive advantage. The success of Alibaba, Tencent, Baidu, and Ctrip encouraged many Chinese entrepreneurs to follow the same path: creatively imitate successful U.S. internet B2C businesses in China. A successful internet B2C business is a disruptive innovation, initiated at the firm level, and its coverage is mainly the countries where it has strong market share. This sequence of cross-region creative imitation in internet B2C businesses created the China internet wave, the second disruptive innovation in China. The coverage of this wave is mainly China and thus contributed to its economic growth. Even though the wave started in late 1990, its impact on economic growth did not appear until around 2005, taking off around 2011.

In the latter years of the first decade of the twenty-first century, many young Chinese entrepreneurs with technology backgrounds and the Chinese venture community both embraced the creative imitation of successful U.S. internet businesses in China, essentially forming a grassroots movement in the young, internet-savvy community. Xiaomi disrupted China's smartphone market in 2010 with an internet model applied to a hardware business: Xiaomi leveraged the internet to interact with technology-savvy youth, encouraging them to participate in the design of a smartphone that would meet most of their needs, and then sold it to them at cost, with the goal of building a community that would buy Xiaomi products and services to serve their daily needs. This was the first internet business model that was not a creative imitation. This triggered the "internet thinking" (*hulianwang siwei*) wave in China, starting in 2013. With Premier Li Keqiang's announcement of the "Internet Plus" action plan in 2015, many traditional business leaders were open to the idea of applying internet thinking, mobile technology, the internet of things, and big data to their businesses. The movement also brought an awareness of how advanced technology can sustain business growth. The Chinese government set up technology parks to support the commercialization of advanced technology, including internet, mobile, biotechnology, advanced materials, alternate energy, robotics, cloud computing, and big data analytics.

Is China Ready for the Third Disruptive Innovation?

The main contribution of internet businesses to economic growth is in value-added service sectors like express delivery, wireless services, data services, and payment services. Government-provided data show that China's exports were essentially flat over the five years 2012–16. In 2016, four Chinese internet companies were among the top ten global internet companies as ranked by revenue (Wikipedia). Combining these facts with the curves in figure 2.4, we can conclude that starting from 2008, many traditional businesses in China were facing stagnation, the growth resulting from the first disruption had plateaued, and the sustained economic growth starting in 2010 came from China's second disruptive innovation in internet-related businesses. In 2012, many economists pointed out that China had encountered the middle-income trap in around 2008 (Cai 2012; Woo 2012; Woo et al. 2012). Their arguments were based on historical industry data and government policies at that time. But they did not see that there was another disruptive innovation brewing in the background.

Deng initiated the practice of giving people some freedom for small-scale experimentation. If the outcomes were positive for society, policies would be created to support large-scale implementation; but if the results were negative, government policies would clamp down very quickly. Since Deng, this seems to have become normal practice in Chinese policymaking. Many initiatives by Chinese government leaders are not policies but rather broad guidelines for people to explore and experiment with. The government provides incentives for people to experiment in line with the initiatives, but supporting policies only follow if the experiments prove successful. Therefore, to assess whether China will avoid the middle-income trap, looking at industry trend data, current policies, and government announcements is not enough. These only provide a picture of the nation's economic trend based on its current status. When a disruptive innovation plateaus, the middle-income trap becomes a possibility. Incremental improvement in policies or industry structure will not allow a country to escape the trap. To avoid it, the country needs to initiate or support another disruptive innovation. Therefore, a better way

FIGURE 2.4 China's GDP and production, 1980–2015 (current prices, US$ billions)

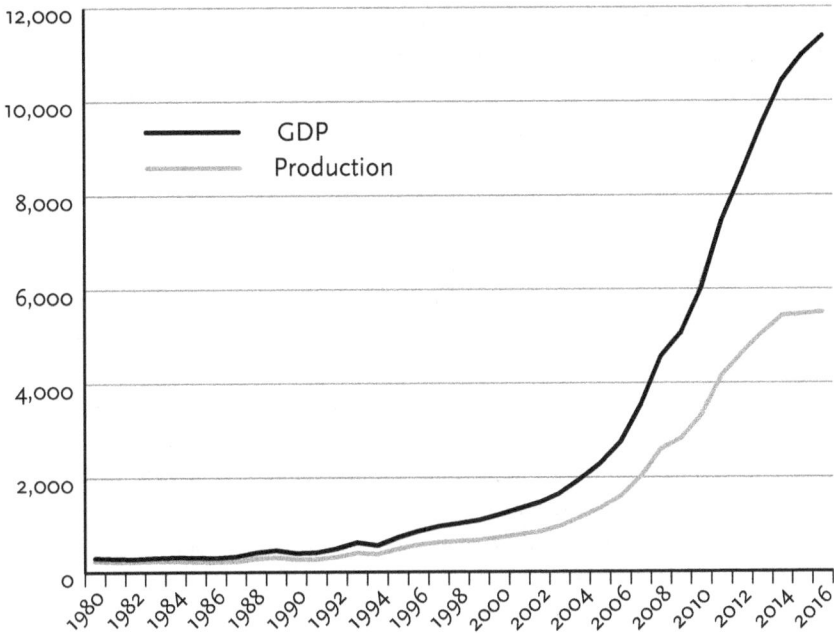

SOURCE: World Bank.
NOTE: GDP = gross domestic product.

to investigate the possibility of China hitting the middle-income trap is to assess whether there is a disruptive innovation brewing in the background. Such an assessment calls for an analysis of the government vision; the mindsets of people and industrialists; industry structure, assets, and abilities; the problems firms are facing; business culture; and so on, all to determine whether the environment is ready to support a certain type of disruptive innovation. If we had applied such an analysis in 2008, the successes of Alibaba, Tencent, and Baidu would have given the indication that an internet-related disruptive innovation was emerging that would enable China to avoid the middle-income trap. In recent years, Chinese internet businesses have been slowing down, and China's GDP growth rate has dropped to between 6 and 7 percent, once again igniting the debate on whether China can avoid the middle-income trap. While most arguments are based on current Chinese government policy, current industry structure, and public statements by Chinese leaders, I shall address the problem by assessing whether there is a third disruptive innovation that is brewing in the background. If so, what is this third wave, and is China ready for it? I shall assess China's current situation from four perspectives: (1) government vision and intentions, (2) industry mindsets and people's mindsets, (3) Chinese industrial structure and problems facing firms, and (4) China's innovation-supporting infrastructure. Based on these, I shall lay out a possible third disruptive innovation path that China is ready to implement.

At the 19th National Congress of the Communist Party of China in October 2017, Xi Jinping put forth a vision of (1) solving basic problems that impact the people's well-being, such as income disparity, environmental pollution, and issues with food safety and healthcare; (2) improving the people's quality of life; (3) building "socialism with Chinese characteristics in a new era"; and (4) the Belt and Road (*yidai yilu*) initiative, which aims to build trade and infrastructure connecting Asia and Europe and Africa along and beyond the Silk Road. There was no concrete policy created to address how to achieve these goals; these were merely guidelines for exploration and experimentation. People and industries that explored and experimented along these guidelines would receive government financial support. Many have made the claim that, due to their culture and educational system, the Chinese people do not excel at creative, outside-the-box thinking. However, this culture and educational system make them very good at thinking creatively in a relatively big box. In 1978, Deng gave the Chinese people a bigger box and mobilized them to think creatively in that box to start China's first disruptive innovation; Xi follows Deng's act, giving the Chinese an even bigger box that hopefully can trigger another disruptive innovation.

Premier Li Keqiang publicly announced the concept of Mass Innovation, Mass Entrepreneurship (*dazhong chuangye, wanzhong chuangxin*) as a new engine for Chinese economic growth in September 2014. Again, this was not a policy but broad guidelines that received government support. More than two thousand incubators (and/or accelerators) were set up in the two years 2014–16 in response to this initiative. It is still not clear whether the Mass Innovation, Mass Entrepreneurship initiative will have much of an effect on China's economic growth. But from my personal interactions with the Chinese people, its impact on their mindsets is clear. In 2008, innovation was considered as a high-risk proposition that, if possible, companies tried to avoid; now every company embraces innovation and is open to the idea of bringing in new technology to find new growth paths. In 2008, the first choice of many young college graduates was to find a stable job in the government or in a large company, and joining a start-up was their last choice when they could not find a job. Parents used to be ashamed to tell others that their children were working in a start-up right after college; now, since Premier Li has told the nation this is the "right path," parents are proud to announce this. This new mindset will have a positive impact on China's preparations for the next disruptive innovation.

Over the last 36 years, three groups of enterprises have been developed in China. The first, SOEs, have access to national resources and have controlled many resource-based businesses and are also strong in infrastructure development and resource management. The second, private enterprises, have engaged in traditional production, manufacturing, and service businesses. They have built up skills in production, technology improvement, incremental innovation, and have developed relationships with value chain members and with the government. The third group, internet-related information technology (IT) businesses, have developed skills in creative imitation (of the United States and across China's regions), overcoming China's institutional void, and developing related businesses with positive network effects. SOEs and private enterprises grew up riding the first wave of disruptive innovation and are mostly practicing incremental innovation. Now facing stagnation, these two groups are actively seeking ways to have a breakthrough. In contrast, internet-related IT businesses grew up by initiating, pushing, and supporting the second wave of disruptive innovation. Many of their leaders feel that the wave may have plateaued and are eager to initiate another new disruptive wave.

To support China's disruptive growth over the past 36 years, an innovation cluster structure was developed. Industrial parks were set up to support the first disruptive innovation in the 1980–90s, while in the 2000s technology parks were set up to support China's second disruptive innovation and high technology commercialization. And most recently, the above-mentioned 2,000-plus incubators were set up in response to Li Keqiang's initiative. These incubators can be broadly categorized into five groups: (1) those supported by local governments, with the objective of fostering regional economic growth; (2) those set up by large enterprises to foster the growth of their ecosystems via innovation; (3) those affiliated with universities and research centers to foster the commercialization of new technologies; (4) those set up by real estate developers, focusing on providing office space and housing for start-ups; and (5) those set up by investors who are imitating the Silicon Valley incubator/accelerator model to source good start-ups. Most incubators provide administrative support, entrepreneurship training, and mentoring, and help in obtaining angel funding. Many of them build linkages with Silicon Valley and other global technology centers in order to source start-ups from overseas Chinese teams with strong technology backgrounds. Many of these incubators, except the second category, are finding that the success rate of new start-ups is low and so are looking at different ways to transform themselves.

With this background, I believe that China is ready to implement a three-pronged disruptive innovation. The first prong continues the practice of the second wave: cross-region creative imitation of successful IT-related disruptive innovations from the United States. More and more young Chinese entrepreneurs with IT backgrounds, not to mention the venture community, have accepted this as a proven model. This momentum will continue and will prolong the economic growth (though slowing) prompted by the second wave, and thus continue to improve people's quality of life. Related activities can be complemented and supported by Chinese incubator clusters and the IT-related device production ecosystem.

There is another trend that is beginning to emerge in China. "Internet thinking" and "Internet Plus" have changed the mindsets of many leaders in traditional businesses facing stagnation. They are eager to find new ways to transform their businesses by adapting new technologies and business model innovations. The new business opportunity open to them is to leverage their core competences, and their understanding of the industry, and to incorporate advanced technologies to solve the basic problems (pollution, food safety, healthcare) created by rapid economic growth over the last nearly four decades. Solutions would require the formation of a dynamic new ecosystem to deal with institutional voids and deliver a new value proposition. This would create opportunities for new start-ups to incrementally innovate new technology products to support the transformation of traditional businesses. It would also stimulate the development of service industries to support a new growth economy. This, then, is the second prong, one that would transform traditional Chinese companies into innovation-based companies. The coverage of this type of disruptive innovation is regional. It would be supported by local governments and would vitalize regional industrial parks, technology parks, and technology incubator clusters, and take around five years for its economic effects to be seen.

The third prong in this third wave of disruption is the promotion of Xi Jinping's grand vision, the Belt and Road initiative. From a purely economic point of view, the initiative's risk is very high. However, the other goal of the initiative is to extend China's influence and enable China to take a larger role in global affairs. Thus, despite the high financial risk, it is expected that China will persist in this initiative. The Belt and Road initiative is similar to China's first disruptive innovation, which drew upon global resources to help China develop its economy; this time China takes the initiative to leverage and extend its experience to draw global resources (including its own) to assist the economic development of other developing countries. In the beginning, large Chinese SOEs in the resource and infrastructure development sectors have been the main players. But the initiative's ultimate success hinges on whether China can gain the trust of these countries, and can extend its skill in cross-region creative imitation and its knowledge in dealing with institutional voids to transfer China's success to countries with different cultural, political, economic, and social environments. One way to achieve this is to establish a platform and encourage local governments, firms, and people to become part of the ecosystem to support this disruptive innovation. This would take more than five years to see economic effects.

China's sustainable economic growth from the first two prongs will give developing countries more confidence in its ability to assist their economic development. If China can successfully help these countries to grow, then their growth will create problems similar to those that China now faces. The solutions developed by Chinese firms in the second prong can be applied to these countries, further strengthening positive network effects to accelerate building the ecosystem needed to support the Belt and Road vision.

Conclusion

Successful economic reform and transformation must occur through structural and institutional change that disrupts the current environment. It is not known from an *ex ante* point of view what structure will be viable under such a disruption. Therefore, the key issue for the reformer is to find out what works, rather than what would be an optimal structure from economic or institutional perspectives. The main difficulty the reformer faces is how to deal with a large group of people who have mindsets contrary to the reformer's vision. Changing their mindsets to align with the reformer's vision is the necessary first step toward successful reform. Changing mindsets is not easy. It cannot be achieved through rational argument, because mindsets are usually based on myths, dogma, ideologies, and past experiences. It can only be achieved gradually after people have positive experiences with the change.

It is interesting to note that Deng Xiaoping successfully changed Chinese mindsets to align with his vision. He then empowered people to use their creativity to implement a local platform that benefits all local players, creating a successful small-scale disruptive innovation. To scale up the success, he implemented national policy to encourage cross-region creative imitation of such solutions and created new institutional structures that steered China slowly from a planned economy to a mix of a planned and market economy. People's mindsets changed gradually as economic growth provided them with positive experiences. Deng developed policy based on proven success rather than formal analysis. In a sense, Deng's success illustrates how an institutional entrepreneur can leverage his political position to change people's mindsets and use small-scale experimentation to overcome institutional pressure and initiate institutional change.

A new business culture slowly formed in China: cross-region creative imitation. This culture naturally led to the second disruptive innovation, as private enterprises with technology backgrounds creatively imitated the internet B2C successes of the United States. In the process, management developed skills and abilities to overcome institutional voids in a developing economy and leapfrog by creating related businesses with positive network effects. Considering the Chinese government's vision, the current world situation, and the Chinese people's mindsets, core assets, and abilities, I believe China is ready to implement a three-pronged disruptive innovation. This would involve, first, creative imitation of successful IT-related disruptive innovations in the United States; second, transforming traditional businesses by adapting new technologies and business model innovations to solve the problems introduced by rapid economic development; and, third, creatively imitating China's first disruptive innovation in developing countries to support the Belt and Road vision.

References

Armstrong, Mark. 2005. "Competition in Two-Sided Markets." Working paper, University College, London.

Cai, Fang. 2012. "Is There a 'Middle Income Trap'? Theories, Experiences and Relevance in China." *China & World Economy* 20, no. 1 (January–February): 49–61.

Chen, Chung, Lawrence Chang, and Yimin Zhang. 1995. "The Role of Foreign Direct Investment in China's Post-1978 Economic Development." *World Development* 23, no. 4 (April): 690–703.

Chen, Xiangming, and Tomas de'Medici. 2009. "The 'Instant City' Coming of Age: China's Shenzhen Special Economic Zone in Thirty Years." Inaugural Working Paper Series No. 2 (Spring), Center for Urban and Global Studies, Trinity College, Hartford, CT.

Christensen, Clayton M. 1997. *The Innovator's Dilemma: When New Technologies Cause Great Firms to Fail.* Boston, MA: Harvard Business Review Press.

———. 2003. *The Innovator's Solution: Creating and Sustaining Successful Growth.* Boston, MA: Harvard Business Press.

DiMaggio, Paul J. 1988. "Interest and Agency in Institutional Theory." In *Institutional Patterns and Organizations: Culture and Environment,* edited by Lynne G. Zucker, 3–21. Cambridge, MA: Ballinger.

Eisenstadt, Shmuel N. 1980. "Cultural Orientations, Institutional Entrepreneurs and Social Change: Comparative Analysis of Traditional Civilization." *American Journal of Sociology* 85, no. 4: 840–69.

Headey, Derek, Ravi Kanbur, and Xiaobo Zhang. 2009. "China's Growth Strategy." In *Governing Rapid Growth in China: Equity and Institutions,* edited by Ravi Kanbur and Xiaobo Zhang. New York: Routledge.

Hu, Zuliu, and Mohsin S. Khan. 1997. "Why Is China Growing So Fast?" *IMF Economic Issues* no. 8, International Monetary Fund, Washington, DC.

Johnson, Mark G., Clayton M. Christensen, and Henning Kagermann. 2008. "Reinventing Your Business Model." *Harvard Business Review* (December).

Kanbur, Rari, and Xiaobo Zhang, eds. 2009. *Governing Growth in China: Equity and Institution.* London: Routlege.

Khanna, Tarun, and Krishna Palepu. 2010. *Winning in Emerging Markets: A Road Map for Strategy and Execution.* Boston, MA: Harvard Business Press.

Lau, Lawrence, Yingyi Qian, and Gérard Roland. 2000. "Reform without Losers: An Interpretation of China's Dual-Track Approach to Transaction." *Journal of Political Economy* 108, no. 1: 120–43.

Lin, Justin Yifu. 1987. "The Household Responsibility System Reform in China: A Peasant's Institutional Choice." *American Journal of Agricultural Economics* 69, no. 2: 410–15.

Lin, Justin Yifu, Fang Cai, and Zhou Li. 1996. *The China Miracle: Developing Strategy and Economic Reform*. Hong Kong: Chinese University Press.

Qian, Yingyi, and Chenggang Xu. 1993. "Why Chinese's Economic Reforms Differ: The M-Form Hierarchy and Entry/Expansion of the Non-State Sector." *Economics of Transition* 1, no. 2: 135–70.

Rochet, Jean-Charles, and Jean Tirole. 2003. "Platform Competition in Two-Sided Markets." *Journal of the European Economic Association* 1, no. 4: 990–1029.

Roson, Roberto. 2005. "Two-Sided Markets: A Tentative Survey." *Review of Network Economics* 4, no. 2: 142–60.

Sachs, Jeffrey D., and Wing Thye Woo. 1997. "Understanding China's Economic Performance." NBER Working Paper 5935, National Bureau of Economic Research, Cambridge, MA, February.

Sun, Mingchun, and Edison Tse. 2007a. "Sustainable Growth of Payment Card Network: A Two-Sided Market Approach." *Journal of Business Strategies* 24, no. 2: 165–91.

———. 2007b. "When Does the Winner Take All in Two-Sided Markets?" *Review of Network Economics* 6, no. 1: 16–40.

Tse, Edison (Desun Xie). 2012. *Yuan chuangxin: Zhuanxing qi de Zhongguo qiye chuangxin zhi dao* [Disruptive innovation]. Beijing: Wuzhou Communication Publishing.

———. 2016. *Chongxin dingyi chuangxin* [Redefining innovation]. Beijing: CITIC Press.

Wang, Yan, and Yudong Yao. 2003. "Sources of China's Economic Growth 1952–1999: Incorporating Human Accumulation." *China Economic Review* 14, no. 1: 32–52.

Woo, Wing Thye. 2012. "China Meets the Middle-Income Trap: The Large Potholes in the Road to Catching-Up." *Journal of Chinese Economic and Business Studies* 10, no. 4: 313–36.

Woo, Wing Thye, Ming Lu, Jeffrey D. Sachs, and Zhao Chen, eds. 2012. *A New Economic Growth Engine for China: Escaping the Middle-Income Trap by Not Doing More of the Same*. London: Imperial College Press.

Zhu, Kangdui. 2010. "Narratives of Wenzhou's Industrial Privatization." In *Narratives of Chinese Economic Reform: How Does China Cross the River*, edited by Xiaobo Zhang, Arjun de Haan, and Shenggen Fan, 91–114. Singapore: World Scientific Pub. Co.

CHAPTER 3

From "Produce and Protect" to Promoting Private Industry

The Indian State's Role in Creating a Domestic Software Industry

Dinsha Mistree

G overnment policies have historically hampered innovation and eco-nomic growth in India. From its independence in 1947 through the 1970s, the Indian government sought to foster a planned economy where state-owned enterprises (SOEs) and a small set of private-sector busi-ness groups would receive market protections.[1] But unlike the developmental states in East Asia, where state-led initiatives resulted in industrialization and new possibilities for innovation, the Indian state ultimately proved unable to direct such an economic transformation.[2] In the early 1980s the government began dismantling the License Raj, and this process culminated in economic liberalization in 1991.

---

1 India suffered slow growth rates from its independence in 1947 until 1980. This is widely considered to be the result of poor government policies brought about through centralized planning. For a review, see Rodrik and Subramanian (2005).
2 Many excellent studies have examined the developmental state miracles of South Korea and Taiwan. For Korea, see Amsden (1989) and Evans (1995); for Taiwan, see Wade (1990). For an insightful comparative perspective on both Korea and India, see Kohli (2004).

The author would like to acknowledge Kris Gopalakrishnan for a helpful conversation as well as the editors of this volume for insightful feedback.

Since that time, the Indian economy has grown fast on balance, yet in an uneven manner. India's working population is mostly employed in an agricultural sector that has experienced anemic growth over this time period, in no small part due to government institutions that continue to discourage market reforms and policies that suppress technological innovation. As a result, the percentage of value added to the economy from agriculture has been going down since 1980, with agriculture being responsible for about 16 percent of the value added to the economy as of 2019 (see figure 3.1). The industrial sector has done slightly better as it has generally kept pace with overall economic growth, but it contributes only about 25 percent of the value added to the economy. Instead of relying on agriculture or industry, however, India has become a service-sector economy, with about 60 percent of the value added to its growing economy coming from services.

FIGURE 3.1 Value added to the Indian economy by sector, 1960–2019

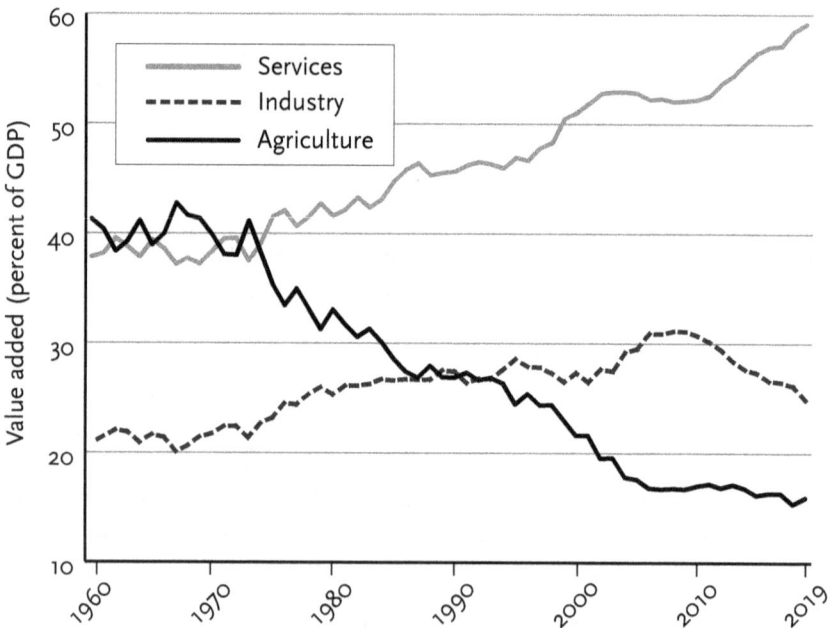

SOURCE: World Bank's World Development Indicators (WDI).
NOTE: Services were calculated by subtracting agriculture and industry from 100. The WDI's services measure was not used as it excludes ISIC divisions 46–49, which cover wholesale trade, retail trade, and land transport or transport via pipeline. These ISIC divisions have traditionally been categorized as services. GDP = gross domestic product.

Why has India's service sector flourished? In this chapter, I examine its crown jewel: India's software industry. As with other Indian industries, innovation and growth in the software industry suffered under government control from the 1960s to the 1980s. When reforms came to the industry in 1984, however, private companies in the software industry—including several independent start-ups that were not affiliated with India's business groups—did not want the state to adopt a laissez-faire approach. While they celebrated the end of *protective* regulations that were designed to aid SOEs, the private software industry successfully pushed for government policies that would *promote* industrywide innovation and growth. Among these promotional policies, the central government expanded its already considerable investment in technical higher education and developed a telecommunications infrastructure that would enable software export services, while state and local governments created technology parks that would provide office space, constant electricity, and clean water. Some of these parks—like Electronic City in Bangalore—also became model innovation clusters along the lines of those described by Lee and Kim later in this volume (chapter 7).

Following the shift in government policy in the 1980s, the growth of the software industry has been profound. Software exports grew at a blistering 33 percent annual compounded rate from 1990 to 2015 (see table 3.1). Today several of India's largest companies are software exporters, including Tata Consultancy Services (TCS), India's largest publicly traded company by market capitalization. Within software exports, the information technology/business process management segment contributes between 8 to 10 percent of the entire country's gross domestic product.[3] Apart from software exports, almost every leading technology company in the world has at least one research and development facility in India. Put simply, a technology services ecosystem has emerged that will probably determine the course of India's economic future in the twenty-first century.

The development of India's software industry is an economic miracle in a country not known for such success stories. What explains its comparative success? I argue that the industry's growth is partly due to the government's decision to shift from a state-led model whose priorities were to "produce and protect," to a pattern of broad-based industry promotion. Following the decision to abandon its produce-and-protect model, the government could have struck a different path: it could have adopted a laissez-faire approach to the industry or it could have identified a few private-sector firms to become national champions. Instead, government policies aided the industry as a whole rather than privileging national champions. As a result, the Indian software industry is a vibrant and innovative ecosystem that potentially provides important lessons for other industries in India and elsewhere.

---

3   National Association of Software and Services Companies (NASSCOM) India, various years, compiled by Statista.

TABLE 3.1 Gross Indian software export earnings

Year	Total exports (US$ millions)	Compounded annual growth rate (%)
1980	4	—
1985	27.7	47.26
1989–90	105.4	30.64
1994–95	480.9	35.47
1999–2000	4,000	52.76
2004–05	17,700	34.64
2009–10	50,000	23.08
2014–15	98,000	14.41
2017–18	125,000*	8.45*

SOURCE: Pre-1995 data come from interviews compiled by Heeks (1996), and from Sharma (1995); post-1995 data come from annual reports of the Department of Economics.
NOTE: *projected figures.

This chapter proceeds as follows. First, I present the history of the software industry from its beginnings to 1984. During this time, the Indian government sought to centrally plan the economy. For the electronics sector (of which the software industry was a part), this meant that the government sought to throttle competition from foreign entities and even from India's own private sector in favor of new SOEs. Next, I present the causes and consequences of the 1984 New Computer Policy. This policy essentially signaled that the government was abandoning the priorities of "produce and protect." Over the next several years, the government would focus on the *promotion* of industry. I conclude with a discussion of why the software industry succeeded. Other scholars have suggested that the success of the industry is due to the government's retreat from policymaking. Even though ending the produce-and-protect model was certainly healthy for the software industry, the government's promotional policies also clearly played an important role in the industry's success. Similar kinds of promotional policies could aid other innovation-driven industries in India and elsewhere.

The 1960s to 1984: Produce and Protect

At a high level, states can pursue any of four strategies for fostering an infant industry. They can directly *produce* by creating an SOE; or they can pick winners, usually by creating *protective* regulations that privilege a specific player or a few players; or they can *promote* the industry as a whole, usually by reducing the costs on input materials or by waiving taxes; or they can simply do nothing (laissez-faire).[4] Postwar industrialization has usually involved government protection. In chapter 9 of this volume, Moon and Lee examine the relationship between firm size and innovation across six East Asian countries. Economies with planned capitalist models like Taiwan, South Korea, and Japan saw their governments protect a few key private-sector players as they pursued industrialization. By contrast, successful free-market economies like Hong Kong and Singapore tend to focus on service sectors like finance and trade. These different starting points carry important implications for firm size and innovation policy.

Government officials in India initially pursued the first two strategies of production and protection in the country's pursuit of economic development. Production and protection manifested in centralized planning, which was initially beneficial to the computing sector as government resources could be steered toward expensive start-up investments. Indeed, it was two technocrats who initially recognized the importance of computing for the future course of the country. In Kolkata (known at the time as Calcutta), the Indian Statistical Institute, under the direction of P.C. Mahalanobis, built an analog computer in 1953 and acquired a digital computer from Britain in 1956, along with another digital computer from the Soviet Union in 1958 (see Menon 2018). These computers would be used for processing government data related to economic planning. In 1960, the Tata Institute for Fundamental Research (TIFR) in Mumbai (known at the time as Bombay) formally commissioned India's first digital computer under the direction of Homi J. Bhabha, a leading atomic scientist working within the Indian government.[5]

At around the same time, the central government also decided to partner with the United Nations Educational, Scientific and Cultural Organization (UNESCO), the Soviet Union, West Germany, the United States, and the United Kingdom to build five Indian Institutes of Technology (IITs) across India. At IIT-Kanpur—the campus that was founded with U.S. support—the U.S. government and the Ford Foundation worked with local academics to create the first educational programs in computing. IIT-Kanpur imported the IBM 1620 in August 1963, becoming the first campus in the country to use a computer with a FORTRAN compiler.[6] Professor Harry Husky of the University

---

4   This framework is adapted from Evans (1992). Evans uses slightly different terms and argues that the Indian state never adopted a laissez-faire approach to the electronics sector, but instead shifted from producing and protecting to promoting private industry.
5   After building its first computer, TIFR decided to buy computers from the foreign private sector instead; see Rajaraman (2015).
6   Because Indian programmers learned FORTRAN, subsequent mainstream computer languages including C were much easier to learn; see Rajaraman (2015).

of California, Berkeley, along with Professors Forman Acton and Irving Rabinowitz from Princeton, came along for the first two years to set up the computer and establish the first programming classes at Kanpur, which were made mandatory for all engineering students. By 1965, there were at least 15 digital computers spread across the country, mostly at central government research agencies and technical institutes.

Because of initiatives like the one at IIT-Kanpur, a growing number of Indians were learning to program computers. An even larger number of Indians were quickly recognizing the potential promise of computing. Among this latter group was Lalit Kanodia, a 1963 graduate of IIT-Bombay. Following his graduation, Kanodia enrolled in an MBA program at the Massachusetts Institute of Technology (MIT). After completing his MBA in 1965, Kanodia went home for the summer before starting the PhD program at MIT. During his break, he fell in love and sought to get married. The priest informed the couple that there were no auspicious dates for marriage in the summer and so Kanodia decided to defer his studies for a term. While waiting in India, he approached P. M. Agerwala, the managing director of Tata Electric Companies, who suggested he write some papers on how the Tata Group could utilize computers. Kanodia suggested that the Electric Companies should automate their load dispatch system, computerize their billing system by buying computer time from TIFR, and launch an enterprise that he called the Tata Computer Centre. After making these three suggestions, Kanodia returned to MIT in January 1966.

The Tata Group decided to act on all three suggestions and recruited Kanodia to start the Tata Computer Centre. Kanodia convinced two of his Indian classmates from MIT to join and together they started the company in 1967 by leasing two IBM computers. In 1968, this company was renamed Tata Consultancy Services (TCS).[7]

TCS would become one of the first indigenous, privately owned companies to operate in the computing space in India, but while other Indian business groups were avoiding the computer sector, foreign companies were also establishing themselves.[8] By the mid-1960s, IBM already had a thriving hardware computer business in the country and was consolidating its position as an industry leader. To get around restrictions on foreign production, IBM and

---

7   Kanodia (2012) suggests that government officials found it difficult to control software exports, discussing how several customs collectors came to his office to understand how software is exported, presumably so that they could interfere in its operations, but were unable to do so.

8   Another private company, Hinditron, was founded by Hemant Sonawala in 1966. Sonawala used to work for Digital Equipment Corporation (DEC) in the United States and his company sold their equipment.

a British company named International Computers Limited applied to the Indian government to produce computers in India. After striking a deal with the Indian government, IBM would import used computers, refurbish them in Mumbai, and then rent them to Indian customers for as much as US$190,000 per year (Rajaraman 2015, 30). As the computers that it was providing were of lower quality than what was available in the United States, IBM was soon accused of profiteering by some government officials. IBM responded by arguing that in the United States they merely sold computers whereas a customer in India would get computing services as well: IBM provided regular maintenance services as well as systems engineers who could analyze data processing and would even assist in programming. IBM recruited and trained Indians to fill these technical roles, generating what would become the first generation of Indian IT consultants.

As a foreign firm, IBM would have to continuously pay close attention to the government officials in charge of centralized planning for the emerging computing industry. As IBM's refurbished computers and domestic IT consultants spread across India, the central government was seeking to craft a comprehensive industrial policy for electronics. There were many factors to consider. Chief among these was whether India should produce computer hardware domestically or import the hardware and focus on software development. In 1963, the central government formed a committee, with Homi Bhabha as its chairman, to craft a government plan for electronics. A subcommittee led by R. Narasimhan was tasked with making a plan for computers; this subcommittee recommended to the government that large computers should be imported, but smaller computers should be manufactured locally. After taking into account the views of academics, military officials, leaders at government laboratories, and a small number of leaders in the private sector, this decision became government policy (Rajaraman 2015).

Official planning reports take time as a variety of constituents have to be consulted, and the Bhabha Committee on Electronics would not complete its report until 1966. But Bhabha was killed in a plane crash before formally submitting the report, delaying the implementation of some recommendations. Apart from shaping a policy on computer imports, the committee also called for the establishment of a new SOE, the Electronics Corporation of India Limited (ECIL). A new Department of Electronics (DOE) would oversee ECIL, which would broadly be in charge of planning the development of the computer industry (Heeks 1996).

As a result of the Bhabha Committee's report, India's electronics policy largely followed the import substitution model being applied in many other Indian industries at the time. The DOE and the central government placed high tariffs on computers and computer parts and enacted cumbersome strictures on the release of foreign exchange for acquiring computers or software. But unlike typical import substitution models, the DOE also put into place policies that hampered private domestic development. Private domestic computer manufacturers faced foreign exchange and capital restrictions, caps on production quotas (to protect against any one player gaining too much market share), government bans on producing the best computers (for instance, private manufacturers were banned from producing 32-bit machines, which could only be manufactured by ECIL until 1984), and private manufacturers were unfavorably considered for government contracts.

This strong preference for SOEs over the private sector was unique. In other sectors, privately owned business groups like Tata, Birla, and Godrej were oftentimes the beneficiaries of such restrictive policies. Such business groups would often be given individual exceptions, enabling them to monopolize certain markets. In the computing industry, on the other hand, the protectionist policies that the government imposed were mostly designed to aid state-owned electronics companies (see Khanna and Palepu 2005).

There were at least two reasons why business groups did not hold the same sway in the computing industry as they enjoyed in the rest of the economy. First, most business groups had not recognized the importance of computing by the 1970s. The only major business group with an electronics company in the 1960s and 1970s was Tata. In the early years of TCS, the company could sustain itself by focusing on computerizing Tata's other companies and was not interested in manufacturing hardware. It relied on IBM machines and eventually partnered with Burroughs, a British computer-manufacturing firm. As a result, TCS was not focused on computer manufacturing so much as it was focused on services. Second and related, the government's main policymakers came from a close and well-connected academic and government network, not from industry. They did not privilege domestic business groups because they did not come from domestic business groups. Instead, they understood and believed in government research agencies like TIFR, academic institutions like the IITs, and SOEs like ECIL.

Unfortunately for India's central planners, coordinating production and promotion efforts across so many different levels of government and across so many different ministries proved difficult. Even though ECIL was intended to be the flagship SOE in the computing space, several other central government ministries and departments also sought to create computer companies (Heeks 1996). By the mid-1980s there were more than a dozen different central government enterprises in this space. Further complicating matters, a number of state governments also set up their own SOEs. For instance, Kerala formed Keltron in 1973—which was supposed to develop semiconductors—and the state of Uttar Pradesh created a data processing company known as Uptron

Powertronics in 1977. State-level initiatives like these drew talented workers and government resources away from companies like ECIL and the Computer Maintenance Corporation (CMC), while also bringing more competition to what was supposed to be a protected industry.

In typical developmental states like South Korea or Taiwan, a regulatory policy that was set by a high-level committee would be followed closely. Coordination between governmental agencies was virtually assured, as there was usually a clear hierarchy of power. As other scholars have noted about state planning in India, however, disparate groups with their own power bases have frequently complicated regulatory policy (Kohli 2004). State-led development of the electronics sector was no different. The plans for supporting state-led computer manufacturing would fall prey to the same problems that afflicted much of the rest of the License Raj. At the same time as the Bhabha Committee was enacting its report, another government committee, initially chaired by R. Venkataraman and then by V. M. Dandekar, warned that automation brought on by computers would threaten employment and the central government. In 1972, this committee introduced strict controls on public or private computer adoption, including a policy requiring labor to approve the introduction of computers in any organization. Such restrictions made the adoption of computers much more difficult, which further reduced the domestic market for computing. It is unlikely that such restrictions would have been implemented in a state with a more coordinated government.

The decisions of the Dandekar Committee reveal how the nascent software industry was unable to check other powerful interests. A simple lack of coordination among government actors clearly affected the infant computing sector. By the early 1970s, computer technology outside of India was progressing rapidly. The Indian central planning approach, with its cumbersome procedures and internal political divisions, was already causing a constant stream of problems. For instance, computer prices outside of India were dramatically falling with the development of large-scale integrated circuits, which are enabled by semiconductors. Government and industry leaders decided that a domestic semiconductor industry would first have to be developed before a hardware computing industry could form. They immediately announced restrictions on the import of semiconductors or integrated circuits. Building an industry would take time, however. The DOE formed a committee to create a semiconductor industry in 1971, and a report was issued two years later, in 1973. Progress on implementing the semiconductor policy was slow and ground to a halt when Indira Gandhi suspended democracy and declared a state of emergency (commonly called "the Emergency" in India) for 19 months, beginning in 1975. As a result, the DOE made no serious step toward fostering a semiconductor industry until

1978 (Subramanian 1992). With government protections in place to create a semiconductor industry—but with no movement toward creating such an industry—private domestic manufacturers could not get integrated circuits. ECIL was given an exception and could use foreign integrated circuits, but it never scaled its production volume. As a result, from 1971 to 1978, ECIL sold 98 computers, with all but four machines being sold to government departments and universities that were required to purchase ECIL machines. Today, India is an international leader in semiconductor research and design, but semiconductor manufacturing is dominated by companies operating in East Asia.

Apart from its own internal failings, international headwinds also hampered the formation of the Indian computing industry in the 1970s. In 1971, India and Pakistan went to war. For a variety of geostrategic reasons that are beyond the scope of this chapter, the United States aligned with Pakistan instead of India. India was already limiting computer imports, but the Nixon administration placed embargoes on electronics and computer imports from the United States. Also, the cooperative relationship that India had enjoyed with American technology experts was dramatically affected. For instance, the Kanpur Indo-American Programme that brought American technology experts to IIT-Kanpur was supposed to be renewed in early 1972 but was instead canceled. India conducted its first nuclear tests in 1974, leading to further embargoes on high-end computers and software.[9]

India also faced a huge currency problem during the 1970s owing to a poorly managed domestic economy, combined with a spike in global oil prices. Indira Gandhi nationalized the country's banks in 1969, which restricted the flow of domestic capital; at the beginning of 1974, the Foreign Exchange Regulation Act also came into effect, basically enabling the government to acquire all foreign exchange in the country (including foreign exchange owned by residents) and requiring the Reserve Bank of India to sign off on all transactions involving foreign exchange. Acquiring computers or computer parts from abroad became almost impossible, although companies did try. Patni Computers, for instance, had partnered with an American firm called Data General to sell that company's minicomputers in India. To get around the foreign exchange restrictions, in the late 1970s Patni hired twelve programmers to add value by writing software on top of Data General's systems. The company's focus shifted from the onerous business of selling minicomputers to software development services and in

---

9   The United Nations Development Programme continued to fund technology initiatives with the central government. This money was used to create the National Centre for Software Development and Computing Techniques in 1972 and the National Informatics Centre in 1975, for instance.

1980, eight of these programmers split off from Patni to form Infosys, one of India's biggest software consulting companies (Yost 2017).

Also, according to the 1974 Act, all international companies that were not considered "essential" by the central government would have to dilute their equity to 40 percent and take an Indian partner. This condition would have a huge impact on IBM (Khanna and Palepu 2005). IBM thought that it would be able to secure "essential" status as its installations were spread across several important public- and private-sector locations. IBM also conveyed to the central government that it would set up exporting operations and would use 26 percent of its in-country profits to develop a research and development center in India (Subramanian 1992). IBM began what it thought would be quick negotiations with the central government in 1974; of course, Indira Gandhi declared Emergency from 1975 to 1977 and subsequently lost the 1977 election. An opposition government led by Morarji Desai came into power, derailing IBM's negotiations with the government. By 1978, it became clear to IBM that it would have to accede to dilution or leave the Indian market. Figuring that problems like these would continue, IBM decided to leave the Indian market.

IBM sold its in-country computers to Indian customers at cut-rate prices. Just as important, the company left behind its maintenance workers and programming consultants as well. Many of IBM's ex–computer maintenance workers went to work for a government company called the Computer Maintenance Corporation (CMC), but ex-IBMers also started their own software companies or went to work for other domestic computer companies.

1984 to the Present: The Promotion Era

The Indian government had sought to create a centrally planned electronics industry, one where SOEs would drive growth for the entire industry. To help these SOEs, the government stifled the domestic private sector and all but eliminated any foreign competition. These policies were ultimately disastrous as the government was unable to effectively coordinate its production and protection policies. Yet poor policies can only be changed when there is political appetite for such reforms. For the electronics sector as a whole—and the software sector in particular—reforms began in 1984, seven years before the rest of the economy would be liberalized. In this section, I present the political circumstances that led to this transition.

Indira Gandhi and the Congress Party came back to power in 1980, this time with her son, Rajiv, prepared to play a prominent role in government. As it would turn out, he would also play a significant role in the growth of the computer industry. In 1982, Rajiv Gandhi oversaw the organization of the Asian Games in Delhi, and he reached out to various technology advisors for help, including several of the leaders of the DOE. The Games—and the computer programs that the organizers utilized—proved to be highly successful, and by the time Rajiv ascended to the prime ministership in October 1984, he was simultaneously aware of the enormous potential of computers as well as the government-generated challenges that the industry was facing.

Rajiv came to power committed to ending centralized economic planning. Unlike many other Indian politicians of the time, Rajiv had traveled extensively through the West. He had studied in Great Britain and had an Italian wife. In 1970, he announced to his family that he would make a career as a commercial pilot for Indian Airlines. For the next ten years, Rajiv would explore the world. This international exposure shaped his economic orientation.

Just as important, Rajiv came to power with no political debts. He was never supposed to enter politics. Instead, his younger brother, Sanjay, was being groomed to inherit the family's political legacy. When Sanjay died in an aircraft accident in 1980, however, Rajiv was thrust into the family business. In 1981, he was given a reliable Congress Party seat and three short years later he found himself the prime minister of India.

Rajiv's quick rise to power was the result of being born to Indira Gandhi, not of shrewd political alignments or even a charismatic ability to move crowds. Riding a wave of sympathy following his mother's assassination, Rajiv's Congress Party won 404 of the 543 seats in Parliament, more than Indira Gandhi or Jawaharlal Nehru had ever managed to win. Kohli eloquently describes the political environment following Rajiv's ascendancy:

> The considerable sense of power, and the hurry in which it had been acquired, must have created a sense among the new rulers that they had hijacked the state. The state suddenly stood quite autonomously, free of societal constraints, ready to be used as a tool for imposing economic rationality on society. Situations of state autonomy like this always encourage the powerful to pursue their ideological whims. (Kohli 1989, 312)

Less than a month after coming to power, in 1984 Rajiv's government announced the New Computer Policy that would end central planning for the industry. Instead of seeking to protect SOEs, the government would now seek to promote private manufacturers and software developers. Private hardware manufacturers would now be able to make 32-bit machines and would no longer be subject to manufacturing limits. Crucially, the new government policy also allowed the importation of assembled boards with microprocessors and boards with interface electronics.

This decision essentially got the Indian state out of the produce-and-protect mode and into private-sector promotion. But the government would now be promoting two industries. In addition to computer hardware, the 1984 New Computer Policy sought to support private companies that were in allied fields, specifically assembly, system integration, and "software development and services," the latter officially becoming a recognized industry. This recognition allowed private companies to get loans from banks and claim duty exemptions; it also exempted software from excise duties. Engineers who went abroad to develop and maintain software for clients, along with the profits they earned, were considered "software exports" and were exempted from duties as well.

Rajiv installed new leaders at the DOE who were much friendlier with the private sector, including foreign firms. From the late 1970s, Indian expats were serving in executive ranks at various U.S. multinational firms and were debating whether to locate computer operations in India. Many of these expats had come from the IITs and knew about the talented workforce in the country, but they also knew the inhospitable political environment that foreign companies faced, especially after IBM's hasty exit from the country in 1978. These political considerations kept American foreign firms out. With the new regime, American firms sought to test Rajiv's appetite for openness. In 1985, Citibank approached the Indian government with a proposal to set up a private satellite link between its U.S. operations and its office in the Santa Cruz Export Processing Zone in Mumbai. The satellite link would be used to help Indian software engineers work remotely with their American counterparts, essentially enabling software outsourcing. The government agreed, and Citibank's software sales began to skyrocket. Shortly afterward, Texas Instruments asked for permission to establish a satellite link between its headquarters in Dallas and a new offshore software development center in Bangalore; again, the government agreed. N. Seshagiri, one of the original Bhabha Committee members who had ultimately become Rajiv's main advisor on electronics, would subsequently boast, "We broke 26 separate rules to accommodate TI's [Texas Instruments'] Bangalore subsidiary and are willing to break more!"[10] Dozens of other multinationals would soon strike similar arrangements.

In 1986, the DOE announced the Computer Software Export, Software Development, and Training Policy. Export-oriented software companies could now import computers duty-free, provided that these could generate 250 percent of their cost within four years, while regulations on the

---

10   Evans 1992, 7, quoting SIPA News (Silicon Valley Indian Professionals Association Newsletter), 1988.

domestic-oriented use of imported hardware were also lightened. Software imports went from a system of quotas to tariff protection, enabling anyone to import if they paid a 60 percent import duty. Such a move maintained some protections on domestic markets but was probably designed to simultaneously enable software exporters to buy and build on foreign software packages. Foreign exchange was made available via annual rather than separate permits for each transaction, reducing the amount of licensing processing that an export-oriented software company would have to undergo. Just as important, the central government allowed software developed in India to be exported using satellite and cable communication systems. Foreign firms had their own dedicated satellite links, and the government decided to build a system to provide domestic firms with satellite access as well. The government also gave software exporters access to Indonet, a network of IBM mainframes across the country that the government would maintain and expand. Almost overnight, the government had switched from strangling private software firms to embracing them.[11]

At least three important factors made these reforms easier to implement, or at least minimized the forces of resistance that derailed reforms in other industries. First and foremost, private software companies sought to remove protections across the board. No individual company or business group wanted protection; indeed, no major business group had a company in computer hardware and only Tata had a stake in the software industry via TCS and Tata Unisys Ltd. But Tata's software companies had never relied on government concessions to the extent that its parent business group had

---

11   Perhaps the only area where the central government showed any continuity with the past was its commitment to educating a growing class of software developers. In 1986, new computer science programs were forming all over the country and the government was training teachers and professors who could instruct in software development. The central government was also continuing to fund academic research, usually in partnership with the United Nations Development Programme. To provide just a few examples, between 1984 and 1986, it funded programs in computer-aided design, computer-assisted management programming, advanced computing, and knowledge-based computer system development. Meanwhile, several research initiatives were taking place in parallel computing and computer networking, which would position Indian software engineers for the meteoric rise of the internet and the World Wide Web.

benefited from in other industries.[12]

By 1984, leaders in the software industry also recognized that the domestic demand for software services was miniscule compared to the enormous potential of foreign markets. Software providers in the domestic market lacked serious piracy or intellectual property protections. Anti-piracy software laws did not exist until 1984 and were likely to go unenforced. At the same time, software firms had experimented with exporting services. When government restrictions were minimized, Indian firms knew that they could offer cheaper services compared to their competitors. Keeping foreign entrants out of the Indian market was not a huge priority for Tata or other software players: the domestic market was simply not that appealing compared to foreign markets. The private sector wanted the government to reduce protective regulations. Rather than substituting an SOE national champion for one from the private sector, it wanted the government to pursue policies that would benefit the industry and the ecosystem as a whole.

For the government's part, there was sincere high-level political commitment to reforming the computing sector. A second factor that led to these reforms was a small set of technocrats within the government who believed that things needed to change. The same DOE that had previously taken nearly nine years to come up with a plan for the semiconductor industry was now run by leaders who would present a new software policy three weeks after Rajiv Gandhi came to power. In Rajiv, these reformers found a politician who was as eager to reform the sector as they were.

Many politicians have come to power promising reform, only to be stymied by larger political forces. However, in his early years, Rajiv was able to pursue a series of reforms because of his strong popularity. Following his mother's assassination, Rajiv won a huge majority in the 1984 national elections and did not have to make many political compromises to rise to power. This allowed him to pursue an ideological agenda that was broadly supportive of economic reform.

Rajiv's eagerness for reform was widely known, but ideological whims had to give way to political exigencies a few short years into his rule. During his

---

12   For the most part, the DOE practices sought to privilege government enterprises at the expense of all private actors, large and small. One such legacy example comes in 1989, after the initial liberalization reforms. TCS and an SOE named CMC Limited were both competing for a bid to computerize the Bombay Stock Exchange. TCS's bid was weakened when the DOE refused to approve the import of the computer hardware that TCS had proposed using, and CMC won the bid. This action was met with some surprise by the Indian industry, but was standard practice before 1984. Indeed, perhaps the only true "loser" from these reforms were state-owned companies, like CMC and ECIL, who had previously benefited the most from market protections.

tenure as prime minister, Rajiv tried to end central planning in other industries—and even spoke of dismantling India's License Raj altogether—but he was otherwise unable to translate desires into policy. The old guard within his own Congress Party was skeptical and Rajiv soon found out that the trade unions—an important Congress ally—also took a strong anti-computerization stance.[13] In the first years of his administration, Rajiv had the popular support and the political power to check these challengers.[14] But following its commanding victory in 1984, Rajiv's Congress Party subsequently lost a series of state elections, including the Haryana elections in May 1987. Additionally, several corruption scandals weakened Rajiv's political standing, including the Bofors scandal, which implicated Rajiv and many members of his inner circle for accepting kickbacks on military equipment. At the time, Haryana was a Congress stronghold and this loss returned India to a "'muddle through' model of economic policymaking" (Kohli 1989, 311). Following this loss, Rajiv and his advisors had to adopt a more populist outlook that was tolerant of central planning. Rajiv increasingly had to rely on the political support of his party, including the old guard, who mostly supported central planning. Pragmatic political considerations would have to trump ideology.

By 1987, Rajiv's focus was on winning elections, but in 1989, the Congress Party lost its majority and was unable to form a government. For just the second time in India's history, the Congress Party was relegated to the opposition. No one political party was able to maintain control despite several attempts, and national elections were called in 1991.

Software industry policymaking from 1987 to 1991 has been likened to a "headless chicken" (Heeks 1996, 331). Because of the larger political circumstances, Rajiv and other politicians would not give the industry much attention. Also, for political reasons, the technocrats who oversaw the DOE were removed and replaced with generalist bureaucrats who had limited understanding of the software space. As a result, policy directives were formed by the strongest coalition of interests with no larger vision or planned direction. Software companies quickly figured out how to successfully

---

13   This decision was made by the Rangarajan Committee, which also recommended that banks adopt UNIX as the standard operating system. Many software companies developed their UNIX skills because of this recommendation, which was fortuitous as the UNIX market would become very large. By 1994 UNIX work was estimated to make up between 15 to 20 percent of India's software exports.

14   The computer industry also received broad public support as well. The galvanizing moment came in 1986, when Indian Railways computerized its ticket reservation systems. The new program was tremendously popular with voters. As a result, popular political support for computers—and for the computer industry—was high.

navigate this new landscape. In addition to direct lobbying, a coalition of large software firms created an industry lobby in 1988 called the National Association of Software and Services Companies (NASSCOM). An industry elite would soon start to emerge in the private sector.

After decades of government policies that had inhibited the industry's growth, the software industry would now use government to promote its interests. The industry started by turning the DOE into an almost unwitting handmaiden. Following private-sector cues, the DOE set up foreign promotional boards and organized marketing conferences in different countries to promote Indian companies, developed insurance schemes to protect computer companies, and ensured that India's domestic banks as well as the Export Import Bank gave preferential treatment to computer firms. Another big win for the software lobbying industry came in late 1990. At a time when the Indian government was facing a balance-of-payments crisis that made it desperate for capital and foreign exchange, the central government somehow decided that the software industry would not have to pay taxes on export profits.

In 1991, Rajiv was assassinated while campaigning in the national elections. The Congress Party was able to form a minority government with the aid of several leftist parties. P. V. Narasimha Rao was able to navigate the Congress Party infighting to become the prime minister. Rao was a polymath who had personally been influenced by the 1984 New Computer Policy. As Rajiv's home minister, he had been present on the day that Rajiv had initially spoken about liberalizing the computer industry in 1984 (Sitapati 2017). Wanting to learn more, Rao immediately acquired a personal computer that he would learn to love. Over the next several years he not only kept a diary on his computer, but also learned two computer languages.

Despite the fact that both Rajiv and Rao came to power following assassinations, the political circumstances that Rao encountered on his ascension were far different from the situation that had greeted Rajiv. Rao was in charge of a party that was divided, with many others in Congress having sought the top position following Rajiv's death. Rao also had to rely on a coalition government to stay in power.

Apart from the political realities, India was also facing a looming economic crisis. When Rao came to power in 1991, India had almost completely exhausted its foreign exchange and was in danger of defaulting. In response to this crisis, most economists encouraged liberalization of the economy. Rao listened to his experts and in the 1991 budget speech delivered by Rao's finance minister, Manmohan Singh, the Indian government announced it was going to end central planning. Buried within this speech, Singh promised to indefinitely extend the tax elimination for software exports, which would hold for much of the rest of the 1990s.

The period following the 1991 liberalization announcement was kind to the Indian software industry, but liberalization should not be mistaken for laissez-faire. Far from leaving the industry to its own devices, the central government sought to aid the software industry's growth such that by the 1990s the DOE started to resemble industry handmaiden government agencies in other developmental states, such as South Korea's Ministry of Communications, which sought to develop the country's indigenous computer industry. In addition to overturning regulations and granting favorable tax concessions, the DOE and allied sectors within the government also made several proactive moves for the private sector (Evans 1992). By this point, the DOE was regularly meeting with software industry lobbyists, sponsoring industry marketing events in India and abroad, recruiting domestic and foreign investors, providing discounted physical infrastructural services, especially in telecommunications, and offering other important benefits to the software sector. And instead of competing with the private sector like they previously had done, SOEs like ECIL and CMC either focused on supplying government software services or on providing government infrastructure that could help the private players.

In contrast to handmaiden agencies in other countries, however, the DOE and the central government did not seek to pick winners. By the early 1990s, companies like TCS, Infosys, HCL, and WIPRO were an emerging class of heavyweights that had special relationships with the DOE, but some of India's biggest contemporary software firms were not formed until the late 1990s. These included companies like Mphasis, Mindtree, and Larsen and Toubro's Infotech. Yet despite the emergence of industry leaders, the Indian software industry has remained relatively fragmented and competitive. As a result, the industry has historically been supportive of start-ups as well as small- and medium-sized firms. With some exceptions, the leading companies have sought promotional benefits that are good for the industry as a whole, not protectionist measures that would give them control over a specific market.

Apart from central government policies, various state and local governments have also pursued promotional policies designed to support the software industry. Perhaps the most successful example is Electronic City in Bangalore. In 1976, a state-level bureaucrat named R. K. Baliga incorporated the Karnataka State Electronics Development Corporation (KEONICS). KEONICS would ultimately build an industrial park that provided an array of free and subsidized infrastructural benefits to public and private electronics firms operating within its campus. The state government of Karnataka constructed office buildings, provided discounted and reliable 24-hour electricity, set up clean water systems, and by the late 1980s, provided firms with access to Indonet and the government-maintained satellite network. Officials who oversaw Electronic City also offered a single government window to make all requests. A foreign software company could register itself with the state government in an afternoon; properly registering any other kind of business would normally take several months. Local government officials—and even some customs officials—would also be kept at bay. This state-level promotion is perhaps the main reason why five of the ten largest software export firms are based in Bangalore and why so many international firms have been drawn to the city.[15]

With favorable central and state government policies, growth followed for the Indian software industry. The spread of computing and the internet during the 1990s and 2000s aided the global demand for new software. There was also a strong demand to "fix" existing software. In 1995, the European Union decided to develop a common currency, requiring all banks to change their denomination systems in their software. This problem required low-level computer fixes, and Indian software firms came to the rescue. Software officials in many parts of the world were also warning of a Y2K problem: essentially most programs had been coded in a DD/MM/YY format; with the year 2000 fast approaching, officials warned that software systems could potentially crash if this formatting was not fixed. Indian software firms again came to the rescue. These kinds of stories have continued until today, with the software industry well positioned for future growth.

Why Did Software Succeed?

The success of the Indian software industry is due in no small part to the promotional policies that the government adopted; however, this reality often goes overlooked, or is altogether undermined by those who suggest that the industry prospered because of government noninvolvement. For instance, Khanna and Palepu (2005, 306) suggest that the software industry succeeded not because of good government involvement, but instead because of minimal government involvement. They point out that because software involves technology that officials did not fully understand, it was able to slip under "the discerning bureaucrat's otherwise omnipresent proverbial radar screen." Also, they claim that because the software industry is neither capital intensive nor involves tangible assets, government entanglement is less likely.

---

15 Further aiding matters, Karnataka is also known to have a closely connected political and economic elite class.

But we should be skeptical that the software industry has thrived simply because of ignorant government officials, low capital requirements, and a business that sells intangible assets. After all, infant software industries in other developing countries share these same features, yet many have been unable to achieve the same success that we observe in India.

It is perhaps more accurate to instead say that the industry succeeded because ideologically committed technocratic reformers came in who ended produce-and-protect policies and sought to promote the private sector. Even though these reformers were quickly removed in favor of generalist bureaucrats, these bureaucrats also sought to do what was best for the private sector. They turned to the industry's leaders for instruction (Evans 1992). If a singular player had dominated the software industry—or if the foreign markets had not been so much more attractive than the domestic market—then these officials might have implemented a "national champion" strategy to protect a private-sector leader. Indeed, domestic business groups in other areas of the economy were able to secure such concessions. But the software industry at the time was made up of multiple private firms who mostly had their sights set on foreign markets. Software industry leaders did not seek protectionist policies, but instead sought policies that would promote the entire industry. As a result, the government continued to make substantial outlays for technical education, reduced barriers to registering new start-ups, provided subsidized and reliable physical and communications infrastructure to all companies, promoted the industry to potential customers and investors at home and abroad, and so forth. India's software industry is a success story in large part because of the promotional strategies that the government has been effectively able to execute. The political origins and the economic effects of these policies deserve greater attention.

References

Amsden, Alice. 1989. *Asia's Next Giant: South Korea and Late Industrialization*. New York: Oxford University Press.

Evans, Peter. 1992. "Indian Informatics in the 1980s: The Changing Character of State Involvement." *World Development* 20, no. 1 (January): 1–18.

———. 1995. *Embedded Autonomy: States and Industrial Transformation*. Princeton, NJ: Princeton University Press.

Heeks, Richard. 1996. *India's Software Industry: State Policy, Liberalisation, and Industrial Development*. New Delhi: Sage Publications.

Kanodia, Lalit. 2012. "The Software Journey of Indian and the Road Going Forward." Indo-American Chamber of Commerce. Accessed May 13, 2018. https://iaccindia.wordpress.com/2012/10/12/the-software-journey-of-india-and-the-road-going-forward.

Khanna, Tarun, and Krishna G. Palepu. 2005. "The Evolution of Concentrated Ownership in India: Broad Patterns and a History of the Indian Software Industry." In *A History of Corporate Governance around the World: Family Business Groups to Professional Managers*, edited by Randall Morck, 283–324. Chicago: University of Chicago Press.

Kohli, Atul. 1989. "Politics of Economic Liberalization in India." *World Development* 17, no. 3: 305–28. See pg. 312.

———. 2004. *State Directed Development: Political Power and Industrialization in the Global Periphery*. New York: Cambridge University Press.

Menon, Nikhil. 2018. "'Fancy Calculating Machine': Computers and Planning in Independent India." *Modern Asian Studies* 52, no. 2: 421–57.

Rajaraman, Vaidyeswaran. 2015. "History of Computing in India: 1955–2010." *IEEE Annals of the History of Computing* 37, no. 1: 24–35.

Rodrik, Dani, and Arvind Subramanian. 2005. "From 'Hindu Growth' to Productivity Surge: The Mystery of the Indian Growth Transition." *IMF Staff Papers* 52, no. 2: 193–228.

Sharma, R. 1995. "Indian Software Firm Seen Maintaining Past Growth." Reuters Wire, March 8.

Sitapati, Vinay. 2017. *Half-Lion: How P.V. Narasimha Rao Transformed India*. Delhi: Penguin Press.

Subramanian, C.R. 1992. *India and the Computer: A Study of Planned Development*. New York: Oxford University Press.

Wade, Robert. 1990. *Governing the Market: Economic Theory and the Role of Government in East Asian Industrialization*. Princeton, NJ: Princeton University Press.

World Bank. Various years. "World Development Indicators." Accessed January 9, 2019. https://databank.worldbank.org/reports.aspx ?source=2&country=IND.

Yost, Jeffrey. 2017. *Making IT Work: A History of the Computer Services Industry*. Cambridge, MA: MIT Press.

CHAPTER 4

Developing Singapore's Innovation and Entrepreneurship Ecosystem

From Internet/Mobile Services to Deep-Technology Commercialization?

Poh Kam Wong

Since its political independence in 1965, the small island-state of Singapore has achieved rapid economic growth and transformed itself into a major global financial, business, and transport/information technology (IT) hub. In terms of gross domestic product (GDP) per capita, Singapore surpassed Japan in 2010 and caught up with the United States in the mid-2010s (World Bank 2018). Despite slowing growth in recent years, Singapore's GDP (purchasing power parity) per capita in 2016 still ranked as the third highest in the world, according to the International Monetary Fund.

The rapid economic development of Singapore from developing to developed country in less than four decades was achieved through a consistent public policy focus on attracting and leveraging direct foreign investments from global multinational corporations (MNCs) to achieve continuous upgrading and productivity growth (Wong 2003). By encouraging global MNCs to transfer increasingly more advanced technologies and know-how to their subsidiary operations in the city-state, and by investing heavily in education and on-the-job training to enable the domestic workforce to rapidly absorb and diffuse new technologies, Singapore has been able to achieve rapid technological catch-up, industrial upgrading, and productivity improvement. This is despite not having substantially invested in public research and development

(R&D) to develop indigenous technological innovation capabilities until late in its economic development, compared with Taiwan and Korea; indeed, even today Singapore lacks a science and technology ministry. Moreover, much of the public R&D spending has been directed at the innovation needs of the global MNCs and some of the large government-linked corporations in strategic sectors, with relatively less going to local small- and medium-sized enterprises—in contrast to, for example, the priorities followed in Taiwan.

While this unique economic development model—an open economy framework combined with strong state intervention—has been the basis for Singapore's remarkable economic success, concerns have been growing among the city-state's intelligentsia, as well as its political leadership, that this development model needs to be significantly changed for the city-state to continue to prosper in the new millennium. With its high developed-country costs, Singapore now needs to compete close to the frontier of the global knowledge economy, as opposed to the earlier, easier task of technological catch-up. Moreover, economic growth and innovations in the global marketplace are increasingly coming from young, entrepreneurial firms, rather than large, incumbent corporations. While the Schumpeterian destruction of large incumbents by new disruptive innovators has been a constant in economic history, the speed at which such disruptions are occurring appears to have increased in recent years as digital transformation intensifies and the so-called fourth industrial revolution begins to take shape. As highlighted by Schwab (2016), while digital technologies have enabled revolutionary advances in internet/mobile applications and e-commerce, it is when digital technologies are applied to rapid advances in technologies that are physical (autonomous vehicles, new materials, 3D printing, advanced robotics, etc.) or biological (genetic engineering, neurotechnology, bioprinting, etc.) that major transformational impacts occur. I describe the advanced physical and biological technologies underlying Industry 4.0 as "deep technologies."

Public policymakers' growing concern with promoting technology entrepreneurship is of course not confined to Singapore; policymakers across the world have announced their intentions to grow their own versions of Silicon Valley (Lerner 2009). Singapore's experience in this regard could therefore offer lessons that would be of interest to other nations and cities as well.

In a number of earlier works (e.g., Wong 2001, 2006; Wong and Singh 2008), I examine the emerging shift of Singapore's economy in the first half of the 2000s toward a more "balanced" development model that reduces its high degree of reliance on large enterprises (both local government-linked corporations and foreign MNCs) by growing the technology entrepreneurship sector. In this chapter, I will examine the progress of this emerging shift in the subsequent decade up to now. In particular, I show that, while there has indeed been significant growth of the technology start-up sector, driven in part by new public policies, this growth has been primarily in internet/ mobile/e-commerce services, with relatively few deep-technology-based start-ups achieving significant scale.

The chapter is organized as follows. First, I provide a stylized institutional analysis of Singapore's public policy approach to developing its innovation and entrepreneurship ecosystem. Next, I provide some salient empirical evidence on how the ecosystem has evolved. Finally, I make some concluding observations and highlight a number of relevant implications for other countries.

Institutional Framework for Policymaking and Implementation

A national institutional framework for the making of innovation and entrepreneurship policy tends to be complex and is often path dependent on historical contexts and political legacies, even as it evolves over time in response to changing global and domestic environments (OECD 2012). As such, the institutional framework of every nation tends to have its own idiosyncratic elements, and Singapore's is no exception.

Lacking an official version of how Singapore's government organizes its innovation and entrepreneurship policy functions, I have created a stylized overview of the institutional framework for innovation and entrepreneurship policymaking and implementation that has emerged over the past decade or so (see figure 4.1). Responsibility is held by four basic groupings of state institutions:

- The **National Research Foundation** (NRF), under the prime minister's office, provides overall funding and broad policy guidance through five-year research, innovation, and enterprise (RIE) plans, the first two being RIE 2011–15 and RIE 2016–20.
- The **Ministry of Education** oversees the education and research activities of the various institutions of higher learning.
- The **Ministry of Trade and Industry** oversees key economic implementation agencies: the Economic Development Board (EDB, responsible for attracting domestic investments); the Agency for Science, Technology and Research (A*STAR, responsible for implementing mission-oriented public R&D); SPRING Singapore (responsible for the promotion of local small- and medium-sized enterprises and start-ups); and International Enterprise (IE) Singapore (responsible for promoting the international

FIGURE 4.1 Singapore's institutional framework for science and technology innovation & entrepreneurship policy, 2017

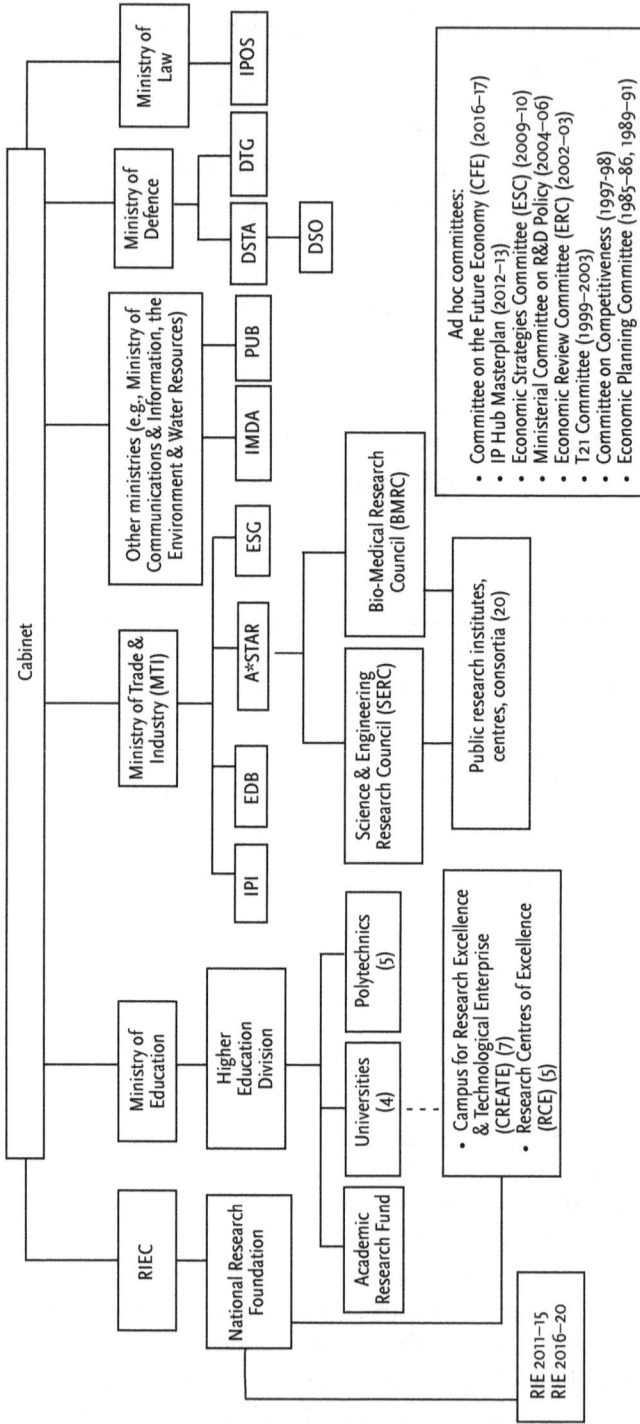

SOURCE: Updated from Wong and Singh (2011).

NOTE: A*STAR = Agency for Science, Technology and Research; DSO = Defence Science Organisation; DSTA = Defence Science and Technology Agency; DTG = Defence Technology Group; EDB = Economic Development Board; ESG = Enterprise Singapore; IDA = Infocomm Development Authority; IMDA = Infocomm Media Development Authority; IPI = Intellectual Property Institute; IPOS = Intellectual Property Office of Singapore; MDA = Media Development Authority; PUB = Public Utilities Board; RIE = research, innovation, and enterprise (plan); RIEC = Research, Innovation and Enterprise Council; SPRING = Standards, Productivity and Innovation Board.

growth of local enterprises).[1]

* **Agencies within other ministries that have significant innovation-promotion mandates** within their specific industry verticals. Figure 4.1 highlights the most important of these: (1) the Infocomm Media Development Authority (IMDA), under the Ministry of Communications and Information, for the information and communication technology (ICT) and media industries; (2) the Public Utilities Board, under the Ministry of the Environment and Water Resources, for the water industry; and (3) the Defence Science and Technology Agency, under the Ministry of Defence, for the defense industry. I also separately highlight the Intellectual Property Office of Singapore, under the Ministry of Law, which does not focus on a specific industry but promotes innovation broadly through enabling legal frameworks for intellectual property protection and transactions.

Collectively, these four groupings of state institutions have been responsible for policies and programs that have had significant impacts—both direct and indirect—on innovation and entrepreneurship activities in Singapore. I highlight the main roles of the key agencies identified in figure 4.1, also using four groupings (see table 4.1).

Unlike many other countries, Singapore does not regularly create five-year economic development plans. Instead, the government convenes *ad hoc* inter-ministerial committees to formulate national economic development strategies as and when deemed necessary, often in response to significant external changes. For example, the Economic Planning Committee 1985, the Committee on Competitiveness 1997, and the Economic Strategies Committee 2009 were convened in response to the severe recession in 1985, the Asian financial crisis in 1997, and the global financial meltdown in 2008, respectively. The latest key output, a report of the Future Economy Council (FEC) released in early 2017, charts new strategies in response to Industry 4.0 disruptions (FEC 2017).

These committees announced new strategic directions related to innovation and entrepreneurship. Subsequent policy and program changes included, on occasion, changes to the institutional framework as well. For example, the 1999–2003 Technopreneurship 21 Committee for the first time identified the promotion of technology entrepreneurship as a key policy goal, which led to a slew of new programs, including the establishment of an SG$1 billion Technopreneurship Investment Fund under A*STAR (then called the National Science and Technology Board) to invest in venture capital (VC) funds and to jump-start the VC industry, and the creation of the SPRING Startup Enterprise

---

1   On April 1, 2018, SPRING and IE Singapore were merged into Enterprise SG.

TABLE 4.1 Key innovation policy roles of Singapore's state institutions

Creating indigenous sources of technological capability	Leveraging foreign sources of technological capabilities	Facilitating diffusion and adoption of new technologies by existing firms	Promoting the formation and growth of tech start-up firms
National Research Foundation			
Funds public R&D	Funds foreign universities to establish R&D in Singapore (through the CREATE program)	Funds university-industry collaboration and entrepreneurship education activities Cofunds corporate venture funds	Cofunds venture capital funds (ESVF) and incubators (TIS) Incubates and invests in tech start-ups through SGInnovate
Ministry of Education: Universities			
Develop technical talents Conduct basic R&D	Attract foreign students to Singapore through scholarships, etc. Recruit foreign scientists through professorships and postdoctoral positions	Transfer R&D results to industry through licensing	Develop entrepreneurial talents Promote R&D commercialization through spin-offs
Ministry of Education: Polytechnics and vocational schools			
Conduct applied research		Assist enterprises to absorb new technologies and innovations Train workforce in relevant skills to absorb new technologies	Develop entrepreneurial talents
Ministry of Trade and Industry (MTI): Agency for Science, Technology and Research (A*STAR)			
Conducts public R&D	Develops local STEM talent through PhD scholarships in prestigious overseas universities	Transfers R&D results to industry through licensing; transfers R&D personnel to local SMEs	Promotes R&D commercialization through spin-offs
Ministry of Trade and Industry (MTI): Economic Development Board (EDB)			
	Attracts foreign MNC R&D and innovation activities to Singapore through tax incentives, etc.	Funds MNCs and large local enterprises to help local SMEs to upgrade (through LIUP program)	Invests in tech start-ups (through VC fund EDBI)
Ministry of Trade and Industry (MTI): SPRING			
		Promotes adoption of new technologies and innovation by local SMEs through grants, subsidies, and technical services Promotes industry networking	Cofunds angel investments and incubators Promotes tech start-ups through various grant schemes
Industry-specific state institutions			
Ministry of Communications and Information (MCI): Infocomm Media Development Authority (IMDA)			
	Attracts foreign MNCs and talent in ICT and media to Singapore	Promotes adoption and diffusion of ICT and digital media innovation	Invests in start-ups in ICT and digital media (through VC fund Infocomm Investments Pte Ltd [IIPL]) and procures from start-ups
Ministry of Defence: Defence Science and Technology Agency (DSTA)			
Funds defense-related R&D	Procures critical defense technologies from overseas	Diffuses defense technologies to local defense industry	Invests in start-ups in defense technologies (through VC fund CapVista)

SOURCE: Author.
NOTE: CREATE = Campus for Research Excellence & Technological Enterprise; ESVF = early stage venture fund; ICT = information and communication technology; MNC = multinational corporation; R&D = research and development; SME = small- and medium-sized enterprise; STEM = science, technology, engineering, and mathematics; TIS = Technology Incubation Scheme; VC = venture capital.

Development Scheme (SEEDS) under EDB to match investment in start-ups from angel investors. The 2002–03 Economic Review Committee further expanded the promotion of tech start-ups by making it a new function for SPRING, which also took over the SEEDS scheme from EDB, while the 2004 Ministerial Committee on R&D Policy led to the establishment of the NRF in 2006 (Wong and Ho 2018). The FEC's 2017 report led to the merger of SPRING with IE Singapore in 2018 to become Enterprise Singapore, addressing a concern that IE Singapore had in the past focused on helping only larger, more established local enterprises to go overseas, not early-stage tech start-ups.

Table 4.2 lists the public funding schemes introduced since 2000 by various state agencies to promote technology entrepreneurship. Even though *ad hoc* inter-ministerial committees and other regular coordination mechanisms (such as cabinet reviews) exist to minimize conflict or the duplication of effort among the various state actors, functions still overlap due to ambiguous jurisdictional boundaries and, at times, institutional rivalries. For example, the Technology Incubation Scheme (TIS) introduced by NRF in 2008 overlapped somewhat with SPRING's SEEDS scheme, and because it was seen as more generous (85 percent of cofunding up to SG$500,000 vs. one-to-one matching), arguably negatively affected the uptake of the latter. Likewise, the Infocomm Investments Pte Ltd (IIPL) fund put forward by the Infocomm Development Authority of Singapore (before it was merged with the Media Development Authority to form the Info-communications Media Development Authority) invested in ICT-related start-ups that were also targeted by the VC funds cofunded by NRF under the Early Stage Venture Fund (ESVF) scheme. More recently, NRF created SGInnovate, a new agency with a broad but vague mandate to promote innovation for the global market ("Build from Singapore, for the World"). With the IIPL fund being transferred to SGInnovate, it is as yet unclear if its current overlap with the ESVF will persist.

Ecosystem Development

Here I attempt to collate relevant empirical evidence from various sources, including my own research, to provide a picture of how Singapore's innovation and entrepreneurship ecosystem developed over the past decade, in view of the plethora of public policy programs introduced. While there are unfortunately glaring information gaps, I believe a number of clear and salient patterns can be discerned, which I will seek to highlight below.

TABLE 4.2 Public-sector funding schemes supporting technology entrepreneurship, 2000–17

Year started	Name of scheme	Type of scheme	Target stakeholders	Support quantum
A*STAR (formerly known as NSTB)				
1999	Technology Investment Fund (TIF)	Fund-of-fund investment	Venture capital funds	Varying amounts; total fund US$1 billion
SPRING				
2000	SPRING Startup Enterprise Development Scheme (SEEDS)	Equity investment	Investors	Up to SG$1 million (dollar-for-dollar matching) per deal
2005	Business Angel Scheme (BAS)	Equity investment	Business angels	Up to SG$2 million (dollar-for-dollar matching) per deal
2008	Technology Enterprise Commercialisation Scheme (TECS)	Grant	Projects of innovators/ entrepreneurs	Up to SG$250,000 per proof-of-concept project/ S$500,000 per proof-of-value project
2008	Young Entrepreneurs Scheme for Schools (YES!)	Grant	Schools	Up to SG$10,000 per school (total SG$4.5 million fund)
2009	Incubator Development Programme (IDP)	Grant	Incubators or venture accelerators	SG$30 million for the whole program in 2009 (up to 70% qualifying costs)
2010	Angel Investment Tax Deduction Scheme	Tax incentive	Business angels	Maximum tax deduction of $250,000
2012	Action Community for Entrepreneurship (ACE) Start-ups Grant	Grant	First-time entrepreneurs	SG$50,000 ($7 for every $3 matching) per start-up
2015	Sector Specific Accelerator (SSA)	Equity investment	Accelerators	SG$70 million for the whole program
National Research Foundation (NRF)				
2008	Early Stage Venture Fund (ESVF)	Equity investment	Venture capital firms	SG$140 million for the whole program
2008	The Technology Incubation Scheme (TIS)	Equity investment	Technology incubators	Up to SG$500,000 (85% of investment) per start-up
2008	Proof-of-Concept (POC)	Grant	Public research/ higher education institutes	Up to SG$250,000 per proof-of-concept project
Infocomm Development Authority (IDA)				
2010	iSTART: ACE scheme (Accelerate and catalyse entrepreneurship)	Grant	Tech start-ups	Up to SG$250,000 (50% of salary of five technical staff)

SOURCE: Compiled from the websites of NRF, SPRING, and Infocomm Media Development Authority (IMDA).

NOTE: A*STAR = Agency for Science, Technology and Research; NSTB = National Science and Technology Board.

Development of the National Innovation System

The size and characteristics of Singapore's national innovation system can be measured through a number of well-established indicators: R&D intensities, scientific publications, and patents.

Investment in R&D

After two decades of rapid growth, gross domestic expenditure on R&D in Singapore grew more moderately over the last fifteen years, as the ratio of this expenditure to GDP stabilized around 2 to 2.5 percent (see figure 4.2). While this puts Singapore comfortably within the middle band of Organisation for Economic Co-operation and Development (OECD) countries, it is notably behind Korea, Japan, and Taiwan in Asia, and the small advanced economies like Switzerland, Denmark, Finland, and Israel.

FIGURE 4.2 Growth in R&D spending, in millions of Singaporean dollars and as a share of GDP, 1978–2015

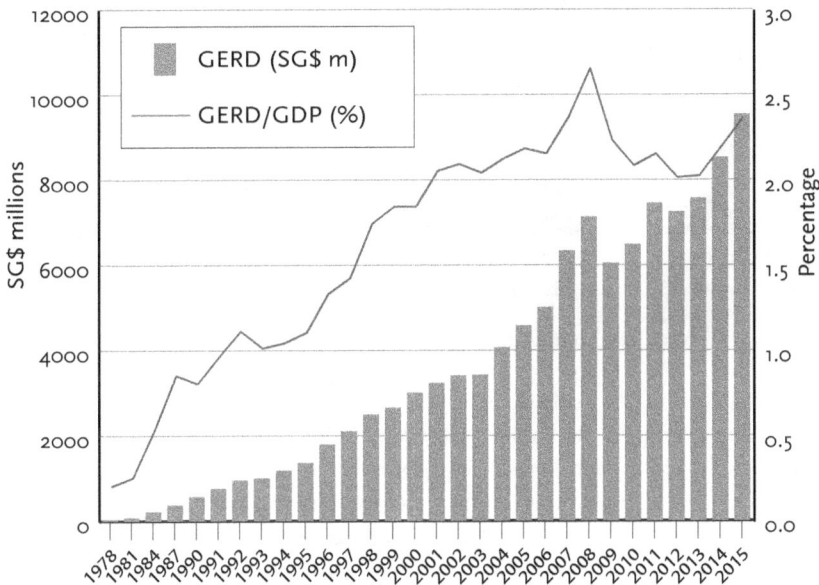

SOURCE: National Survey of R&D Expenditure and Manpower (various years), Science Council of Singapore (prior to 1990), National Survey of R&D in Singapore (various years), National Science and Technology Board (for 1990–2000), and Agency for Science, Technology and Research (2001–15).

NOTE: GDP = gross domestic product; GERD = gross domestic expenditure on R&D; R&D = research and development.

The private sector's share of Singaporean R&D investment was also relatively stable, at around 60 percent over the last decade (figure 4.3). That said, local firms' share of this spending steadily decreased after 2000 to less than one-quarter in 2015, suggesting that Singapore's indigenous firms continue to have little engagement in innovation activities. These firms' share declined the most in manufacturing, falling to just 20 percent.

FIGURE 4.3 Share of R&D expenditure, by origin, 1996–2015

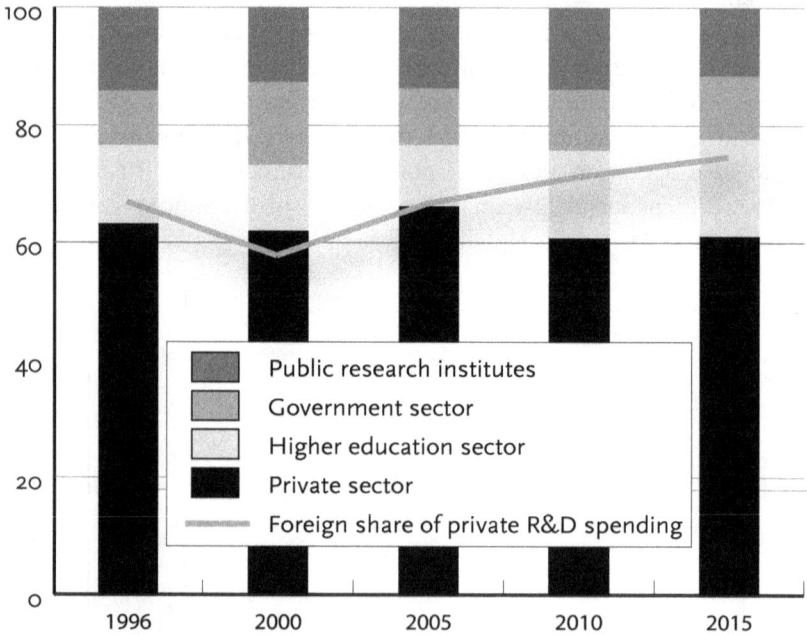

SOURCE: National Science and Technology Board (for 1996–2000); Agency for Science, Technology and Research (2005–15).
NOTE: PRI = public research institutes; R&D = research and development.

The sectoral composition of private R&D also changed rapidly over these years. For example, the share devoted to manufacturing declined steadily from nearly 90 percent in 1996 to 54 percent by 2015 (figure 4.4). Over the same time period, there was a moderate rise in the share of R&D in the deep-tech-related sector (defined narrowly as biomedical, cleantech/energy, and advanced engineering) to over 25 percent, while that in ICT-related services stabilized around 17 percent.

FIGURE 4.4 Private-sector R&D expenditure, by industry, 1996–2015 (%)

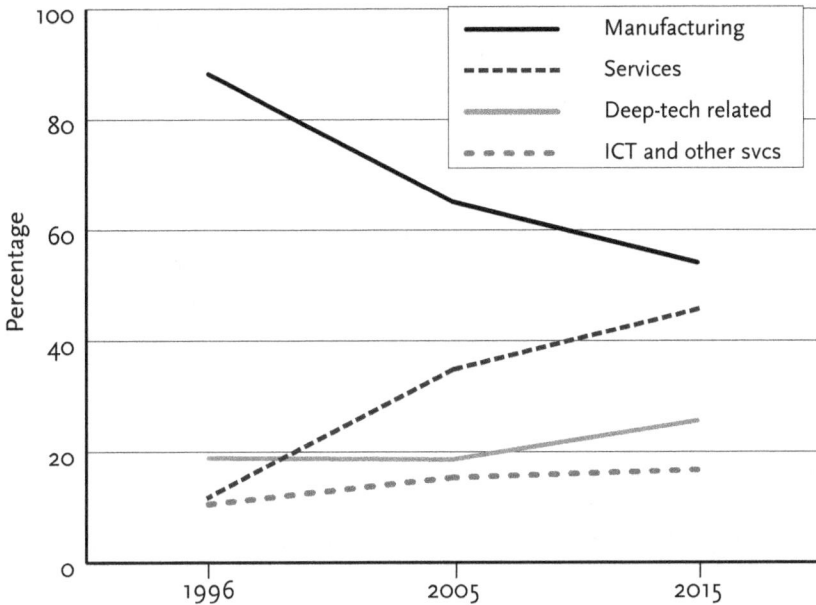

SOURCE: National Science and Technology Board (for 1996–2000); Agency for Science, Technology and Research (2005–15).

NOTE: "Deep-tech related" comprises biomedical sciences, chemicals, and R&D services. ICT = information and communication technology; R&D = research and development; svcs = services.

Scientific Publications

The number of scientific publications grew steadily over the past decade, and at a higher rate than in earlier periods. Measured in terms of number of publications per million people, Singapore ranked among the highest in the world by 2013 (NSF 2016). This quantitative growth was accompanied by a moderate increase in quality, as measured by Web of Science (WOS) citation impacts.

Further analysis of this steady improvement in scientific publication outputs suggests that public-sector research organizations, particularly Singapore's two universities, the National University of Singapore (NUS) and Nanyang Technological University (NTU), along with A*STAR, contributed disproportionately to the increase in both quantity and quality. Over the past twenty years, NUS and NTU steadily rose in various annual rankings of universities in the world; in 2016–17, NUS was ranked twenty-fourth and fifteenth in the world by Times Higher Education and Quacquarelli Symonds, respectively, and the top in Asia according to both. If we remove publications from public research organizations, and look only at the scientific publication outputs of Singapore's private firms, the picture becomes much less impressive. While no available studies disaggregate these outputs by local vs. foreign firms, a study I am conducting on university-industry co-publications (involving at least one co-author from NUS and one from a private-sector organization) over the period 2005–14 suggests that the majority of the collaborating firms are of foreign origin (Wong, Singh, and Tijssen 2018).

Patents

In contrast to scientific publications and R&D spending, Singapore's patent outputs (as measured by patents granted by the United States Patent and Trademark Office to inventors based in Singapore) increased sharply, from 943 in the period 1996–2000 to 7,171 in 2011–16 (Wong and Singh 2018). This increase is more dramatic among foreign than local organizations; indeed, if we remove public-sector organizations, including public research institutes and universities, the growth of patents among local private-sector firms is significantly slower than for foreign firms, confirming a substantially lower rate of technological innovation. As of the end of 2016, only four among the top twenty U.S. patent owners in Singapore were Singaporean owned, and of these, three were public organizations (A*STAR, a public research institute, and the two universities NUS and NTU). With the exception of Creative Technology, no indigenous firm in Singapore owned more than one hundred patents. In particular, none of the large government-linked corporations, including the three large telecommunications firms and those in advanced engineering (ST Engineering) and offshore engineering (Keppel, Sembawang), had more than thirty patents (Wong and Singh 2018).

Taken together, the above indicators strongly suggest that Singapore's innovation system continues to be highly dominated by foreign firms and public-sector research organizations. This underscores the slow progress made by Singapore toward developing the innovation capability of its indigenous firms.

Contribution of R&D Investments to Singapore's Economic Development

To further examine the implications of the empirical observations discussed above, I conducted an econometric analysis of the contribution of R&D investment to Singapore's economic growth over the period 1978–2012 (Ho and Wong 2017). My results, summarized in table 4.3, show that the short-run impact of R&D on productivity (as measured by the elasticity of total factor productivity changes to R&D changes) over this period was comparable to that seen in smaller advanced economies in the OECD. However, in terms of long-run R&D productivity, Singapore lags behind these smaller OECD countries and far behind the large G7 countries. I further tested for possible changes in R&D-related productivity in the last decade or so versus earlier years but found no evidence of significant structural breaks. Last, my analysis finds that the direct productivity effect of public-sector R&D is weaker than that of private, although additional Granger causality analysis reveals that public R&D stimulates private-sector R&D over the course of years.

TABLE 4.3   Estimates of R&D-TFP elasticities in Singapore vs. OECD countries

	Singapore[a]	Singapore[b]	Greece[c]	16 OECD countries[d]	22 OECD countries[e]
Dependent variable	TFP*	TFP*	TFP*	Private-sector TFP	Private-sector TFP
Period	1978–2012	1978–2011	1987–2007	1980–98	1971–90
Short-term elasticity[†]	0.025	0.013	Nonsignificant	0.024 (private R&D) 0.028 (public R&D)	NA
Long-run elasticity[†]	0.091	0.081	0.038 (total R&D) 0.075 (public R&D)	0.13 (private R&D) 0.17 (public R&D)	0.078 (non-G7) 0.234 (G7)

SOURCE: Ho and Wong 2017.
NOTE: *TFP is based on GDP; [†]elasticity is with respect to R&D; G7 = Group of Seven; GDP = gross domestic product; OECD = Organisation for Economic Co-operation and Development; R&D = research and development; TFP = total factor productivity; NA = not available. Referenced studies: [a]Ho and Wong 2017; [b]Ho, Wong, and Toh 2009; [c]Voutsinas and Tsamadias 2014; [d]Guellec and van Pottelsberghe de la Potterie 2002; [e]Coe and Helpman 1995.

In view of the large share of Singapore's R&D spending due by foreign firms and public research institutions, the above findings suggest (1) the leakage of value capture from R&D, possibly made worse by the greater propensity of foreign firms to commercialize their R&D knowledge outside Singapore; and (2) frictions in transferring public R&D knowledge to private firms, possibly made worse by the low absorptive capacity of local firms. The finding that overall R&D productivity has not improved much in recent years also suggests that there have been no significant structural changes in Singapore's innovation system, despite various public policy changes over the last ten years.

To the extent that the above interpretations of my econometric findings are valid, they highlight the urgency of significant policy changes to address this fundamental weakness in Singapore's innovation system—the underdevelopment of the innovation capability of indigenous firms.

Development of the Technology Entrepreneurship Ecosystem

To complement the above analysis on innovation outputs, I now turn to the development of technology entrepreneurship, based on data from two research projects I recently conducted. The first (Wong, Ho, and Ng 2017) involves a compilation of unpublished census data from the Singapore Department of Statistics (DOS) on new firm formation in Singapore over the period 2004–15, as well as primary data on 530 tech start-ups under ten years of age (of which 80 percent were five years of age or younger) collected through a questionnaire survey in 2016. The sectoral composition of the survey respondents was found to be representative of the DOS census data. The second study (Wong and Ho 2018) draws on an ongoing online database of start-ups called TechSG that I initiated in 2015. The project identifies Singapore-based tech start-up entities and their founders/investors by periodically crawling the most popular websites of business news and start-up social media (e.g., e27, TechinAsia); the home pages of VC funds, incubators, and government agencies; as well as data on the crowdsourcing of inputs from the start-up community. Further information about these start-ups is gathered from their websites and in some cases their company registration records, to remove start-ups that have deregistered and other nonrelevant cases and to provide more finely grained classification. Despite possible biases in coverage (e.g., start-ups that do not have their own websites are usually excluded), TechSG has been widely acknowledged as the most comprehensive repository of publicly available information on Singapore's tech start-up ecosystem; as of early 2018, it contained information on over 2,600 start-ups and their founders, over 230 investors, 42 incubators, and 50 other facilitators.

I start with an overview of the aggregate growth trend of start-ups and their share of total employment in the economy (Wong, Ho, and Ng 2017). For the purpose of this analysis, start-ups are defined as young firms, ages five and under, with at least 50 percent of capital individually owned (to remove young firms that are subsidiaries of other firms). As can be seen from figure 4.5, the number of start-ups in Singapore more than doubled, from about 22,800 in 2004 to over 48,000 in 2015, while total employment likewise more than doubled from 156,500 to 345,300. Start-ups' share of total employment also increased from 7.1 percent in 2004 to 9.4 percent in 2015 (note that a temporary peak of around 10 percent over 2008–10 was due to slower employment growth among existing firms, especially large firms, caused by the global financial crisis in 2008).

The above trend pertains to all start-ups, not just tech start-ups. Following other scholars, I define tech start-ups as those in industries (using three-digit International Standard Industrial Classification [ISIC] levels where available) that have above-average R&D intensities. As shown in figure 4.6, the total number of tech start-ups increased at a lower rate than total start-ups, from around 2,760 in 2004 to over 5,100 in 2015. However, this is due to a decline in the high-tech manufacturing sector since 2007, while start-ups in high-tech services more than doubled from around 1,540 in 2004 to over 3,900 in 2015.

FIGURE 4.5 Growth in Singapore start-up employment, 2004–15

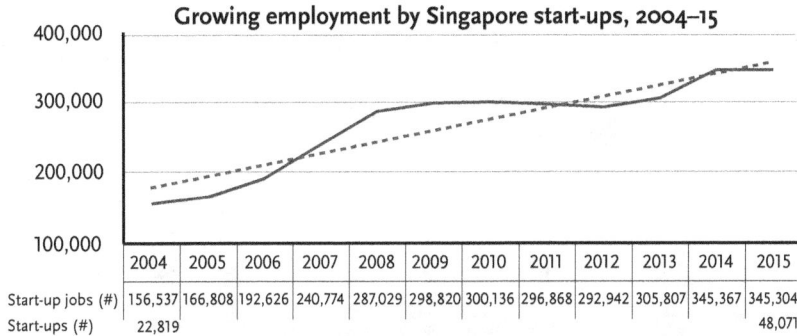

Growing employment by Singapore start-ups, 2004–15

	2004	2005	2006	2007	2008	2009	2010	2011	2012	2013	2014	2015
Start-up jobs (#)	156,537	166,808	192,626	240,774	287,029	298,820	300,136	296,868	292,942	305,807	345,367	345,304
Start-ups (#)	22,819											48,071

Growing contribution of start-ups to total employment in Singapore , 2004–15

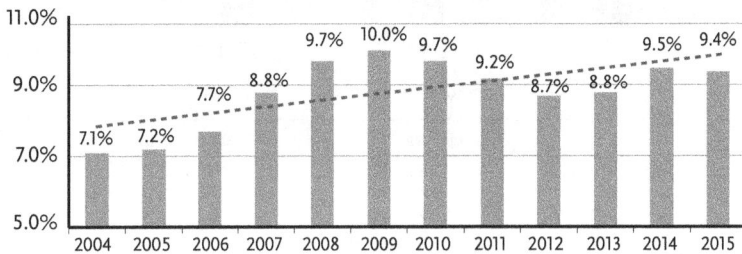

Values by year: 7.1% (2004), 7.2% (2005), 7.7% (2006), 8.8% (2007), 9.7% (2008), 10.0% (2009), 9.7% (2010), 9.2% (2011), 8.7% (2012), 8.8% (2013), 9.5% (2014), 9.4% (2015)

SOURCE: Singapore Department of Statistics (DOS).
NOTE: Start-ups defined as firms five years of age of younger and with at least 50 percent individually owned capital.

A more detailed breakdown of the sectoral composition of tech start-ups suggests that the biggest growth is in ICT-related sectors, with the share of deep-technology sectors (defined more narrowly as biomedical, cleantech/energy, and advanced engineering) largely stagnating at around 6 percent (see figure 4.7).

The above data from the DOS do not provide a meaningful breakdown of the ICT sector into specific subsectors. To obtain more insights into the internet/mobile app subsector, I utilize data from the TechSG database (Wong and Ho 2018). Looking at data on 1,300 verified tech start-ups' year of establishment, extracted in March 2016 from TechSG, I find a significant increase in the share of tech start-ups in the ICT sector, much of them focused on internet/mobile services (see figure 4.8a). The shares of start-ups in "deep technology" and other high-tech sectors either stagnated or declined.

FIGURE 4.6 Growth in number of tech start-ups in Singapore, by sector and in total, 2004–15

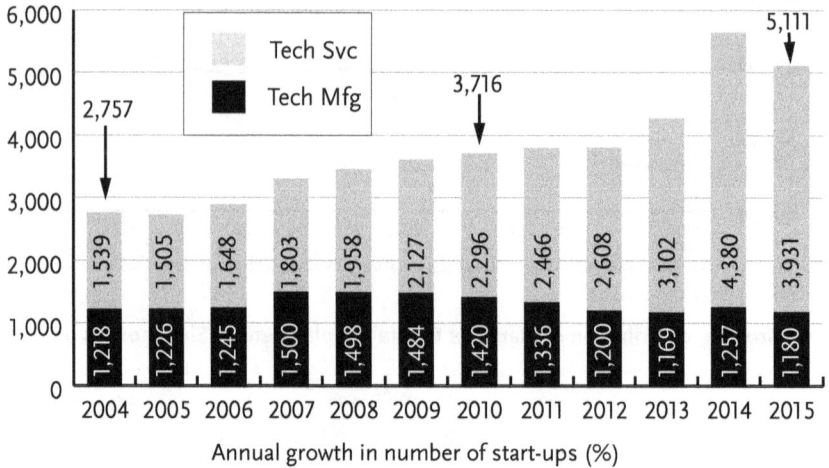

Annual growth in number of start-ups (%)

	Tech mfg	Tech svc	All tech start-ups
2004–10	2.59	6.89	5.10
2010–15	–3.64	11.35	6.58

SOURCE: Singapore Department of Statistics (DOS); Accounting and Corporate Regulatory Authority (ACRA).
NOTE: Mfg = manufacturing; Svc = services.

Data from the 2016 survey of 530 tech start-ups in Singapore (Wong, Ho, and Ng 2017) further indicate that the majority of Singaporean ICT start-ups in general and internet/mobile start-ups in particular are mostly founded by relatively young university graduates; this is in contrast to the founders of deep-tech start-ups, a larger proportion of which have master's degrees or doctorates. In addition, founders of tech start-ups outside the ICT sector tend to be older and a larger proportion have significant professional/ managerial work experience.

Figure 4.8b provides further insights into the sectoral composition of tech start-ups in Singapore (as listed in TechSG) by comparing these with data on start-ups in London and New York City, which were compiled using a similar methodology. Interestingly, the share of ICT start-ups in Singapore is comparable to those in London and New York City (76 vs. 79 vs. 70 percent), and the same trend holds for internet/mobile start-ups (43 vs. 50 vs. 48 percent). The share of deep-tech sectors in Singapore is larger than New York City and London (12 vs. 8 percent and 6 percent, respectively).

FIGURE 4.7 Sectoral composition of tech start-ups in Singapore, 2004–15 (census data)

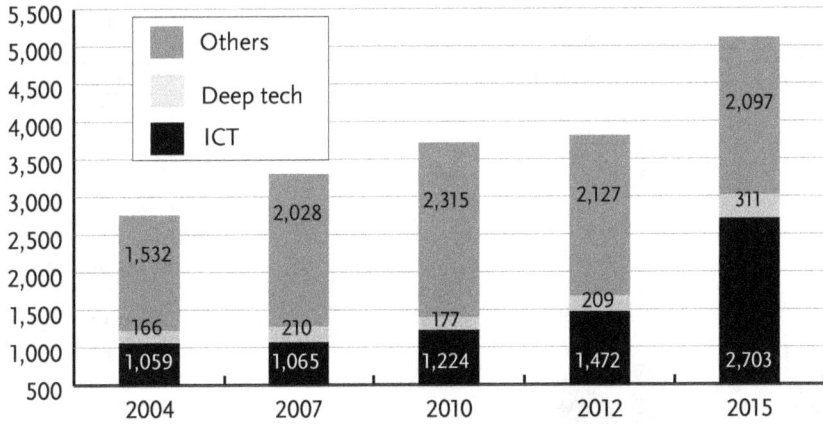

Composition (%)					
	2004	2007	2010	2012	2015
ICT	38.4	32.2	32.9	38.7	52.9
Deep tech	6.0	6.4	4.8	5.5	6.1
Others	55.6	61.4	62.3	55.9	41.0
n	2,757	3,303	3,716	3,808	5,111

SOURCE: Singapore Department of Statistics (DOS); Accounting and Corporate Regulatory Authority (ACRA).
NOTE: ICT = information and communication techology.

The above comparative analysis suggests that Singapore's tech start-up pattern reflects that of other global financial, business, and information service hubs such as London and New York City, with a significant focus on internet/mobile services that leverage off these cities' role as digital information hubs. Despite significant R&D investment in various deep-technology fields, Singapore still lacks the depth and specialization of other high-tech start-up hubs, such as Boston and San Diego in life sciences; Silicon Valley in semiconductor/digital devices, big data, cleantech, and energy; and Munich in advanced engineering and manufacturing. Indeed, while several internet/ mobile ecommerce start-ups from Singapore have successfully scaled up regionally and achieved valuation of above SG$500 million in recent years (e.g., SEA, Grab, PropertyGuru, Carousell), no deep-tech start-up has successfully taken a place among the global leaders in its chosen niche.

FIGURE 4.8A   Change in tech start-ups' business activities in Singapore, pre-2005–16

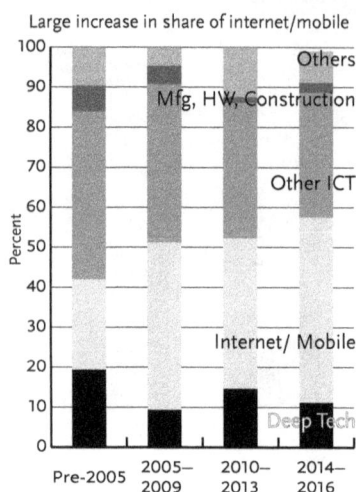

Large increase in share of internet/mobile

% distribution	Year of start-up founding			
	Pre-2005	2005–2009	2010–2013	2014–2016
Deep technology	19.35	9.3	14.58	11.19
Biomedical	12.90	4.65	9.33	7.26
Cleantech, energy, env.	6.45	3.49	4.08	2.26
Advanced engineering	0.00	1.16	1.17	1.67
Internet / mobile	22.58	41.86	37.61	46.19
Internet, mob., e-comm.	9.68	22.09	20.7	22.62
Internet applications in media & lifestyle	12.90	19.77	16.91	23.57
Other ICT-related	41.94	39.53	33.82	31.19
Software, IT services & solutions	16.13	25.58	11.08	11.90
ICT in financial & business services	25.81	13.95	22.74	19.29
Mfg, HW, & const.	6.45	4.65	1.46	2.50
Others	9.68	4.65	12.54	7.98
TOTAL (n)	100%	100%	100%	100%
	(31)	(86)	(343)	(840)

SOURCE: Calculated from TechSG database (www.TechSg.io).
NOTE: ICT = information and communication techology; env. = environment; mob. = mobile; mfg. = manufacturing; HW = hardware; const. = construction.

FIGURE 4.8B   Business activities of tech start-ups in Singapore vs. London and New York City

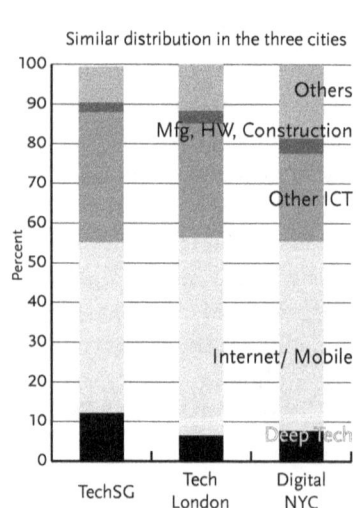

Similar distribution in the three cities

% distribution	TechSG	Tech London	Digital NYC
Deep Technology	12.15	6.47	7.66
Biomedical	7.77	4.17	5.30
Clean tech, energy, env.	2.92	2.13	2.13
Advanced engineering	1.46	0.17	0.23
Internet / mobile	43.08	49.88	47.75
Internet, mob., e-comm.	21.77	24.51	23.11
Internet applications in media & lifestyle	21.31	25.37	24.64
Other ICT-related	32.69	28.73	22.12
Software, IT services & solutions	12.69	10.54	8.04
ICT in financial & business services	20.00	18.19	14.08
Mfg, HW, & const.	2.46	3.25	3.74
Others	9.00	11.76	18.73
TOTAL (n)	100%	100%	100%
	(1,300)	(1,726)	(5,264)

SOURCE: Calculated from TechSG database (www.TechSg.io), and Digital NYC and TechLondon sites.
NOTE: See figure 4.8a for abbreviation key.

Possible Effects of Public Policy on Technology Entrepreneurship

In the absence of randomized trials and tracer studies with control groups and longitudinal tracking, it is difficult to rigorously assess the efficacy and impact of individual public policies or schemes on the development of technology entrepreneurship in Singapore. However, a comparison of data from the 2016 survey with an earlier survey I conducted in 2010 (Wong, Ho, and Singh 2011) suggests that the degree of support that tech start-ups received from their ecosystem increased significantly between these years (Wong, Ho, and Ng 2017). In particular, the proportion of young tech start-ups that reported participating in at least one government support scheme (including university incubation programs) or receiving angel investment/VC funding increased substantially. A significantly larger proportion of young tech start-ups also reported cooperating with other parties in the ecosystem to foster innovation. The degree of innovation among start-ups in 2016 also appears to be higher than in 2010, as is the proportion of start-ups with overseas operations. Interestingly, in 2016 a significant proportion of tech start-up entrepreneurs (43 percent) were foreigners, suggesting that the Singaporean tech start-up ecosystem was relatively successful in attracting immigrant entrepreneurs, especially in the ICT sector.

The significant increase in young tech start-ups participating in university incubation programs over the period 2010–16 appears to be consistent with data from TechSG, which show a sharp increase in tech start-ups (40 percent as of May 2016) that are spin-offs from universities/A*STAR or that have participated in university entrepreneurship education/incubation support programs (Wong and Ho 2018).

Further analysis of the 2016 survey data also suggests that the growth performance of tech start-ups is positively correlated with their participation in university incubation programs, as well as with receiving angel investment and/or VC funding (Wong, Ho, and Ng 2017). While participation in other government schemes has no direct association with growth performance, it is likely that the effect of the various public cofunding schemes for angel investment and VC would have been captured by the amount of investment received.

Last, but not least, the survey findings suggest that deep-tech start-ups face different challenges than do ICT start-ups: obtaining financing is identified as the most critical challenge in deep-tech, versus recruiting and retaining key personnel in ICT. Consistent with this observation, the bulk of the start-up funding schemes provided by government agencies involve early-stage grants or cofunding of equity investments of small amounts (SG$50,000–500,000), sufficient for most internet/mobile start-ups to develop their products/ services but often inadequate for deep-tech start-ups. This public policy bias is likely to have resulted in an oversupply of venture funding for low-capital, short-gestation start-ups, but an undersupply of venture funding for higher-capital, longer-gestation start-ups in the Singaporean tech start-up ecosystem. For example, the NRF TIS cofunding program was copied from the Israeli Technology Incubation Model, which was originally created to incubate high-risk technology development by highly trained scientists and engineers who migrated to Israel from the former Soviet Union after the fall of the Berlin Wall. To attract private investors to back such risky ventures, the program offered very generous public cofunding of 85 percent. Unfortunately, when implemented in Singapore, the TIS did not restrict the type of tech start-ups that could be funded, and as a result, virtually all the investors awarded the TIS utilized it to invest in ICT and internet/mobile start-ups, with few going into the intended deep-tech sector. In addition, the ESVFs cofunded by NRF also underinvested in deep-tech start-ups, because the matching fund for each of these ESVFs was too small (up to SG$10 million), resulting in small-sized funds (SG$20 million or less) that could not support a portfolio with too many high-risk deals.

Concluding Observations

It has been more than ten years since the publication of the book *Making IT: The Rise of Asia in High Tech*. My chapter in that volume assessed the development of Singapore's innovation and entrepreneurship ecosystem from the early 1990s to the early 2000s. Here, I have sought to provide some empirical evidence on the changes in this ecosystem since. The following conclusions can be drawn:

Despite significant quantitative growth, a fundamental weakness remains in Singapore's innovation system: the underdevelopment of indigenous firms' innovation capability. This underdevelopment is particularly manifest among local small- and medium-sized enterprises, although some of the large government-linked corporations are also slow to invest in innovation capability development.

While tech start-up activities increased substantially over the last decade, these are predominantly in the internet/mobile/IT services sector. Deep-tech start-ups remain small in number, and few have the potential to be global leaders.

Public policy changes over the last decade to support technology entrepreneurship have largely focused on enabling start-ups in the digital innovation space, particularly internet/mobile/IT services, where start-up capital require-ments and the required gestation time for product development are relatively modest. Going forward, the challenge will be to nurture deep-tech start-ups, particularly those seeking to commercialize R&D outputs from public research institutes and universities. Greater policy focus to address the hurdles in university-industry knowledge transfer, as well as more technology-cluster-specific policies, are likely to be needed. So is a deliberate strategy to push the various quasi-state-owned enterprises or government-linked corporations to invest more in innovation—by, for example, reducing their traditional reliance on the domestic market and forcing them to compete in the global market. Greater policy attention is also needed to address tech start-ups' obstacles to scaling up, including so as to penetrate the emerging markets of the Association of Southeast Asian Nations (ASEAN).

My findings on Singapore's experience in developing its innovation and entrepreneurship ecosystem hold a number of implications for other newly industrialized economies. First, policies fostering the national innovation system need to be better integrated with policies promoting technology entrepreneurship. In the case of Singapore, the two sets of policies appear to be poorly integrated: much of the investment in public R&D has not been translated into technology commercialization, because the absorptive capacities of existing local enterprises have not been sufficiently developed. At the same time, the many new start-ups being supported are mainly in the internet/mobile subsector, which actually did not draw much on the public R&D investment.

Second, as late-industrializing Asian economies intensify their efforts to catch up with advanced economies through the development of more indig-enous firms with capabilities in the advanced technology sector, Singapore's mixed experience in this regard suggests the need for policymakers to take a holistic approach toward nurturing indigenous capacity. As highlighted earlier, commercializing advanced technologies can be achieved through new start-ups or existing enterprises, so public policy needs to be framed broadly to encompass the facilitation of both pathways. In Singapore, policymakers have paid much attention to the entrepreneurial start-up pathway, but perhaps not enough to increasing the innovative capability of existing firms, especially the large incumbent government-linked corporations. In contrast, Korea may have overemphasized the second pathway to the detriment of the first.

Third, for latecomer economies with small domestic markets and limited supplies of indigenous talent, Singapore's experience highlights the critical importance of building strong international connectivity to attract talent, access markets, and absorb VC. Policy-wise, Singapore has done relatively well in attracting both overseas R&D and entrepreneurial talent (and to a certain degree, overseas VC funding), and not as well in facilitating indigenous start-ups to scale up internationally.

Last but not least, Singapore's case suggests that universities can play a potentially significant role in fostering technology entrepreneurship. While venture funding facilitated by public grants and cofunding has clearly contributed, the proactive role of local universities in providing start-up incubation support appears to have been important as well. It is also likely that the increased emphasis on entrepreneurship seen over the past fifteen years in Singapore's universities, particularly the NUS, may have enlarged the supply of young university graduates predisposed to pursue start-ups versus working in large companies and the public sector (Wong, Ho, and Singh 2014).

References

Agency for Science, Technology and Research (A*STAR). Various years. "National Survey of R&D in Singapore." A*STAR, Singapore.

Coe, David T., and Elhanan Helpman. 1995. "International R&D Spillovers." *European Economic Review* 39, no. 5: 859–87.

Future Economy Council (FEC). 2017. *Report of the Committee on the Future Economy*. Singapore: FEC.

Guellec, Dominique, and Bruno van Pottelsberghe De La Potterie. 2002. "R&D and Productivity Growth: Panel Data Analysis of 16 OECD Countries." *OECD Economic Studies* 2001, no. 2: 103–26.

Ho, Yuen Ping, and Poh Kam Wong. 2017. "The Impact of R&D on the Singaporean Economy." *STI Policy Review* 8, no. 1: 1–22.

Ho, Yuen Ping, Poh Kam Wong, and Mun Heng Toh. 2009. "The Impact of R&D on the Singapore Economy: An Empirical Evaluation." *The Singapore Economic Review* 54, no. 1: 1–20.

Lerner, Josh. 2009. *The Boulevard of Broken Dreams: Why Public Efforts to Boost Entrepreneurship and Venture Capital Have Failed—and What to Do about It*. Princeton: Princeton University Press.

National Science Foundation (NSF). 2016. "Science & Engineering Indicators 2016." NSF, United States.

National Science and Technology Board. Various years. "National Survey of R&D in Singapore." National Science and Technology Board, Singapore.

Organisation for Economic Co-operation and Development (OECD). 2012. *Innovation for Development*. Paris: OECD.

Schwab, Klaus. 2016. *The Fourth Industrial Revolution*. Geneva: World Economic Forum.

Science Council of Singapore. Various years. "National Survey of R&D Expenditure and Manpower." Science Council of Singapore, Singapore.

Voutsinas, Ioannis, and Constantinos Tsamadias. 2014. "Does Research and Development Capital Affect Total Factor Productivity? Evidence from Greece." *Economics of Innovation and New Technology* 23, no. 7: 631–51.

Wong, Poh Kam. 2001. "Leveraging Multinational Corporations, Fostering Technopreneurship: The Changing Role of S&T Policy in Singapore." *International Journal of Technology Management* 22, no. 5/6: 539–67.

―――. 2003. "From Using to Creating Technology: The Evolution of Singapore's National Innovation System and the Changing Role of Public Policy." Chapter 8 in *Competitiveness, FDI and Technological Activity in East Asia*, edited by Sanjaya Lall and Shūjirō Urata. Cheltenham: Edward Elgar.

―――. 2006. "The Re-making of Singapore's High Tech Enterprise Ecosystem." Chapter 5 in *Making IT: The Rise of Asia in High Tech*, edited by Henry Rowen, William Miller, and Marguerite Hancock. Stanford: Stanford University Press.

Wong, Poh Kam, and Annette Singh. 2008. "From Technology Adopter to Innovator: The Dynamics of Change in the National System of Innovation in Singapore." Chapter 3 in *Small Economy Innovation Systems: Comparing Globalization, Change and Policy in Asia and Europe*, edited by Charles Edquist and Leif Hommen. Cheltenham: Edward Elgar.

―――. 2011. OECD *Review of Innovation in Southeast Asia: Country Profile of Singapore*. Research report commissioned by OECD. April.

―――. 2018. "The Changing Structure of Singapore's National Innovation System: Evidence from Patenting Data." NUS Enterprise working paper, National University of Singapore, Singapore.

Wong, Poh Kam, and Yuen Ping Ho. 2018. "The Changing Structure of Singapore's Technology StartUp Ecosystem: Evidence from the TechSG Project." NUS Enterprise working paper, National University of Singapore, Singapore.

Wong, Poh Kam, Annette Singh, and Robert Tijssen. 2018. "Studying the Role of University in Knowledge Creation vs Commercialization Using Stokes' Typology: Evidence from the National University of Singapore." NUS Enterprise working paper, National University of Singapore, Singapore.

Wong, Poh Kam, Yuen Ping Ho, and Annette Singh 2011. *Study on High-Tech Start-Ups in Singapore. Final Report*. Prepared for the National Research Foundation.

―――. 2014. "Toward a 'Global Knowledge Enterprise': The Entrepreneurial University Model of the National University of Singapore." Chapter 12 in *Building Technology Transfer within Research Universities: An Entrepreneurial Approach*, edited by Thomas J. Allen and Rory P. O'Shea. Cambridge: Cambridge University Press.

Wong, Poh Kam, Yuen Ping Ho, and Crystal Su Juan Ng. 2017. *Growth Dynamics of High-Tech Start-Ups in Singapore: A Longitudinal Study*. Research report prepared for the National Research Foundation.

World Bank. 2018. "World Development Indicators: Size of the
   Economy." Accessed April 2018. http://wdi.worldbank.org/table/WV.1.

CHAPTER 5

Taiwan's Quest for an Innovation Economy
A Tale of Two Transformations
Michelle F. Hsieh

A distinctive feature of East Asian postwar development is the state's active involvement in the economy. This involvement has stimulated a series of research studies on the so-called developmental state. The literature emphasizes the state's capacities to nurture new industries and induce entrepreneurs to invest in sectors they might not otherwise have considered (Johnson 1982; Woo 1991; Amsden 1989; Wade 1990; Weiss 1998). The successes of the information technology (IT) industry in Taiwan and South Korea, for example, have made these economies poster children and models for emulation (Evans 1995; Rowen, Hancock, and Miller 2007).

Latecomer economies are in a race, trying to keep up with advanced economies while they are in turn being pursued by other, late-latecomer, economies. East Asia's latecomer economies, like Taiwan and South Korea, are constantly searching for a template that will induce entrepreneurial growth and create new innovative industries to keep ahead of the competition. The recommendations they receive along the way often derive from the experiences of the IT industry. Thus, the priority is to develop new capabilities that are more flexible, skill intensive, and innovation driven. The new economy is believed to require the coordination of complex yet flexible institutions in meeting shifting challenges and demands. This setup would be a departure from most developmental states' current practice of scaling up investment policies from a centralized bureaucracy with strong leadership.

Creating the next Silicon Valley is a hot topic dominating policy debates and performance assessments, as is identifying the institutional arrangements that can induce public-private synergy in generating knowledge diffusion and collaboration. To this end, common policy practices are to increase investment in education, to encourage innovation by subsidizing research and development (R&D) (see chapter 6 on Japan and chapter 7 on Korea in this volume), and to encourage entrepreneurship through incubating start-up policies (see chapter 4 on Singapore).

In this chapter, I consider the question of innovation and entrepreneurship clusters. Here I present an overlooked model, proven to be equally successful as the celebrated model common in the IT industry: namely, a model of network-based, innovation-focused small- and medium-sized enterprises (SMEs), as seen in the upgrade of Taiwan's machinery industry. I refer to this alternative as the less-celebrated model.

This chapter demonstrates that Taiwan's SME-based machinery industry has adapted well and shown more resilience in the ongoing quest for innovation than the celebrated model of the IT sector. The chapter is organized as follows: I first give working definitions of innovation and entrepreneurship and show their relationship to the notion of clusters. I then examine the performance of manufacturing subsectors and their innovative capacities by using indicators such as industrial and commerce census data to support the claim that the less-celebrated model of Taiwan's SME-based machinery industry has done just as well if not better than the widely acclaimed IT-based model. A section is devoted to explaining how learning and innovation in the machinery industry have contributed to its resilience. I bring the role of public technology support institutions to the forefront and discuss the specifics of how orchestrating cross-cutting ties and thereby facilitating learning and cross-industry fertilization has been conducive to the collective learning and capacity building that sustain cluster dynamism. By juxtaposing the transformation of Taiwan's IT sector with that of its machinery industry, I conclude with a reconceptualization of development strategies and policy implications.

Defining Innovation, Entrepreneurship, and Clusters

Despite being buzzwords in headlines and among Asian policymakers discussing the next stage of national development, the concepts "innovation" and "entrepreneurship" tend to be vaguely defined, and their implications can be elusive. The term "innovation" is often associated with rapid-speed knowledge and research-intensive industries like IT and biotechnology that involve high entry barriers. In this chapter, I adopt Schumpeter's position on innovation, which considers entrepreneurship as innovation (Swedberg 2002; originally Schumpeter 1934). In his view, entrepreneurship/innovation can be best understood as the recombination of existing means. Innovation is about entrepreneurial activities that break existing routines through recombination and create added value. This might be through introducing new materials, production methods, products, or a new degree of quality; a new market; or even a new organization setup of any industry through a combination of existing means (Schumpeter 1934, 66). Therefore, innovation and the creation of additional value are about an active recombination of people, resources, knowledge, and social networks, as well as about creating new opportunities by pooling previously unconnected resources for an economic purpose (Granovetter 2005). It follows that entrepreneurship and innovation form a dynamic process, rather than a static one measured by the number of new firm entries or a focus on personal characteristics (Imai 2007; Aldrich 2005, 454). This kind of innovative activity may not easily be captured by statistical indicators such as R&D expenditures or number of patents. It demands a qualitative understanding and exploration of the concrete social relationships and interactions among actors. Thus, the focus centers on the interactions among firms/actors instead of on a single actor.

It follows that the analytical questions should move from deliberating whether large or small firms will triumph to investigating the specifics of how an ecosystem or regional economies can link actors and firms of various sizes and competencies together (Castilla et al. 2000, 246). The specific ways in which connections are made among various actors in a system account for the variations in outcomes (Block and Evans 2005). It is in this sense that networks of firms, the linkages among them, and the concept of clustering become relevant to understanding how entrepreneurship and innovation occur. The literature on networks postulates that a social network helps to transmit information and knowledge, and that this in turn generates innovation (Castilla et al. 2000; Smith-Doerr and Powell 2005; Saxenian and Hsu 2001). In particular, networks of social relations embedded in a geographical region are believed to be conducive to new ideas. This is because geographical proximity increases frequent interpersonal contacts that facilitate information exchange and speed up information flow.

Lastly, the kind of innovation I refer to is related to technology development and the potential growth resulting from technological advancements. It follows that manufacturing is important in the so-called knowledge economy because it inspires technological advancement and adds value, creates jobs, and promotes more equitable growth. The effects can be seen by comparing the situations around restructuring in western European countries and the United States. For instance, Germany and small countries like Denmark, instead of deindustrializing, have simply restructured and continued to thrive in high-quality and high-value-added advanced manufacturing, even in the face of competition from Asia (Herrigel 2010). In contrast, studies reveal that increasing inequality in the United States over the past three decades has to do with deindustrialization and increasing financialization, whereby firms do not invest in productive goods but downsize and focus on maximizing short-term profits for their shareholders (Lazonick 2009; Lin and Tomaskovic-Devey 2013). Moreover, the recent efforts to establish many innovation platforms working with SMEs and various incentives and policies aimed at bringing manufacturing back to the United States suggest that innovation cannot take place in a vacuum or the research lab but needs to be close to the shop floor. All in all, manufacturing matters for innovation (Block and Keller 2011; Berger 2013; Locke and Wellhausen 2014).

This chapter builds on these concepts by examining the case of Taiwan and offering an explanation of its resilient SME clusters.

Decentralized Industrialization and Taiwan's Postwar Development

A distinctive feature of Taiwan's postwar economic development was decentralized industrialization, which consists of a system of SMEs clustered in a geographical locale where numerous small firms complement one another in the production process, with each specialized in one phase of production. Together as a whole, they formed the foundation of the "Taiwan miracle," in which various industries claimed world-class distinction by inserting themselves successfully into the global production network and thrived by being international subcontractors for industries ranging from shoes, apparel, bicycles, and machine tools in the 1980s to IT industries from the 1990s onward.

Various industries within Taiwan's decentralized industrial system have the following general characteristics in common:

- The SME-based production system encompasses an extensive division of labor in which firms complement one another in the production process. They cluster in a geographical locale, or "industrial district" (Piore and Sabel 1984), where numerous firms compete and cooperate in the same industry. Many of the SME network-based industries in

Taiwan focus on (a) assembling or (b) parts. The assembling industry involves an extensive system of subcontracting and a high degree of specialization. Extensive subcontracting is also exercised within the parts industry. The various components of a part are subcontracted to small factories that specialize in manufacturing them.

- The SME production network consists of numerous independent parts makers and processing specialists who focus on intermediate input and do not make the final product.

- Production networks are decentralized in the sense that they are open networks in which suppliers and specialist firms are usually not tied to particular assemblers. They can supply several firms within the industry or sell to other industries.

- Parts makers and specialist firms are incorporated into the global production network and compete directly in the world market rather than being completely dependent on domestic assemblers. The ability of SMEs to export directly—since the start of export-led industrialization in the 1970s—has been exceptional when compared to neighboring countries like Japan and Korea, where large conglomerates handle most of the exports.

One immediate consequence of such decentralized industrialization is that interindustry linkages are high. In an open and independent network, information not only travels within the industry but cascades among industries. Workshops that perform some processing jobs for bicycle assemblers and parts suppliers—such as drilling, lathing, milling, metal surface finishing, and anodizing—are not locked into one particular supplier or one industry. They perform processing jobs for a variety of industries. Moreover, the ability of parts makers to connect with the global market means that their points of access to information are multiple, so they have multiple sources of learning. This means that knowledge and ideas cross industry boundaries and are not contained under a single roof. As will be discussed later, these characteristics affect how one understands where breakthroughs and technological learning come from and how innovation occurs.

Highlighting Taiwan's decentralized development sets the groundwork for a discussion of innovation and industrial upgrading, by identifying key innovation actors and driving forces. A dominant view in the literature on latecomer economies is that Taiwan's decentralized SME system may have already run its course in the current quest for innovation, and that production, organizations, and resources should be scaled up to capture technological rents. As can be seen in the global value chain literature, it is lead firms, which are usually large firms, that will orchestrate innovation activities and the capture of rents (Amsden and Chu 2003; Gereffi, Humphrey, and Sturgeon

2005; Gereffi 2013). On the other hand, an increasing body of literature suggests that networks of firms will prevail in the current quest for innovation, in light of the transformation that took place in Silicon Valley (this might be termed a continuity thesis). Here, interindustry connections prove to be an advantage. The idea of interindustry learning is pertinent because connecting to different clusters and different supply chains in different industries creates opportunities for the recombination of valuable new information and thus better learning. Having access to multiple, nonredundant information sources is conducive to learning and innovation because moving in different circles connects one to a wider world, whereas a closed network might lead to a locked-in effect (Burt 2004).

Where Do Innovations Come from?
A Tale of Two Transformations

Indicators of Innovative Capacities

The following section sketches an overall picture of Taiwan's technological development since 2000. The empirical task here is to identify which sector has been driving Taiwan's innovation and industrial transformation in the past two decades. Over this period, Taiwan, like Japan and Korea, increased its R&D. For instance, in 2001, national R&D expenditures were about 2.02 percent of gross domestic product (GDP), a remarkable increase from 1.7 percent in 1990. By 2006, they were 2.43 percent of GDP, reaching 2.90 percent in 2011 and 3.16 percent in 2016. At the same time, the key spenders on R&D shifted from the public to the private sector. For instance, the government was responsible for over 50 percent of R&D expenditures in 1990; this figure went down to 30.10 percent in 2001, then steadily declined to 28.68 percent in 2006, 23.85 percent in 2011, and 19.66 percent in 2016. In contrast, R&D expenditures by private companies went from 64.86 percent in 2001 to 67.15 percent, to 72.60 percent, to 77.74 percent in the respective periods (see table 5.1).[1] IT industries (including various electronic components, computer and computer peripheral equipment, and semiconductors) continued to consume a large bulk of national R&D expenditures, moving from 40.57 percent in 2001 to 56.64 percent in 2016.[2] In contrast, the metal and machinery industries,

---

1   The figures are from the National Science and Technology Survey: https://wsts .most.gov.tw/stsweb/technology/TechnologyStatisticsList.aspx?language=E, retrieved March 30, 2018.

2   The data were retrieved from the National Science and Technology Survey and calculated by the author.

TABLE 5.1 Major R&D indicators in Taiwan (in millions of New Taiwan dollars)

	2001		2006		2011		2016	
	Value	Percentage	Value	Percentage	Value	Percentage	Value	Percentage
R&D expenditures	204,974	100.00	307,037	100.00	414,412	100.00	541,360	100.00
Funds from business enterprise sector	132,950	64.86	206,177	67.15	300,874	72.60	420,873	77.74
Funds from government	61,702	30.10	88,044	28.68	98,840	23.85	106,444	19.66
Funds from university fund	6,636	3.24	8,399	4.07	9,624	3.20	8,991	2.14
Funds from higher education sector	2,719	1.33	3,257	1.06	3,918	0.95	3,590	0.66
Funds from private nonprofit sector	931	0.45	1,071	0.35	1,007	0.24	995	0.18
Funds from abroad	35	0.02	91	0.03	148	0.04	466	0.09
R&D expenditures as a percentage of GDP								
(R&D expenditure/GDP)	204,974	2.02	307,037	2.43	414,412	2.90	541,360	3.16
	2001		2006		2011		2016	
R&D expenditures by industries' manufacturing sector (aggregated)								
Total R&D expenditures	119,898		190,744		278,669		384,701	
R&D expenditures/sales (%)	—		1.21		1.60		2.36	
R&D expenditures/national R&D expenditures (%)	58.49		62.12		67.24		71.06	
IT industries								
Total R&D expenditures	83,164		143,884		218,719		306,646	
R&D expenditures/sales (%)	—		5.53		8.73		13.88	
R&D expenditures/national R&D expenditures (%)	40.57		46.86		52.78		56.64	
Metal and machinery sector								
Total R&D expenditures	19,052		25,896		31,440		38,703	
R&D expenditures/sales (%)	—		4.24		5.11		5.86	
R&D expenditures/national R&D expenditures (%)	9.29		8.43		7.59		7.15	

SOURCE: National Science and Technology Survey, Taiwan, https://wsts.most.gov.tw/stsweb/technology/TechnologyStatisticsList.aspx?language=E.
NOTE: GDP = gross domestic product; R&D = research and development.

constituting less than 10 percent of national R&D expenditures, went from 9.29 percent in 2001 to 7.15 percent in 2016.

Using patents as a proxy for innovation and technological capacities, Taiwan has consistently ranked fifth—as measured by the number of patents among all countries filed at the U.S. Patent and Trade Office (USPTO)—since 2000. The total number of patents increased from 4,667 in 2000 to 6,128 in 2008 to 8,781 in 2011 to 11,690 in 2015. According to patents filed at the USPTO, the semiconductor industry (under the IT sector) has been the key patent generator among all industries from Taiwan (and also South Korea). Yet at the individual firm level, the Taiwan Semiconductor Manufacturing Corporation (TSMC), Taiwan's top generator of patents awarded by the USPTO, contributed 7 percent of Taiwan's total patents in 2007 and about 15 percent in 2015.[3] At the same time, the top ten patent-holding organizations are from the IT sector, and half of them are semiconductor industries, but they constituted only 41 percent of patents within the IT sector and about 24 percent of Taiwan's total patents from the 2000–07 period (Wang 2010, 297).

To sum up, the IT sector has continued to be the key driver of Taiwan's innovation in the past two decades, according to the indicators of R&D expenditures and patents. Looking at patent distributions, IT innovation activities continue to be relatively diffused across firms in the IT sector when compared to South Korea, where Samsung Electronics prevails. That company alone created about one-third of the USPTO-registered patents coming from Korea in 2015.

Sectoral Transformation Reconsidered, 1996–2011

Employing industrial and commerce census data,[4] figure 5.1 presents the transformation in Taiwan's manufacturing sector from 1996 to 2011, a period when Taiwan allegedly went through major restructuring, both economically and politically. Conventionally, this period is associated with the dominance of high-tech IT exports as a key driver of Taiwan's economy, replacing labor-intensive industries. There was increased internationalization of production by Taiwanese firms through an arrangement called "triangle manufacturing," whereby transactions between foreign buyers and Taiwanese producers were conducted in Taiwan, while the final products, ranging from those of light industries to IT production, were exported through another country, for example, from offshore factories in China and Vietnam. Lastly, large firms gained an increasingly strong foothold in the manufacturing sector.

---

3   The patent figures are from USPTO (2000, 2007, 2011, and 2015). The percentages were calculated by the author.

4   The data from the 2016 industrial census had not been released as of the date of this writing; the discussion is therefore based on data collected from 1996 to 2011.

FIGURE 5.1 The contribution of revenue and value added of the four major industries in Taiwan's manufacturing sector

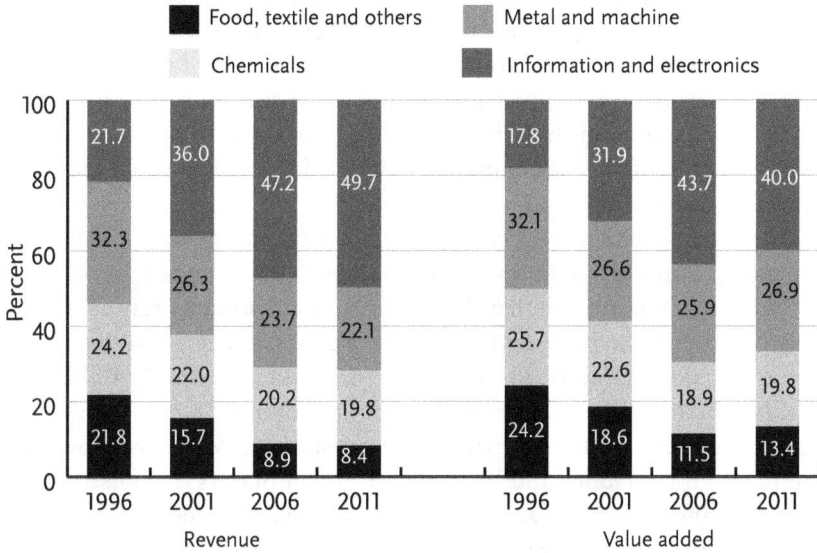

SOURCE: Directorate-General of Budget, Accounting and Statistics. Industry, Commerce and Service Census Taiwan-Fukien area, the Republic of China, 1996–2011, https://wsts.most.gov.tw/stsweb/technology/TechnologyStatisticsList.aspx?language=E.

The industrial and commerce census data reveal that the IT sector created the most revenue and value added in Taiwan's manufacturing sector, constituting almost 50 percent (49.7 percent) in 2011, up from 21.7 percent in 1996. This sector generated 40 percent of the total value added in the manufacturing sector, up from 17.8 percent in 1996.[5] In contrast, the aggregated metal and machinery industries made up 22.1 percent of revenue in the manufacturing sector but generated over 26.9 percent of the total value added in the manufacturing sector in 2011 (see figure 5.1). Examining the composition of the industries within the IT sector, the picture looks slightly different. The semiconductor industry constituted 6.2 percent of the total revenue of the manufacturing sector in 2011 but generated 17 percent of the manufacturing sector's total value added. In contrast, computer and computer peripheral equipment industries gobbled up 26.5 percent of revenue in the manufacturing sector but created only 5.6 percent of the value added. In other words, the metal and machinery industries (26.9 percent of the total

5   The value added is calculated as total gross output minus intermediate input consumption. Basically, it is about the value created by the economic activities undertaken by each firm. The reason that the computer and peripheral sectors generated much revenue but low value added is partly a result of triangle manufacturing, where the value created for the Taiwanese parent company relates only to the outsourcing processing fees.

value added) performed as well as the IT sector (23 percent of the total value added, excluding the semiconductor industry) in Taiwan's economy in the last decade. Moreover, the metal and machinery industries predominantly consist of SMEs and operate on the basis of decentralized networks. Over 60 percent of the total value added by the metal and machinery industries results from work done by firms with fewer than 200 employees, compared to 78.5 percent of the total value added by the IT sector, in which the work is done by firms with over 500 employees.[6]

The data reveal that the acclaimed high-tech transformation based on the experience of the IT sector distorts the understanding of what has occurred in Taiwan's economy, and that this sector's contribution to Taiwan's economy has been misrepresented. Also, the SME-based metal and machinery industries, despite receiving less attention, performed equally well in the last decade. Moreover, in the face of concerns over the demise of the SME network system, empirical evidence suggests that SMEs have moved up the value-added ladder and become key global players or indispensable upstream and midstream global suppliers for several industries. SMEs have continued to be strong exporters, including of parts; and export diversification has been integral to upgrading strategies. Export-oriented industries like bicycles, machine tools, auto parts, and fasteners have continued to be strong exporters, and statistics suggest that total export values doubled or even tripled in the last decade, as illustrated in figure 5.2. Moreover, parts suppliers have been strong exporters by inserting themselves into various global production networks, as exemplified by the increasing export shares of bicycle parts, auto parts, and fasteners. Lastly, unlike European industrial districts that went into decline in the face of globalization and from Asian competition in the 1980s, Taiwan's clusters and accompanying decentralized network-based production have continued to be resilient locally, even with internationalization. Central Taiwan has continued to be the hub for the domestic machine-tool industry as well as the bicycle industry and related machinery parts; Hsinchu has continued to be the hub for the IT industry, the semiconductor industry, and IT-related industries; and southern Taiwan has continued to be the hub for steel- and metal-related industries.

In short, SME-based entrepreneurship has continued to thrive and has played an important role in Taiwan's quest for an innovative economy. If one invokes the conventional proxy (i.e., patents) used to measure innovative or technological capacity, this reaffirms the relative importance of the machinery industry in driving Taiwan's transformation over the past decade. Three

---

6   The data on the transformation of the manufacturing sector are drawn from Hsieh (2014).

FIGURE 5.2 Export value of selected subindustries, 2000–18 (US$ millions)

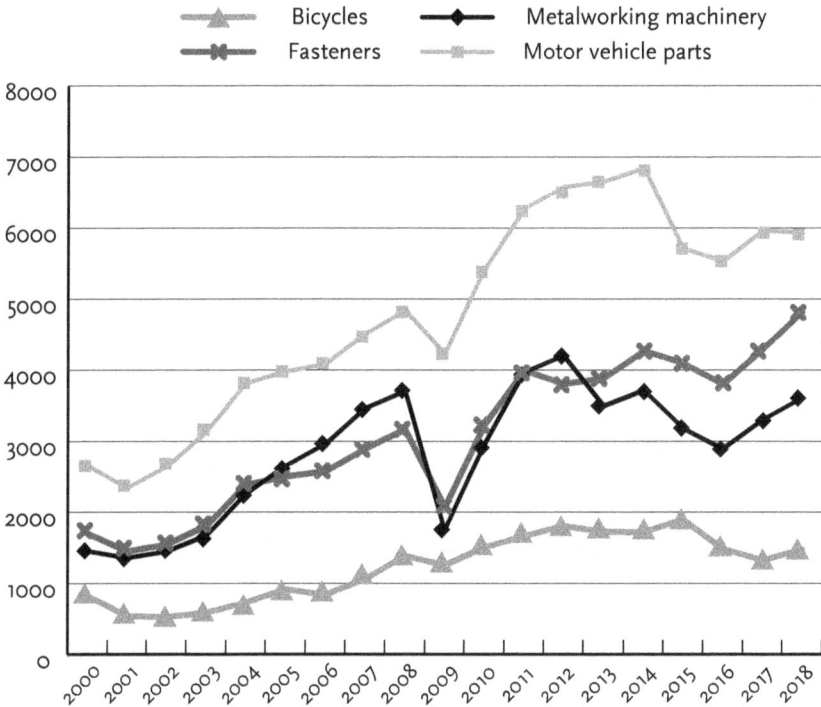

SOURCE: Bureau of Foreign Trade: http://cus93.trade.gov.tw/fsci.

of its subindustries—machine tools, transportation equipment, and sports equipment—also ranked among the top ten patent-holding subindustries in Taiwan (Wang 2010, 301). The fact that half of patent holders in Taiwan's machinery industry were registered as individuals as opposed to organizations suggests that SMEs have continued to be sources of innovation.

Sources of Growth in the Celebrated IT Model vs. the Less-Celebrated SME Ecosystem

Taiwan's SME-based decentralized network production is conventionally perceived as growing independent of the state, contrary to the celebrated IT model, in which the Industrial Technology Research Institute (ITRI) and the government have been considered the key drivers of technological development and diffusion.

In what follows, I compare and contrast the organizational principles of the two ecosystems, with special attention to the less-celebrated model, whose merits are underexplored. The data for the celebrated model build upon the extensive research that has arisen from attempts to explain the well-known achievements of Taiwan's IT industries. The sources of data for the SME-network ecosystem include my more than fifteen years of fieldwork and interviews with various actors related to manufacturing activities in the machinery industry, from assemblers and parts makers to various specialist firms in bicycles, auto parts, machine tools, fasteners, and hardware industries to engineers in public research institutes (PRIS) and government representatives. The interviews conducted focused on the question of how SMEs have adapted their processes so as to retain production in Taiwan while also successfully ascending to higher-value-added production. Because I have observed these cases over a long period of time and tracked their transformations, I have been able to verify that the lessons gleaned from them are both valid and representative. While the statistical indicators outlined above provide an overview of the structural changes in Taiwan's industrial transformation and technological advancement, the qualitative data from selected interviews cited in this chapter illustrate the common themes and dynamics of the learning processes, centering on the interactions of actors, and allow a reconstruction of the worldview of entrepreneurs. The interviewees presented carefully considered positions and qualitative evaluations.[7]

The Celebrated IT Ecosystem Model

The transformation of the IT sector in Taiwan is often attributed to the role of the state in creating new industry. The Hsinchu Science-Based Industrial Park (HSIP, established in 1980) is a prominent example of a government-created cluster, where most IT-related high-tech firms and start-ups are located. The region—with its connections to California and its similar dynamism—is often thought of as the Silicon Valley of the East. Yet, Shih, Wang, and Wei (2007) point out that a crucial difference between HSIP and Silicon Valley is the pivotal role of PRIS as the driving force for technology creation and diffusion. In particular, ITRI (established in 1973), located close to HSIP, plays a pivotal role in developing integrated circuit (IC) technologies and creating spin-off firms. Therefore, the public-private linkages and the IT high-tech cluster in the Taiwanese context center on the role of state-funded research institutions, such as ITRI, and their collaboration with the private sector. And these are often invoked in accounts of Taiwan's success in moving to high-tech industrialization (Wang 2010; Amsden and Chu 2003;

---

7   My interview sources cited below are roughly anonymized—these citations consist of "Interview" plus the surname of the interviewee and the year the interview took place.

Chen 2003; Shih, Wang, and Wei 2007; Fuller, Akinwande, and Sodini 2003; Breznitz 2007). Most of the narratives have agreed that a functional division of labor between the state and industry players contributed to the ascent of Taiwan's IT sector. Unlike what occurred in Korea's IT sector, where large firms such as Samsung and LG did much of the technology acquisition and development, Taiwan relied on PRIs such as ITRI to acquire and absorb new technologies and conduct most of the R&D, especially initially. In turn, ITRI introduced needed technologies, through technology transfer, to the private sector or spin-off firms (Shih, Wang, and Wei 2007).

The other key element of technology diffusion was through the movement of Taiwanese returnees from Silicon Valley to ITRI and to HSIP companies, and personnel moving from ITRI to the private sector.[8] The latter, for example, have constituted an important channel for technology diffusion. Of the more than 16,000 employees who have trained at ITRI since 1973 and subsequently left, 81 percent have gone on to private industry, with more than 5,000 going on to HSIP, especially in the semiconductor and computer peripheral industries (Shih, Wang, and Wei 2007, 111). Job mobility from ITRI to the private sector differentiates ITRI significantly from its Korean and Japanese counterparts, where mobility between researchers in PRIs and the private sector remains limited (Interview Lee 2015; Hashimoto 2013).[9]

While ITRI played a pivotal role at the initial stage of technology development, the private sector has shifted into the driver's seat over the last two decades, as illustrated by the rise and growth of numerous IT companies in HSIP and by the aforementioned R&D indicators. Nevertheless, ITRI has continued to be R&D intensive and plays an important role in Taiwan's high-tech development and dissemination. For instance, it has ranked fourth in patents granted by the USPTO among all Taiwanese organizations over the past two decades. Meanwhile, since the mid-1990s, collaborations between ITRI and the private sector have evolved from an earlier approach of PRIs leading most of the research, and a technology spin-off model, to a joint collaboration between PRIs and the private sector, with research funding shared by both sectors as a way to push ITRI closer to industry (Wang 2010; Shih, Wang, and

---

8   For a detailed discussion of the role of linkages between Silicon Valley and Taiwan's IT development, see Saxenian (2006). Shih, Wang, and Wei (2007) write a detailed account of the role of returnees in the origins of Taiwan's IT industry and their involvement in establishing ITRI.

9   In my comparative research of PRIs in Taiwan, South Korea, and Japan, the Korean interviewees remarked that they were impressed with the level of mobility between ITRI and private industries, whereas job mobility and the level of interaction between the Korean PRI and the private sector is much more limited. Researchers at the Japanese PRI also concurred that the interaction between the PRI and the private sector is largely formal and cases of job mobility are rare.

Wei 2007). ITRI has become a technology-supporting institution, playing a role similar to PRIS in the less-celebrated model (discussed below).

While many IT firms started small, many have grown much larger in scale and become leading global players. However, it is important to highlight that the network-based system has persisted even in the IT sector, especially in the semiconductor industry, Taiwan's leader in technological innovation. For instance, firms insert themselves in the semiconductor industry's global production, with many firms focusing on manufacturing application-specific integrated circuits (ASICs), as opposed to mass-producing dynamic random-access memory (DRAM), in which Korea has prevailed. In fact, the creation of pure foundry manufacturing by TSMC,[10] a spin-off from ITRI, in 1987 was an organizational innovation in the industry and from that time established a new business model for the global semiconductor industry (Chen 2003). The presence of TSMC and other specialized foundry manufacturing firms that focused on midstream wafer manufacturing has induced many local IC chip-design SMEs to insert themselves into the value chain by focusing on upstream design. IC chip design firms have proliferated, from 56 companies in 1990 to 140 in 2000, and to over 250 companies since 2003 (ITRI, various years). There are specialized firms focusing on downstream packing and testing. As a whole, firms have tapped into the highly specialized network in HSIP to work closely with related IT industries to develop end products, mostly electronics and IT components. The growth in ASIC chip design and manufacturing has contributed to the scope of IT-related products/components coming out of Taiwan because most IT components require ASIC chips.

The Ecosystem of the Less-Celebrated SME Model

The transformation of the metal and machinery industries raises the question of how SMEs could have performed so well. The adaptation and upgrading of SME-based metal and machinery industries resemble the flexible specialization production capitalism that Piore and Sabel (1984) characterize as a historical alternative to the mass production system associated with modern industrial capitalism. The SMEs in the flexible specialization production system manufacture a wide range of customized products using flexible, general-purpose machines that require skilled labor capable of multitasking and who are adaptive to changing demands (Zeitlin 2008; Sabel and Zeitlin 1997). In this alternative model, firms focus on niche markets and compete in the quality

---

10   TSMC started as a joint venture between the government and Phillips. The government (through a national development fund) continues to be the second-largest institutional shareholder (6.38 percent), next to TSMC (20.68 percent), with one seat on the board.

segment of the value chain rather than in the price-sensitive segment of mass production of standardized items. Thus, value is added through quality as opposed to efficiency, which is about making things cheaper by producing more of them. On the other hand, the flexible specialization system can be conducive to permanent technological innovation because firms need to redesign products and methods to address growing competition and find new ways to reduce the cost of customized production. This motivation, in turn, encourages technological sophistication and innovation (Piore and Sabel 1984, 207). Often involved are innovations through recombination, such as the reorganization of production, new material applications, innovation in manufacturing processes, the introduction of products to a new market, export diversification, and improvements in the quality of trade.

Contrary to the celebrated model, which attributes responsibility for incubating new technology to the ITRI and the government, Taiwan's SME-based, decentralized industries are often seen to grow independent of the state. For instance, while the state was crucial in orchestrating the formation of the IT cluster, various export-oriented, SME-based industries and clusters in the machinery sector organically evolved in central Taiwan, such as the bicycle industry, machine tools, hand tools, auto parts, hardware, and various machinery accessories. A resilient and vibrant network of SMEs in the metal and machinery industries renewed interest in studying these hidden champions.

The dynamism of the clusters in central Taiwan resembles Marshall's notion of industrial agglomeration and contemporary industrial districts, discussed in the literature in the 1980s and 1990s (examples include Third Italy, southern Germany, and Denmark; see Piore and Sabel 1984; Herrigel 1996; Kristensen 1995). Many interviewees, when asked how they started their business, stated that they worked for firms in similar industries and decided to set up their production focusing on one stage of the production process and supporting others. As one interviewee put it, "You may change jobs, but you never leave the industry" (Interview Chou 2010). Another interviewee's remark captured the role of geography: "All suppliers are within a radius of 60 km and this is how our business operates" (Interview Hsu 2004). The existing network-centered, market-responsive approach suggests that trust and kinship contribute to entrepreneurship as firms spin off in response to the call of export-led industrialization. As the story goes, SMEs successfully connect to the world market and assert themselves in global production networks through original equipment manufacturing (OEM) and respond to demand from buyers (Chen 1994; Hamilton and Kao 2011; Gereffi 1994).

The literature on clusters emphasizes the advantage of agglomeration economies as "collective efficiencies," for agglomeration helps to reach economies of scale. Moreover, trust and cooperation through frequent interactions and kinship account for the flexibility of the clusters and their network-based organizational setup (Powell 1990). Yet, trust and dense ties do not say much about upgrading and capability building. Learning is relevant in understanding innovative capabilities because it induces entrepreneurship and self-discovery/exploration. Self-discovery is largely a problem of complex coordination (Sabel 2012). However, in a context of decentralized clusters, learning can be a problem; decentralization often generates competition and thus diminishes the returns on self-discovery, not to mention that individual SMEs may not have the resources and manpower needed to develop innovation and learning capacities. Therefore, the question is: How do these Taiwanese SMEs learn to improve their quality, given that their R&D expenditure is relatively low (as indicated in table 5.1)? Put differently, how can a system of SMEs build the technical capacities necessary to meet the stringent quality requirements of export markets and succeed in the world market, given their small-scale R&D expenditures and size?

Contrary to a conventional view that assumes that the growth of a network of SMEs is independent of the state, the following section unpacks the black box of learning in a decentralized system. I show how the state could expand the limits of self-learning by addressing collective problems and building external economies and public goods that each individual SME could not realize on its own, so as to induce entrepreneurs to engage in exploration and capability building. This kind of support focuses on an overarching plan to solve collective problems, alleviate the R&D burden of SMEs, and shorten their learning curves to induce firms to engage in complementary learning and investment in a context of decentralized production. It includes a variety of widely practiced but unrecognized initiatives, including manufacturing extension programs, export promotion services, and quality and capability building by the state, that address collective problems and build external economies (public goods) for firms to tap into Taiwan's decentralized setting. Such initiatives have been crucial in accounting for the upgrading of SMEs. In other words, the state builds the hidden infrastructure of those export-led economies that have facilitated SMEs' technology learning and success in the world market. These initiatives are considered hidden infrastructure because they are loosely connected with the economy. Here the role of para-state institutions, such as PRIs (focusing on applied research), are embedded in the ecosystem of the less-celebrated model and serve as the institutional linkages that connect the various actors.

Building an Innovation Ecosystem:
Connecting Decentralized Networks of Firms with Public Institutions that Support Technology

The transformation of SMEs in the metal and machinery industries suggests that decentralized, broad, but overlapping ties among different actors were constructed to facilitate learning and establish the quality and technological capabilities needed to succeed in the global market. The actors involved included relatively low-ranked state agencies (such as the Industrial Development Bureau [IDB] under the Ministry of Economic Affairs), engineers from a variety of technology support institutions (such as industry--specific R&D centers, which receive much less funding than does ITRI), industry associations, and SMEs; each actor is connected with the others in multiple ways. Cases from the machinery industry, including bicycles, auto parts, machine tools, and fasteners, illustrate how building capability by constructing cross-cutting ties can help induce export-oriented entrepreneurship and innovation.

The state's quest to upgrade and overcome the problems of decentralized production in SME-dominant industries, starting in the 1990s, can be exemplified by IDB's Program for the Development of Critical Components and Parts. Several industry-specific research centers were established in central Taiwan, where various machinery industries are located, including the Automotive Research and Testing Center (ARTC), the Bicycle R&D Center (BIRDC), the Precision Machinery Research and Development Center (PMC), the Plastic Industry Development Center (PIDC), and the Footwear Technology Research Center (FTRC). These industry-specific R&D centers are considered public-private partnerships, since funding comes from both government and industry, and board members include firm representatives, Ministry of Economic Affairs' representatives, and university professors. IDB's programs in the 1990s stressed that assistance and research should be more responsive to the private sector and practically applicable. Despite an initial goal to develop critical components and parts, studies have revealed that services (such as establishing industry-specific testing labs) that provide external economies applicable to all firms in an industry do the most to help firms move up to a higher-value-added trade segment in the global market. So do services that bridge production networks and facilitate cross-industry fertilization to help induce entrepreneurship and innovation through recombination.

Providing External Economies and Fostering Collective Problem Solving
The aforementioned industry-specific R&D centers build internationally accredited independent/professional R&D testing labs for each industry and

provide testing and certification of products for designated markets. These services have been fundamental (though their effect is often underestimated) in fostering R&D for SME's high-value-added production and export diversification, and in meeting the stringent quality control standards of advanced economies.[11]

R&D-related testing has been crucial in solving problems related to complex product development and is fundamental to innovation. The services provided by industry-specific R&D centers and the Metal Industries Research and Development Center (MIRDC) have encouraged self-discovery and learning by inducing firms to explore more creative ways to develop their products than they might otherwise have undertaken. Engineers of industry-specific R&D centers see their research labs as functioning to entice firms into exploratory research and to disseminate the knowledge gained. The following remarks by an interviewee capture the necessity of collective problem solving provided by an industry R&D center:

> SMEs tend to expect the industry R&D center to solve collective problems.... You can consider the PMC as a place to incubate technical skills and a think tank for collective problem solving. For instance, we provide training of skilled technicians for new technologies, disseminate those technologies and develop new testing methodologies as technologies evolve. It is like sowing seed. (Interview Chan 2011)

The testing services of industry R&D centers can also mitigate undue risks because firms can take advantage of their testing facilities without having to make unnecessary investments. One interviewee reiterated the importance of working with research labs like the MIRDC, as it bypasses the limits of self-learning: "It is imperative that we work with the R&D lab at the stage of product development because we can use their facilities for testing, so we don't have to invest in testing equipment in advance for something that we don't even know is going to work" (Interview Lee 2010). The following remark by another interviewee highlights the necessity of collective technology support services to shorten the learning curve and induce exploration:

> You can't just tell them to buy advanced equipment that, for all they know, might not even work. No SME owners dare to break their banks to purchase advanced technological equipment unless they are certain this will work. Moreover, exploring this new technology may involve a lengthy self-learning

---

11   Interviewees from the metal hardware and bicycle industries reiterate the importance of meeting industrial standards for export markets because these items belong to a niche market in which European countries and the United States may have completely different specifications and standards (interview info).

curve. This is why I urge the association to purchase the machine so that we can explore it together. Without these kinds of collective technology support programs, no one is going to try new things out. (Interview Wu 2016)

Each industry R&D center has built a database of worldwide industrial standards for its export-oriented industry and specific testing methodologies. These are used to not only certify the testing results but also provide feedback regarding improvements and solutions. They foster collective problem solving, such as in testing and standards compliance, have alleviated the burdens of SMEs by reducing entry barriers for exports, support R&D, and bolster SMEs' place in the world market. For instance, even though Taiwan does not have a strong auto assembly industry, it has developed a vibrant and export-oriented auto parts industry in which component suppliers have successfully inserted themselves into the global supply chain as aftermarket suppliers in the U.S. and European markets. Having access to collective testing facilities provided by ARTC in central Taiwan facilitates such entry into global markets. A veteran engineer at PMC acknowledged that one of the R&D center's first tasks was to develop testing technology that would enhance quality and innovation in the machine tool industry (Interview Huang 2011). Compliance with CE standards (for products sold in the European Economic Area)[12] and the U.S. Fastener Quality Act in the 1990s were crucial for machinery exports and metal products like fasteners and hardware. The PMC and MIRDC proactively responded to potential changes in export market standards, and studied and disseminated the changes needed for testing methodologies and manufacturing methods for the machine tool industry and fasteners to ensure that firms were not shut out of the export market (Interview Chan 2011; Lin 2013). MIRDC established internationally accredited testing and research labs for various small-metal industries, such as for fastener testing or plumbing research and testing. All industry R&D centers actively study and follow the changing regulations and acts of the designated export market, as these changes might affect new material applications, new manufacturing technologies, and involve new testing methodologies.

Having access to industry-specific R&D centers and labs in central Taiwan means that SMEs, especially parts makers, can tap into the external economies provided by public technology support agencies, whereas an individual SME is unlikely to be able to function effectively on its own. This is particularly the case where these SMEs thrive in a niche market in which each export

---

12   European safety standards demand that goods entering the European Union meet the requirements of applicable European Commission regulations and directives. They came into effect in 1995.

destination may require different specifications and standards. The result has been export diversification among SMEs in the machinery industry and transportation sector. For instance, in the past decade, about half the total exports went to the top five destinations in the aggregated transportation industries, while over one-third of the total exports went to destinations outside the top ten countries. In the machinery industry, over 50 percent of the total export value went to countries outside the top ten export destinations, while the top five export destinations received less than 50 percent of the total exports (Hsieh 2014).

Inducing Innovation and Entrepreneurship through Cross-Cutting Ties

As discussed, a key feature of Taiwan's decentralized network production is that firms have multiple channels of access to information. Yet decentralization requires coordination to turn access to information into enhanced capability and innovation without producing chaos. Public technology support agencies can induce firms to explore possibilities in complementary areas by bridging different networks and resources. They connect SMEs from various production networks and facilitate cross-industry fertilization, through which innovation and breakthroughs occur by recombining existing means. In other words, innovation occurs when technology and knowledge diffusion induce collaboration in exploring possibilities.[13] The following examples of the technology support offered by the MIRDC and industry-specific R&D centers illustrate this.

Industry R&D centers help to develop and disseminate particular manufacturing technologies by working with SMEs to improve the entire supply chain for a specific technology, including through fostering locally built equipment. In fact, technology adaptation and breakthroughs often occur at the level of intermediate input (meaning the parts subindustry) and work upward and downward along the supply chain to create backward linkages.[14] For instance, in an initiative to apply hydroforming manufacturing technologies to bicycle tubes, the MIRDC first developed locally built equipment

---

13   Hsieh (2015) provides a detailed case study of how breakthroughs in manufacturing technology occur through cross-industry fertilization and collaboration.

14   The following section draws extensively from the case of the bicycle subindustry. This may not be a big component of the machinery industry in terms of the total value added, but its upgrading process is representative inasmuch as it used to be a labor-intensive industry and was expected to be one of the first industries that would migrate completely to low-wage countries, following their European and Japanese predecessors. Contrary to the predictions, the bicycle cluster in central Taiwan has continued to be vibrant, showing no signs of hollowing out. Moreover, its organization of production and its connections to the wider machinery industry are typical of Taiwan's SME network system and, thus, make it a representative case to illustrate their transformation.

for manufacturing this technology, although the technology was initially applied in heavy industries with equipment acquired from Germany. The MIRDC formed a research consortium and connected firms from different production networks, including materials suppliers, mold-making specialists, processing specialists, equipment builders, bicycle-tube makers, and bicycle assemblers. The MIRDC engineer responsible for the project explained that the rationale for bringing other industries on board to develop a particular technology is to broaden the application of this technology and encourage technology spillover. He observed: "Once we can build the equipment for this manufacturing technology locally at a modest cost that fulfills the functions, we are able to induce others to apply this new production technology. We then broaden the impact of [the] application of this technology" (Interview Chung 2016).

A-Team, an alliance within the bicycle industry established by two leading assemblers and parts suppliers in the 2000s, is an example of the industry's collective effort to move to high-value-added production and sustain a cluster in Taiwan—when the industry faced a potential hollowing-out crisis after a number of firms migrated to low-wage countries. This case exemplifies how innovation in a decentralized setting involves collaborative learning and the bridging of networks. One of the first tasks in A-Team's upgrading process was to adopt the Toyota Production System (TPS, a just-in-time system) for bicycle production. When asked whether the alliance was an attempt at supply chain integration by bringing suppliers into the orbit of leading assemblers, the president of the assembling company stated with no hesitation, "The team was about 'learning,' not about supply-chain integration. They are not our exclusive suppliers" (Interview Tseng 2010). When another leading assembler was asked why his firm invited its competitor to participate in the alliance (it involved team members visiting one another's factories), his response illustrated quite well the problems of coordination in a decentralized network: "Even if we are considered the biggest bicycle manufacturer in Taiwan, we alone could not capture the whole export market, and we need some commitment from other assemblers to induce suppliers to participate" (Interview Hsu 2004). The parts suppliers all gave credit to the advantages of collaborative learning, even though their competitors also participated in the alliance. The members acknowledged that individual firms had considered adapting the TPS and associated methodologies in their own factories, but their attempts had not been successful. The TPS system requires coordination and improvement from the upstream to the downstream of supply networks (Interview Chen 2010).

While SMEs initiated the consortium, IDB acted as a mediator by connecting Toyota Taiwan to the bicycle A-Team for implementing TPS. The IDB officer in charge of industrial development programs in the machinery industry considered these alliances as sowing a seed, as he explained: "Once these parts suppliers learn the trick they will pass on the information to their downstream suppliers, as they all need to meet the requirements set by the A-Team. We thought to use this to bring about some transformation in the industry, given the limited resources we have"[15] (Interview Yeh 2014).[16] The Bicycle R&D Center also participated in this project and went on to work with other firms (not included in the alliance) in the bicycle industry. These efforts helped the industry to become the key player in the high-end quality segment of the bicycle trade, where the total export values increased almost four times to US$1.9 billion in 2015 from its lowest point of US$0.5 billion in 2002 (see figure 5.2). The average price of a bicycle coming out of Taiwan in 2017 was over US$550 (Free on Board, FOB), up from US$290 (FOB) in 2009 and US$120 (FOB) in 2002, when the alliance was first formed amid serious concerns about declining export values and a hollowing out of the industrial base in central Taiwan.[17] In fact, the resilience and dynamism of the clusters actually persuaded firms that had closed their operations and moved production offshore to return production to Taiwan to tap into the external economies and technological prowess provided by the region.

Subsequently, a similar alliance (M-Team) was introduced into the machine tool industry while exploring how TPS could be applied to that industry and other machinery industries in their quest for quality innovation. Recent efforts to move into advanced manufacturing (or smart manufacturing), such as by exploring Industry 4.0, have continued to run according to these institutional arrangements (Interview Chen 2016). The aim is to promote cross-industry fertilization and build a platform that can connect different industries and industry-specific R&D centers and IDB, even as multiple actors are loosely connected in an ecosystem of machinery clusters.

One might question if these industry-specific R&D centers are in tune with the world market and are capable of connecting suppliers from different fields, since they are not firms competing in the market. This is especially true when the R&D done by PRIs have frequently been criticized for resulting in technologies that have no commercial value or are so advanced that they cannot be easily commercialized when working with SMEs. How could these parastate agencies be able to identify partners for product development and capability building?

---

15   The implication is that the resources, in monetary terms, could easily be dissipated without making a dent, given the decentralized industrial structure.

16   Other assemblers who were not in the alliance also concur that their parts suppliers who participated in the alliance shared their experience and advised them to speed up their restructuring (Interview Liang 2011).

17   The data are from Bureau of Foreign Trade: http://cus93.trade.gov.tw/fsci.

These case studies reveal that learning and capability do not simply flow from a mentor to mentees, but in both directions. In the case of the A-Team, Toyota Taiwan acknowledged that it learned a great deal from the project. The general manager of Toyota Taiwan, who actively participated in the project, perceived the alliance as an experiment, as Toyota was not sure whether a production system designed for the automobile industry organized in a closed network could be applied to the decentralized/open network production system of Taiwan's bicycle industry. The engineer who coordinated the hydroforming project emphasized that Toyota learned tremendously from working with bicycle manufacturers and, in turn, by applying that experience to working with firms in other industries. Engineers from the MIRDC credit the variety of industrial training, new technology development, problem solving, technology extension, and testing services they provide for connecting them with SMEs in various industries, especially in the parts sector. In particular, testing services provided for various industries have helped them create knowledge and gain access to industries (Interview Chung 2008; Wang 2013; Lin 2013; Kao 2013).

Lastly, not all industrial development programs or research consortia work equally well under the arrangements seen in a decentralized network. For instance, engineers from public technology support agencies acknowledged that projects connecting different PRIs and the machinery industry to explore the application of a new lightweight material, magnesium alloy, fell short because of difficulties in commercialized production presented by the material's highly explosive nature. Nevertheless, each exploration and collaboration is about building technological capabilities, and this was agreed upon by most of the people I interviewed (Interview Chung 2008; Chiang 2011; Cheng 2016).

In the ecosystem of Taiwan's machinery industry, exploring a new technology or the application of new materials often involves trying to find collaborators by connecting firms from upstream material suppliers to downstream final producers and varieties of specialist firms, possibly from different industries, for collaboration and discussion. Most of my interviewees concurred that innovation and product development for SMEs is often about searching for ideas and tapping into external economies in central Taiwan beyond their own industry boundary: "I frequently visited different trade shows, like machine tool industry and even aerospace industry trade shows, to get ideas to see if we can apply some technology to our industry…" (Interview Wu 2016). A senior engineer from the MIRDC illustrated how the dynamics of technology development in Taiwan center on working with networks of SMEs rather than trying to do everything solo:

I have visited a lot of companies, and I know whom to contact if I am developing a new product/process technology. How can these companies realize the project? We know that their supply networks could assist them (such as numerous specialist firms). When we call the meeting, the companies usually call their suppliers and friends to join the discussion to explore solutions and possibilities. We often end up with a solution beyond my original imagination. (Interview Cheng 2016)

In other words, technology support services and on-site factory visits are not about troubleshooting and top-down assistance, but about exploring manufacturing methods and searching for potential collaborators when new development projects and ideas arise.

These initiatives fly under the radar and are conducive to broad-based entrepreneurship as opposed to the industrial targeting described in literature on the developmental state. The technological support offered by PRIs is not about targeting R&D subsidies to selected, individual firms but about inducing exploration among a network of firms. The responses of my interviewees illustrate these dynamics well. In the interviews, if I asked the question whether they received support from the government, the answer was usually no. But if I reframed the question by asking if they had used the testing services provided by an industry-specific R&D center, the answer was yes. One interviewee said: "I don't think R&D subsidies to individual firms are effective. Instead, it is imperative for the government to construct ties among different industries and the government can establish a platform for firms to tap into" (Interview Wu 2016). Another interviewee thought that his company's participation in the MIRDC's research consortium connecting different industries was about learning: "You asked me how I participated in the project that connects firms across different industries to explore a new manufacturing technology. MIRDC's engineer approached me on this case. It is not really about the amount of R&D subsidies I can get; but as long as there is an opportunity for learning and exploration, I will join" (Interview Chen 2014).

To sum up, in the context of a decentralized industrial system, technology extension services focus on enhancing local spillover effects, integration, and developing the technical capabilities of an entire supply chain as opposed to a top-down technology transfer to selected firms. This explains why, despite relatively low R&D expenditures, a system of SMEs has been able to tap into external economies, and how through recombination and cross-industry fertilization, SMEs have thrived in higher-value-added production chains.

Conclusions and Implications

This chapter takes a network approach to understanding innovation and entrepreneurship. It demonstrates the qualitative aspect of innovation, which often occurs through interactions among different actors (e.g., interfirm linkages). The transformations of Taiwan's SME-based machinery industry suggest alternative possibilities to innovation and prosperity in which collaborative learning and technology diffusion can be conducive to new kinds of entrepreneurship, rather than reliance upon the hefty R&D expenditures of individual firms. These initiatives tend to be invisible and decentralized in the sense that they deploy relatively flattened resources and low budgets. This is contrary to common policy practices that focus on promoting innovation by increasing investment in R&D by focusing subsidies on selected firms, or policies that encourage entrepreneurship by increasing the number of firms in targeted clusters or government subsidies to an increasing number of start-ups, as in Japan and Singapore, respectively. Case studies of innovation clusters using these common practices reveal the poor performance of their firms in terms of both production and technological capabilities—due to a top-down selection process or a decoupling of policies focused on entrepreneurship vs. science and technology (chapters 4 and 6 in this volume; Lee 2000).

Taiwan's less-celebrated model raises a question regarding the proper unit of analysis for studying innovation. This distinction matters because it affects the policy choices for nurturing ecosystems for entrepreneurship and innovation, which entail completely different notions of clustering and ways of constructing cross-cutting ties. In Taiwan's SME network, the unit of analysis is a system comprising networks of firms that complement one another and tap into external economies. Thus, capability building is about (1) bridging different production networks to create technological advancement along an entire supply chain, and (2) sustaining clusters. Success or failure is not measured by the size, number of patents, or performance of an individual firm, but by the viability of the system overall. On the other hand, in a firm-centered innovation system, cross-cutting ties are created in a different way; state agencies connect a variety of governmental resources and PRIs to nurture individual, selected firms. In this case, capability is fostered by bringing different resources to individual firms, as can be seen in the Korean experience of constructing regional innovation clusters (Hsieh 2018).

Lastly, the lessons from the less-celebrated model of Taiwan's machinery industry suggest that what makes a cluster tick is not the size of its firms, but the specific ways in which networks of firms and PRIs are linked in a decentralized system. Each actor is connected in multiple ways to tap into external economies so as to pursue collaborative learning. Even in the celebrated model of the semiconductor industry, firms have continued to tap into decentralized networks to enhance production and spark innovation despite having grown in size and scale. State institutions and a variety of parastate institutions, such as PRIs, are loosely connected in the system; this bypasses the limits of self-learning by bridging different networks to induce collective learning and innovation. This kind of a flexible and dynamic ecosystem is one way for clusters to remain resilient, territorially rooted, and globally connected in the face of globalization.

References

Aldrich, Howard E. 2005. "Entrepreneurship." In *The Handbook of Economic Sociology*, edited by Neil J. Smelser and Richard Swedberg. Princeton, NJ: Princeton University Press.

Amsden, Alice H. 1989. *Asia's Next Giant: South Korea and Late Industrialization*. New York: Oxford University Press.

Amsden, Alice H., and Wan-wen Chu. 2003. *Beyond Late Development: Taiwan's Upgrading Policies*. Cambridge, MA: MIT Press.

Berger, Suzanne. 2013. *Making in America: From Innovation to Market*. Cambridge, MA: MIT Press.

Block, Fred, and Peter Evans. 2005. "The State and the Economy." In *The Handbook of Economic Sociology, Second Edition*, edited by Neil J. Smelser and Richard Swedberg. Princeton, NJ: Princeton University Press.

Block, Fred, and Matthew R. Keller, eds. 2011. *State of Innovation: The U.S. Government's Role in Technology Development*. Boulder, CO: Paradigm Publishers.

Breznitz, Dan. 2007. *Innovation and the State: Political Choice and Strategies for Growth in Israel, Taiwan, and Ireland*. New Haven and London: Yale University Press.

Bureau of Foreign Trade. N.d. "Statistics of Import and Export of Republic of China." http://cus93.trade.gov.tw/fsci. Retrieved May 8, 2018.

Burt, Ronald S. 2004. "Structural Holes and Good Ideas." *American Journal of Sociology* 110, no. 2: 349–99.

Castilla, Emilio J., Hokyu Hwang, Ellen Granovetter, and Mark Granovetter. 2000. "Social Networks in Silicon Valley." In *The Silicon Valley Edge: A Habitat for Innovation and Entrepreneurship*, edited by Chong-Moon Lee, William F. Miller, Marguerite Gong Hancock, and Henry S. Rowen. Stanford, CA: Stanford University Press.

Chen, Chieh-Hsuan. 1994. *Flexible Network and Common Life Structure: Social Economic Analysis of Taiwanese Small-Medium Business*. [In Chinese.] Taipei City: Linking Publishing Company.

Chen, Dongsheng. 2003. *Making It Integrated: Organizational Networks in Taiwan's Integrated-Circuit Industry*. [In Chinese.] Taipei: Socio Publishing.

Evans, Peter. 1995. *Embedded Autonomy: States and Industrial Transformation*. Princeton, NJ: Princeton University Press.

Fuller, Douglas B., Akintunde Akinwande, and Charles Sodini. 2003. "Leading, Following or Cooked Goose? Innovation Successes and

Failures in Taiwan's Electronics Industry." *Industry and Innnovation* 10, no. 2: 176–96.

Gereffi, Gary. 1994. "The Organization of Buyer-Driven Global Commodity Chains: How U.S. Retailers Shape Overseas Production Networks." In *Commodity Chains and Global Capitalism*, edited by Gary Gereffi and Miguel Korzeniewicz. Westport, Conn.: Greenwood Press.

———. 2013. "Global Value Chains in a Post-Washington Consensus World." *Review of International Political Economy* 21, no. 1: 9–37.

Gereffi, Gary, John Humphrey, and Timothy Sturgeon. 2005. "The Governance of Global Value Chains." *Review of International Political Economy* 12, no. 1: 78–104.

Granovetter, Mark. 2005. "The Impact of Social Structure on Economic Outcomes." *Journal of Economic Perspectives* 19, no. 1: 33–50.

Hamilton, Gary G., and Cheng-shu Kao. 2011. "The Asia Miracle and the Rise of Demand-Responsive Economies." In *The Market Makers: How Retailers Are Reshaping the Global Economy*, edited by Gary G. Hamilton, Benjamin Senauer, and Misha Petrovic. New York: Oxford University Press.

Herrigel, Gary. 1996. *Industrial Constructions: The Sources of German Industrial Power*. Cambridge: Cambridge University Press.

———. 2010. *Manufacturing Possibilities: Creative Action and Industrial Recomposition in the United States, Germany, and Japan*. Oxford, New York: Oxford University Press.

Hsieh, Michelle F. 2014. "Hollowing Out or Sustaining? Taiwan's SME Network-Based Production System Reconsidered, 1996–2011." *Taiwanese Sociology*, no. 28: 149–91.

———. 2015. "Learning by Manufacturing Parts: Explaining Technological Change in Taiwan's Decentralized Industrialization." *East Asian Science, Technology and Society: An International Journal* 9, no. 4: 331–58.

———. 2018. "South Korean SMEs and the Quest for an Innovation Economy." In *Beyond the Miracle: Strategic, Policy and Social Innovations for a Post-Industrial Korea,* edited by Joon-Nak Choi, Yong Suk Lee, and Gi-Wook Shin. New York: Routledge.

Imai, Ken-ichi. 2007. "Stability and Change in the Japanese System." In *Making IT: The Rise of Asia in High Tech*, edited by Henry S. Rowen, Marguerite Gong Hancock, and William F. Miller. Stanford, CA: Stanford University Press.

Industrial Technology Research Institute (ITRI). Various years. *Semiconductor Industry Yearbook*. [In Chinese.] Taipei: Industrial Technology Research Institute.

Johnson, Chalmers. 1982. *MITI and the Japanese Miracle: The Growth of Industrial Policy, 1925–1975*. Stanford, CA: Stanford University Press.

Kristensen, Peer Hull. 1995. "Denmark: Many Small Worlds." In *Small and Medium-Size Enterprises*, edited by Arnaldo Bagnasco and Charles Sabel. London: Pinter Publishers.

Lazonick, William. 2009. *Sustainable Prosperity in the New Economy? Business Organization and High-Tech Employment in the United States*. Kalamazoo, MI: W.E. Upjohn Institute for Employment Research.

Lee, Won-Young. 2000. "The Role of Science and Technology Policy in Korea's Industrial Development." In *Technology, Learning and Innovation: Experiences of Newly Industrializing Economies*, edited by Linsu Kim and Richard R. Nelson. Cambridge, United Kingdom: Cambridge University Press.

Lin, Ken-Hou, and Donald Tomaskovic-Devey. 2013. "Financialization and US Income Inequality, 1970–2008." *American Journal of Sociology* 118, no. 5: 1284–329.

Locke, Richard M., and Rachel L. Wellhausen. 2014. *Production in the Innovation Economy*. Cambridge, MA: MIT Press.

Ministry of Science and Technology. N.d. "National Science and Technology Survey." https://wsts.most.gov.tw/stsweb/technology/TechnologyStatisticsList.aspx?language=E. Retrieved March 30, 2018.

Piore, Michael J., and Charles F. Sabel. 1984. *The Second Industrial Divide: Possibilities for Prosperity*. New York: Basic Books.

Powell, Walter W. 1990. "Neither Market nor Hierarchy: Networks Forms of Organization." *Research in Organizational Behavior* 12, no. 2: 295–336.

Rowen, Henry S., Marguerite Gong Hancock, and William F. Miller, eds. 2007. *Making IT: The Rise of Asia in High Tech*. Stanford, CA: Stanford University Press.

Sabel, Charles. 2012. "Self-Discovery as a Coordination Problem." In *Export Pioneers in Latin America*, edited by Charles Sabel, Andrés Rodríguez-Clare, Ernesto H. Stein, Ricardo Hausmann, and Eduardo Fernández-Arias. Washington, DC: Inter-American Development Bank.

Sabel, Charles. F., and Jonathan Zeitlin, eds. 1997. *World of Possibilities: Flexibility and Mass Production in Western Industrialization.* Cambridge: Cambridge University Press.

Saxenian, AnnaLee. 2006. *The New Argonauts: Regional Advantage in a Global Economy.* London, England: Harvard University Press.

Saxenian, AnnaLee, and Jinn-Yuh Hsu. 2001. "The Silicon Valley– Hsinchu Connection: Technical Communities and Industrial Upgrading." *Industrial and Corporate Change* 10, no. 4: 893–920.

Schumpeter, Joseph Alois. 1934. *The Theory of Economic Development: An Inquiry into Profits, Capital, Credit, Interest, and the Business Cycle.* Cambridge: Harvard University Press.

Shih, Chintay, Kung Wang, and Yi-Ling Wei. 2007. "Hsinchu, Taiwan: Asia's Pioneering High-Tech Park." In *Making IT: The Rise of Asia in High Tech*, edited by Henry S. Rowen, Marguerite Gong Hancock, and William F. Miller. Stanford, CA: Stanford University Press.

Smith-Doerr, Laurel, and Walter W. Powell. 2005. "Networks and Economic Life." In *The Handbook of Economic Sociology*, edited by Neil Smelser and Richard Swedberg. Princeton, NJ: Princeton University Press.

Swedberg, Richard, ed. 2002. *Entrepreneurship: The Social Science View (Oxford Management Readers).* New York: Oxford University Press.

U.S. Patent and Trademark Office (USPTO). 2000, 2007, 2011, and 2015. *General Patent Statistics Report: Patenting by Organizations.* https:// www.uspto.gov/web/offices/ac/ido/oeip/taf/reports.htm. Retrieved March 31, 2018.

Wade, Robert. 1990. *Governing the Market: Economic Theory and the Role of Government in East Asian Industrialization.* Princeton, NJ: Princeton University Press.

Wang, Jenn-Hwan. 2010. *The Limits of Fast Follower: Taiwan's Economic Transition and Innovation.* [In Chinese.] Kaohsiung: Chuliu.

Weiss, Linda 1998. *The Myth of the Powerless State.* Ithaca: Cornell University Press.

Woo, Jung-en. 1991. *Race to the Swift: State and Finance in Korean Industrialization.* New York: Columbia University Press.

Zeitlin, Jonathan. 2008. "The Historical Alternatives Approach." In *The Oxford Handbook of Business History*, edited by G. Jones and J. Zeitlin. New York: Oxford University Press.

CHAPTER 6

Innovative Cluster Policies

Evidence from Japan

Toshihiro Okubo

Amid the huge wave of globalization in recent decades, trade costs, including tariff and nontariff barriers, have dropped worldwide. Communication costs have also decreased dramatically through the development of information technology. Today, capital and labor are highly mobile across countries and regions. Consequently, the globalization wave has resulted in intense global competition. In order to survive, many developed countries—such as France, Germany, and Japan—have sought to enhance productivity by creating innovative industrial clusters. These build on economic theories and models such as Marshallian externality and Porter's diamond (Porter 2000), which consider industrial clusters as sources of innovation and economic growth.

Regardless of the policies behind them, industrial clusters in reality seem to lack both innovation and success. While it is hard to find a successful industrial cluster, the large variety of subsidy programs inherent to them require high management costs and sufficient budgets. Yet governments have adopted many cluster policies over recent decades without carefully evaluating their viability through econometric analysis. Only recently have such policy evaluations, using microdata from academic research and advanced econometrics to measure the impact of cluster policies on productivity and firm location, been rigorously carried out.

The impact of cluster policies on innovation and research and development (R&D) has been investigated by some studies (Falck, Heblich, and Kipar [2010] for Germany; Viladecans-Màrsal and Arauzo-Carod [2012] for Spain; and Nishimura and Okamuro [2011a, 2018] for Japan). More closely related to this chapter are several econometric investigations on the impact of subsidies on firm productivity (Devereux, Griffith, and Simpson [2007] for the United Kingdom; Duranton et al. [2010], Martin, Mayer, and Mayneris [2011], and Fontagné et al. [2013] for France; and Okubo and Tomiura [2010, 2012] for Japan) and on local employment (Bondonio and Engberg [2000] for U.S. enterprise zones). These studies find that the impacts of cluster policies on productivity, sales growth, and exports are generally very weak or insignificant, and they conclude that the policies were not effective in attracting productive firms to the targeted regions.[1]

Theoretically, Baldwin and Okubo (2006) propose spatial sorting to explain this unsuccessful outcome in a simple economic geography model. Baldwin and Okubo (2006, section 4) and Okubo (2012) provide a testable theory on the impact of regional subsidy policies.[2] When firms are heterogeneous in terms of productivity, they are geographically sorted by their own productivity. Subsidies are aimed at the relocation of firms from core regions to peripheral ones. In many cases, once a firm relocates from a core region to a peripheral one, it receives a certain amount of subsidy. Such a subsidy tends to attract the least efficient firms, since unproductive firms make smaller profits and thus would value the subsidy received for relocating more than a highly profitable firm. This could explain why relocation subsidies in peripheral regions are considered so ineffective in improving the

---

1   For instance, Martin, Mayer, and Mayneris (2011) report that French cluster firms are large, but their productivity shows a declining trend.

2   Dupont and Martin (2006) provide an economic geography model of the impact of regional subsidies.

Baldwin and Okubo (2006) and Okubo, Picard, and Thisse (2010) build an economic geography model depicting when firms are heterogeneous. The model is a marriage of the international trade model with the firm heterogeneity of Melitz (2003) and the simplest economic geography model of Martin and Rogers (1995). Forslid and Okubo (2014) find several types of sorting/selection patterns in an agglomeration economy.

competitiveness of those regions.[3]

This chapter provides an overview of recent academic research on Japanese cluster policies. Japan, which has a long history of industrial cluster policies, is a highly centralized country and has large fiscal deficits, which reduce the available budget for regional development policies. On the other hand, since peripheral regions are drastically depopulated and deindustrialized, regional development policies—including industrial cluster policies—are inevitable in such regions. This chapter considers how Japanese cluster policies did or did not attract innovative firms and boost regional productivity. Of the several policy issues related to industrial clusters, our main focus is the impact of these policies on the (re)location of firms and on productivity, based on the economic geography literature.

Overview of Japanese Cluster Policies

Japan has a long tradition of regional development policies.[4] The population of its two largest cities, Tokyo and Osaka, grew rapidly from the prewar period (1920s and 1930s). Urbanization concentrated both people and manufacturing in Tokyo and Osaka, and a Tokyo-Osaka bipolar circuit emerged. Over-agglomeration at both poles, and the income gap between these and peripheral regions, were long matters of concern. To reduce over-agglomeration, regional development policies supported the construction of large-scale infrastructure in rural regions in the postwar period. The aim was to balance the development of the high-density and peripheral regions.

---

3   Using the analogy of Baldwin and Okubo (2006), Okubo (2012) models proportional subsidies in which firms receive relocation subsidies proportional to their profits, and finds that peripheral regions can attract the most productive firms. The reason is that the most productive firms receive the largest subsidies. However, since productive firms make the largest profits, the amount of the subsidy would be infinite in peripheral regions. As long as subsidies are financed by taxation, this scheme is not feasible, or it leads to an enormous amount of government budget deficit. In a related finding, Midelfart-Knarvik et al. (2002) report that the EU Structural Fund supports are generally not effective except in Ireland, where the share of highly skilled workers is higher than other targeted countries.

4   Japan's regional industrial development policies and plans date back to the 1890s. From the 1890s to the 1920s, many peripheral regions (towns and villages) took part in the Village-Town Improvement Movement (*soncho ze undo*). The development strategy for regional industries and their structure was formulated based on data obtained from surveys conducted in each town and village. Later, the regional movement was formalized by the central government.

According to Fujita and Tabuchi (1997), the postwar regional economy in Japan experienced two major transformations touching on regional development policies and urban planning schemes. The first was the shift from the Tokyo-Osaka bipolar circuit to the Pacific Industrial Belt during the high-growth period of the 1960s. This transformation witnessed a substantial labor inflow to Tokyo and Osaka and resource reallocation from the agricultural sector in peripheral regions toward manufacturing industries on the Pacific Industrial Belt. The second transformation was a shift to a Tokyo-centered monopolar system after the oil crisis in the mid-1970s. Tokyo attracted firms' central management functions—e.g., headquarters and R&D centers—in manufacturing sectors as well as service industries. Behind these two transformations, Japan experienced a drastic change of industrial structure from agriculture, light industries, and heavy industries to knowledge-intensive or high-tech industries. This structural change is associated with the transformation of geographical location patterns and cluster policies.

These transformations, it is important to note, were to some extent driven by large-scale governmental regional policies fostering highway networks, high-speed railways, and firm clusters. In particular, the Japanese government undertook many initiatives designed to encourage firms' relocation from core to peripheral regions. Amid the low economic growth following the 1970s, a large income gap between core and peripheral regions persisted. Social concerns such as air and water pollution, traffic congestion, and soaring housing prices in core regions prompted public policies for nationwide industrial repositioning. The government's Long-term Regional Development Plan was established to emphasize balanced development across regions. Under the strong initiative of the central government, a variety of industrial cluster policy programs in peripheral regions were developed during the postwar period.

Characterizing Subsidy Programs

Before I consider Japanese cluster policies in detail, policies in postwar Japan can be summarized in the form of a simple subsidy chart (see figure 6.1) proposed by Okubo (2016).

The vertical axis of figure 6.1 indicates the goal and target of the subsidies—either innovation and growth by fostering new and high-tech industries in clusters (upward) or equalization/adjustment/dispersion to reduce the gap between core and peripheral regions by relocating firms and repositioning industries (downward). The horizontal axis indicates whether the subsidy scheme is project based (leftward) or targets a specific village or town (rightward). All the policies discussed below can be categorized by their position on this subsidy chart. For example, the Technopolis and Intelligent Location programs in the 1980s were aimed at creating innovative clusters and developing new industries by targeting specific towns and villages. Thus, these policies are located in the upper-right quadrant. The Industrial Relocation Subsidy policy in the 1970s, on the other hand, intended to relocate manufacturing firms to peripheral regions in order to reduce congestion in core regions. Thus, the policy is located in the lower-right quadrant. The cluster policy in the 2000s (e.g., Industrial Cluster project) was project based and sought to foster elements such as transaction network formation and R&D collaboration among universities and firms. Thus, this policy is located on the left side of the chart. Japanese regional cluster policies historically began in the lower-right quadrant and have migrated counterclockwise toward the upper-left quadrant. The current policy is shifting toward a project-based, targeted model, and is associated with indirect policies such as network formation and research collaboration.

FIGURE 6.1 Categorizing subsidies by their focus: A four-quadrant visualization

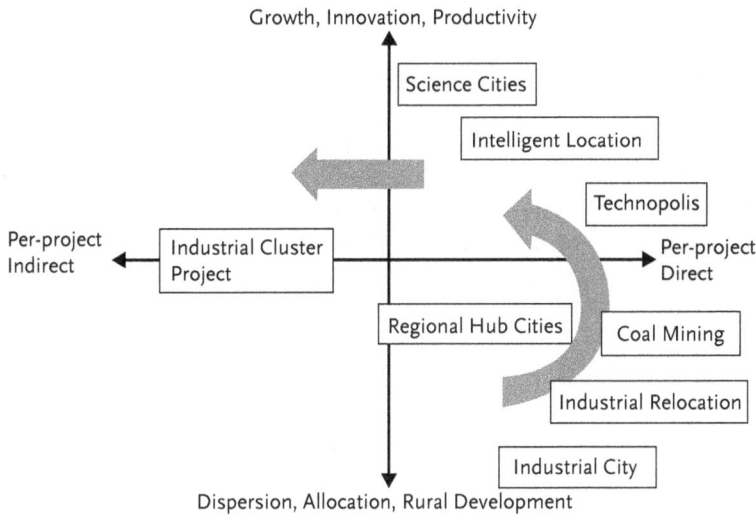

SOURCE: Okubo 2016.

Subsidy Policy Programs in the Postwar Period

I shall now move on to describe representative regional development policies in the postwar period in more detail.

Cluster Policies and Regional Development in the 1960s to 1970s

Overall, industrial cluster policy in the 1960s and 1970s had the main purpose of mitigating over-agglomeration in core regions by promoting relocation to peripheral ones. First, the new Industrial City policy (*shin-sangyo toshi*) was initiated in 1962. It was aimed at relocating industrial complexes (e.g., petrochemical complexes) and clusters of heavy industries from core regions to peripheral ones. Fifteen peripheral regions were nominated out of forty-four candidate regions as regional hubs for peripheral development in 1964. Firms in the regions were allowed tax deductions and subsidies.

Then, the adjustment of the regional industrial structure was supported by the Coal Mining policy (*san tan chi-iki*). This policy program started in 1961 and was intended to foster industries and employment in former coal-mining regions. Japan had traditionally depended on coal as its primary energy source until the late 1950s and 1960s. Coal-mining towns and villages used to be rich and populous, but the drastic shift of energy resource demand brought about by the energy revolution meant that coal-mining regions began to decline rather than grow. The government strongly supported these declining regions by providing regional subsidies to reduce unemployment and shift to new industries.

The Industrial Relocation Subsidy policy (*kojo sai-haichi*) was intended to subsidize manufacturing plants' move out of those regions where the policy was promoted (*iten-sokushin chi-iki*) to those where relocation was encouraged (*yudo chi-iki*).[5] These regions were defined by national government orders. Since almost all regions in Japan were categorized as one type or the other, this policy program had a substantial impact on firms' relocation from core regions to peripheral ones. This subsidy program started in 1972 and mitigated serious congestion in urban regions and industrial regions during a high economic growth period.

Innovative Clusters in the 1980s

After the oil crisis of the 1970s, the Japanese economy entered a low-growth phase. The central government intended to create new innovative clusters in

---

5   The regions from which plants were encouraged to leave (*iten-sokushin chi-iki*) were mainly around three major cities: Tokyo, Osaka, and Nagoya. Plants in these regions were encouraged to relocate to other regions (*yudo chi-iki*), almost all of them outside the three major cities.

peripheral regions. The Technopolis policy, initiated in 1983, was designed to create high-tech industrial complexes, targeting twenty-six regions.[6] The low-growth period led to a shift of the country's industrial structure from heavy to high-tech industries. The Technopolis policy was expected to play a crucial role in encouraging more balanced growth across regions. Also, the policy foresaw the development of new high-tech industries such as precision machinery (semiconductors) and biochemical industries as a result of research collaboration between firms and local universities.

Launched in 1988, the Intelligent Location policy (*zuno ritti*) was designed to attract software and information service industries to fifteen regions that were already targeted by the Technopolis policy. This policy highlighted the support of high-tech-intensive manufacturing and its related industries in peripheral regions.

Originally started in the early 1970s, Science Cities (*gakuen toshi*) was an urban planning policy that aimed to foster clusters of academic and research facilities. One example is Tsukuba City in Ibaraki Prefecture, to which a national university was relocated from central Tokyo as part of a comprehensive development plan for a new city.[7] As Japanese economic planning in the 1980s began to focus more on R&D, science, and technology than on production, Science Cities functioned as an industrial cluster policy.[8]

In sum, all these regional cluster policies, including the early ones of the 1960s and 1970s, were mandated by national law. More important, all targeted regions (and their cities, towns, and villages) explicitly defined by public ordinance documents. Firms in the targeted regions were eligible for subsidies and some government support.

In spite of their similarities, however, there is a sharp contrast in the emphasis of the early cluster policies and those of the 1980s. The latter were aimed at creating high-tech industry clusters and promoting innovation and economic growth, while the early policies were aimed at relocating firms from core regions to peripheral ones, to mitigate urban congestion and reduce the income gap between core and peripheral regions.

New Policy Perspective, 1990s

In the 1990s, the characteristics of regional policies altered slightly, to focus on nonmanufacturing activities, new business initiatives of small firms, and specific functions of a firm's organization, such as software programming,

---

6   The nominated regions were peripheral ones but with relatively good access to Tokyo or Osaka.

7   Keihanna Science City in the suburbs of Osaka is another example.

8   For example, Technopolis requires at least one university with engineering departments in each targeted region.

R&D, and management functions (e.g., headquarters location). The targeted regions included urban areas, while all previous policies had targeted peripheral regions. The change of policy perspective reflected the declining share of manufacturing in the Japanese economy as well as the loosening of agglomerations in core regions (i.e., a hollowing out). This was in sharp contrast to cluster policies before the 1980s, which targeted manufacturing firms in peripheral regions.

The Regional Hub Cities policy (*chiho kyoten toshi*) began in 1992 and sought to attract regional headquarters.[9] It had an indirect and weak effect on the location of manufacturing plants, because only the locations of headquarters changed. Next, the Activating Industrial Clusters policy (*sangyo shuseki kasseika*), launched in 1997, aimed to assist small firms in existing industrial clusters, including in Tokyo, Osaka, and Nagoya, with R&D and sales promotion. Finally, the New Business Creation policy (*shin jigyo soshutsu sokushin*), which started in 1999, aimed at promoting venture capital in regional development.

Toward Indirect Policies, 2000s

From the 2000s onward, regional policies drastically changed. Policies shifted to more indirect policy schemes (assistance in creating networks rather than subsidies and public infrastructure). The targeted regions were far broader, and included core regions (i.e., across several prefectures), and targeted firms needed to apply for assistance. Policies focused less on regions and were oriented toward promoting R&D. The Industrial Cluster project was initiated in 2001 by the Ministry of Economy, Trade, and Industry (METI). Simultaneously, the Ministry of Education, Culture, Sports, Science, and Technology (MEXT) undertook a similar cluster policy, named Knowledge Cluster. This policy aimed at fostering research collaboration between local universities or public research institutions and the private sector.

Since this section discusses regional cluster policy, I focus here on the Industrial Cluster project. The government invested approximately ¥55 billion in supporting R&D under this policy between 2001 and 2004, and ¥2 billion was spent to indirectly support networking and coordination. The duration of the policy was split into three periods (2001–05, 2006–10, and 2011–20) and included midterm reviews. The first period was envisioned as the start-up of clusters, the second period consisted of development, and the third was called the fiscal independence phase. The policy in the second period defined eighteen projects, each of which targeted specific

---

9   Okubo and Tomiura (2016) and Matsuura (2012) study location patterns of headquarters and multiple plants in Japan.

geographical zones (some prefectures, and regions broader than a city or town) and specific industries (e.g., information technology, biotechnology, and ecological technology).

The formation of intrafirm networks was high on the project's agenda. The main policy tools used to this end included holding exchange meetings, seminars, and exhibitions; dispatching coordinators; developing overseas sales channels; and facilitating business matching between firms in different sectors, and matching them with financial institutions.

This policy is different from any of its predecessors in three respects. First, the priority is to facilitate networking rather than to enhance production and productivity. Compared with previous cluster policies, the available direct subsidies are very limited. Second, the regions targeted by this policy are not strictly defined as geographic units with clear boundaries, i.e., they are regions across several prefectures. Third, groups of local firms must apply for assistance: firms no longer automatically receive subsidies just by relocating to the targeted region.

Empirical Evidence

I will now turn to an empirical analysis of Japanese cluster policies using microdata. Based on the availability of microdata, I look at several representative subsidy policies: Industrial Relocation Subsidy, Regional Hub Cities, Science Cities, Coal Mining, Technopolis, Intelligent Location, and the Industrial Cluster project. All these policies are discussed together below, save the latter one, which is discussed separately.

Subsidy Policies, Relocation, and Spatial Sorting

Data
Okubo and Tomiura (2010, 2012) estimate the impact of postwar cluster subsidies using plant-level data from Japan's Census of Manufacturers, conducted by METI.[10] The basic plant characteristics are output, employment (the number of regular workers), and material costs for all plants in all manufacturing sectors. The data are for plants with no less than five employees. My sample includes 48,000 plants in 1978 and then steadily grows to 66,000 by 1990 (table 6.1, number of observations). The sample period consists of six years: 1978, 1980, 1983, 1985, 1988, and 1990.

---

10   This subsection is based on Okubo and Tomiura (2010, 2012).

TABLE 6.1 Basic plant statistics

	Variable	Observations	Mean	Std. Dev.	Min	Max
1978	PROD	48,040	5.844501	1.05994	0	10.59039
	SIZE	48,040	3.316469	1.280155	1.386294	9.781207
	LABOR	48,040	0.23458	0.161315	0	3.793714
	MAT	48,040	0.386597	0.17278	0	5.542666
1980	PROD	48,559	5.979857	1.116493	0	10.81911
	SIZE	48,559	3.310036	1.272666	1.386294	9.795791
	LABOR	48,559	0.225541	0.159418	0	2.939515
	MAT	48,559	0.394448	0.173685	0	3.026459
1983	PROD	53,655	6.051981	1.130118	0	11.66635
	SIZE	53,655	3.276194	1.264586	1.386294	10.05096
	LABOR	53,655	0.238533	0.166984	0	3.813525
	MAT	53,655	0.384374	0.173988	0	2.918972
1985	PROD	57,942	6.138449	1.120561	0	11.59249
	SIZE	57,942	3.31352	1.244825	1.386294	10.1092
	LABOR	57,942	0.238984	0.165001	0	4.167595
	MAT	57,942	0.382028	0.17362	0	4.973279
1988	PROD	61,726	6.237205	1.125369	0	11.79964
	SIZE	61,726	3.302714	1.230873	1.386294	9.922604
	LABOR	61,726	0.242994	0.175535	0	8.39841
	MAT	61,726	0.371382	0.17677	0	11.35772
1990	PROD	66,093	6.347178	1.155394	0	12.44145
	SIZE	66,093	3.299687	1.21973	1.386294	9.943429
	LABOR	66,093	0.238326	0.172053	0	7.920083
	MAT	66,093	0.368006	0.172908	0	3.832807

SOURCE: Okubo and Tomiura 2010.
NOTE: PROD = value added per worker; SIZE = number of workers; LABOR = total wage per output; MAT = expenditure on materials per output.

As table 6.2 shows, the number of plants located in targeted regions substantially increased over the sample period, and at a rate higher than the national average.

TABLE 6.2 Number of firms in targeted areas

Policy		1978	1980	1983	1985	1988	1990
Industrial Relocation	(1)	10,723	10,377	11,059	11,847	11,662	12,187
	(2)	16,839	17,302	18,958	20,935	22,839	24,746
	(3)	3,076	3,175	3,845	3,623	11,077	8,477
Coal Mining		1,263	1,258	1,430	1,339	1,375	1,455
Technopolis					3,423	6,210	4,053
Intelligent Location						536	6,159
Science Cities		234	222	233	277	285	295
Total		48,040	48,559	53,655	57,942	61,726	66,093

SOURCE: Okubo and Tomiura 2010.
NOTE: Industrial Relocation subcategories: (1) areas where moving out was promoted; (2) inducement areas; (3) subsidized inducement areas.

Policy Premium

To estimate the policy premium on plant productivity, Okubo and Tomiura (2010) conduct the following plant-level reduced-form by ordinary least squares (OLS) regression:

$$PRODj = const + \alpha_1 SIZE_j + \alpha_2 MAT_j + \alpha_3 LABOR_j \qquad (1)$$
$$+ \beta_k POLICY_k + \gamma_l + \delta_m + \varepsilon_j.$$

The plant is indexed by j. Since a longitudinal plant identifier linking plants is not available over time in the 1980s and early 1990s, all the regressions are cross-sectional. The dependent variable is the productivity $PROD$, which is defined by the value added per worker.[11] The independent variables are plant characteristics such as industry dummies (γ), prefecture dummies (δ), and relocation policy dummies ($POLICY$). Industries are at a two-digit level. The dummies for forty-seven prefectures are included to control for region-specific determinants of plant productivity. Plant-level variables in equation (1) are the plant size, $SIZE$ (the number of workers), the intensity of material used, MAT (expenditures on materials per output), and labor intensity $LABOR$ (total wage per output). Note that all variables are in logarithmic form. The error term is expressed by ε. $POLICY$ is a dummy variable, which takes 1 if the plant is located in the region (city, town, or village) targeted by the relocation policy program being analyzed.[12] Table

---

11   The denominator is the number of regular employees. The numerator is output (shipment) plus the consumption tax and depreciation, less the raw material costs.
12   The policy dummy is defined as time invariant, irrespective of the start and finish of each policy.

6.1 reports basic statistics. If the coefficient on a policy dummy, β, is positive (negative), we can interpret that the plants located in the regions targeted by the policy are *on average* more (less) productive than those located in other regions after controlling for plant characteristics, industry effects, and prefecture-specific factors.[13]

Results

Table 6.3 shows the regression results. Due to space limitations, only coefficients of *POLICY* are reported. This regression is to examine whether targeted regions tend to have an average productivity that is significantly higher than that of other regions. First, I estimate regressions for all years in the sample period, irrespective of the starting period of each policy.

TABLE 6.3 Policy impact 1

Policy	1978	1980	1983	1985	1988	1990
Technopolis	0.0984	0.0897	0.0241	0.0543	0.0505	0.0507
	7.62 **	6.56 **	1.82 *	4.23 **	3.94 **	4.2 **
Intelligent Location	0.1244	0.0989	0.0684	0.0952	0.0888	0.0875
	9.74 **	7.48 **	5.34 **	7.58 **	7.1 **	7.41 **
Industrial Relocation Subsidy (Inducement area)	−0.1487	−0.1401	−0.117	−0.1314	−0.141	−0.117
	−12.5 **	−11.23 **	−9.64 **	−11.01 **	−11.88 **	−10.44 **
Coal Mining	−0.0452	0.0085	0.1045	0.065	0.0521	0.0666
	−1.31	0.23	2.97 **	1.77 *	1.4	1.91 *
Science Cities	0.0281	−0.0901	−0.0834	−0.1358	0.0081	−0.0148
	0.55	−1.63	−1.53	−2.65 **	0.15	−0.29
Regional Hub Cities	−0.0129	−0.0088	−0.0061	−0.0121	−0.0158	−0.0158
	−1.37	−0.9	−0.65	−1.33	−1.74 *	−1.84 *

SOURCE: Okubo and Tomiura 2010.
NOTE: T-statistics are reported under the coefficient estimates and statistical significance is denoted by asterisks: ** = 5%, * = 10%.

The results shown in table 6.3 demonstrate that the plants located in the targeted regions by most relocation policy programs tend to have significantly lower productivity or to be insignificantly different from plants located in regions not promoted by the policy. Negative coefficients are found in the cases of the Industrial Relocation Policy (inducement area), Regional Hub Cities, and Science Cities. The regions targeted by these policy programs

---

13   We should not interpret equation (1) as indicating the direction of causality. Since my sample is constrained in the form of repeated cross-sections, dynamics or causality are not discussed.

appear to attract low-productivity plants. However, this negative effect on manufacturing productivity should not be immediately regarded as a policy failure, because Regional Hub Cities and Science Cities are in particular intended to attract regional headquarter offices and academic/research facilities, respectively, not productive manufacturing plants. In addition, the ordinary least squares regression results do not necessarily show the causal effects of policy.

By contrast, the Technopolis and Intelligent Location policies have a positive productivity premium. However, I cannot assert on the basis of this regression result that these two policy schemes are successful in attracting high-productivity firms. By comparing the productivity premium of the targeted regions before and after the start of the policy program, we can infer the policy effect. As reported in table 6.3, the magnitude remains the same over time and the gap had been significant even *before* these policy programs started (Technopolis from 1983, Intelligent Location from 1988). Thus, the results indicate that these two programs have selected regions in which higher-productivity plants were *already* concentrated and/or average productivity was higher than the total for Japan. In this sense, we should be cautious in concluding that these two programs succeed in attracting productive plants.

With the specific intention of investigating the impacts of the Technopolis and Intelligent Location policies in more detail, I introduce an alternative definition of targeted regions. In the previous regression (table 6.3), I defined targeted regions as those targeted consistently through the sample period since the start of the policy program. Now, the alternative definition is that of regions targeted each year (and not necessarily targeted in other years). The former definition concentrates on the narrower groups of regions targeted consistently over the years, but the latter definition includes newly targeted regions in regressions on later years. The estimated results based on this alternative definition are shown in table 6.4. The regressions based on the latter definition are naturally limited to the years after the start of each policy program, though the regression based on the former (table 6.3) can be estimated in any year during the sample period. For both the Technopolis and Intelligent Location policies, the productivity of firms in the targeted regions are now significantly lower on average at the beginning of the policies, though the premium changes to become positive in later years.

TABLE 6.4 Policy impact 2

Policy	1983	1985	1988	1990
Technopolis (subsidized only)	−0.3406	0.0412	0.0429	0.0261
	−3.37 **	2.46 **	3.27 **	1.69 *
Intelligent Location (subsidized only)			−0.0694	0.0768
			−1.43	4.9 **

SOURCE: Okubo and Tomiura 2010.
NOTE: T-statistics are reported under the coefficient estimates and statistical significance is denoted by asterisks: ** = 5%, * = 10%.

Spatial Sorting in the Technopolis and Intelligent Location Policies

Okubo and Tomiura (2012) display spatial sorting more directly by providing distributional information based on plant-level data. Table 6.5 shows cumulative frequency distribution, which is an empirical counterpart of the cumulative distribution function (CDF) of productivity across plants. The regions targeted by the Technopolis or Intelligent Location programs are compared with the core regions, which are defined as three major cities— Tokyo, Osaka, and Aichi—and the surrounding prefectures ("Core" in the table). Productivity is measured by deviation from the industry's productivity mean, "DPROD." Negative (positive) values of "DPROD" indicate productivity levels lower (higher) than the average. The column "Gap" implies the CDF difference of core and targeted regions. To highlight transitional change, the distributions are shown only for 1980, 1985, and 1990.

There are two main findings. First, the productivity of firms in regions targeted by the Technopolis or Intelligent Location policies is densely distributed within relatively narrow ranges around the mean, although the core region tends to attract firms at widely ranging productivity levels. In other words, the core region sees not only productive firms due to agglomeration externality and urbanization but also unproductive firms. This is the so-called co-agglomeration of productive and unproductive firms (Okubo, Picard, and Thisse 2010). By contrast, the productivity levels are so low that no firms with comparable productivity are found in targeted regions.[14] This contrast is evident in earlier years. This observation indicates that these regional policy programs were designed to promote regions where most firms had a middle level of productivity.

Second, I find that the gap between productivity distribution in the targeted regions and in the core regions becomes smaller in later years (the "Gap" column in table 6.5). As the distribution in the core regions is stable over the

---

14   Okubo and Tomiura (2014) show the distribution of firm productivity and find that core regions foster not only productive but also unproductive firms.

TABLE 6.5 Distributional information for the Technopolis and Intelligent Location policies

	Technopolis								
	1980			1985			1990		
DPROD	Core	Tech.	Gap	Core	Tech.	Gap	Core	Tech.	Gap
−5.5	0	0	0	0.01	0	−0.01	0	0	0
−5	0.09	0	0.09	0.04	0.06	−0.02	0.01	0.05	−0.04
−4.5	0.11	0	0.11	0.08	0.11	−0.03	0.01	0.14	−0.13
−4	0.15	0	0.15	0.15	0.11	0.04	0.03	0.23	−0.2
−3.5	0.18	0	0.18	0.22	0.11	0.11	0.15	0.27	−0.12
−3	0.4	0.16	0.24	0.35	0.28	0.07	0.33	0.73	−0.4
−2.5	0.57	0.82	−0.25	0.56	0.56	0	0.6	1.14	−0.54
−2	0.94	1.55	−0.61	1.25	1.68	−0.43	1.2	2.36	−1.16
−1.5	2.51	4.98	−2.47	3.14	5.84	−2.7	3.52	8.14	−4.62
−1	8.35	17.81	−9.46	9.77	17.45	−7.68	10.69	22.42	−11.73
−0.5	26.44	44.44	−18	27.94	43.27	−15.33	28.08	45.93	−17.85
0	58.45	70.75	−12.3	58.57	70.54	−11.97	57.61	71.71	−14.1
0.5	83.09	87.75	−4.66	82.89	89.28	−6.39	83.28	88.86	−5.58
1	94.37	95.59	−1.22	94.28	95.85	−1.57	94.2	95.73	−1.53
1.5	98.17	98.45	−0.28	98.19	98.54	−0.35	98.23	98.5	−0.27
2	99.58	99.51	0.07	99.36	99.49	−0.13	99.44	99.41	0.03
2.5	99.91	99.67	0.24	99.89	99.83	0.06	99.87	99.95	−0.08
3	99.98	100	−0.02	99.93	99.94	−0.01	99.93	100	−0.07
3.5	100	100	0	99.97	100	−0.03	99.99	100	−0.01
4.5	100	100	0	100	100	0	100	100	0
	Intelligent Location								
	1980			1985			1990		
DPROD	Core	Intel. Loc.	Gap	Core	Intel. Loc.	Gap	Core	Intel. Loc	Gap
−5.5	0	0	0	0.01	0	0.01	0	0	0
−5	0.09	0	0.09	0.06	0.04	0.02	0.01	0.03	−0.02
−4.5	0.11	0.05	0.06	0.1	0.11	−0.01	0.01	0.06	−0.05
−4	0.14	0.05	0.09	0.17	0.11	0.06	0.03	0.13	−0.1
−3.5	0.18	0.16	0.02	0.23	0.15	0.08	0.16	0.32	−0.16
−3	0.4	0.36	0.04	0.36	0.29	0.07	0.35	0.6	−0.25
−2.5	0.56	0.68	−0.12	0.58	0.55	0.03	0.63	1.13	−0.5
−2	0.94	1.93	−0.99	1.26	1.69	−0.43	1.26	2.24	−0.98
−1.5	2.59	4.68	−2.09	3.2	5.44	−2.24	3.68	6.74	−3.06
−1	8.7	16.96	−8.26	9.92	17.3	−7.38	11.01	20.45	−9.44
−0.5	26.92	41.94	−15.02	28.33	41.81	−13.58	28.65	41.87	−13.22
0	58.74	69.67	−10.93	58.81	69.80	−10.99	57.99	69.19	−11.2
0.5	83.14	87.77	−4.63	83.00	88.02	−5.02	83.41	86.80	−3.39
1	94.40	96.15	−1.75	94.31	95.59	−1.28	94.19	95.27	−1.08
1.5	98.2	98.75	−0.55	98.19	98.53	−0.34	98.22	98.27	−0.05
2	99.59	99.38	0.21	99.37	99.45	−0.08	99.41	99.53	−0.12
2.5	99.91	99.69	0.22	99.89	99.63	0.26	99.87	99.87	0
3	99.98	99.84	0.14	99.93	99.96	−0.03	99.93	99.91	0.02
3.5	100	99.95	0.05	99.97	100	−0.03	99.99	100	−0.01
4	100	99.95	0.05	100	100	0	99.99	100	−0.01
4.5	100	100	0	100	100	0	100	100	0

Source: Okubo and Tomiura 2012, table 5, 237.
Note: Tech. = Technopolis; Intel. Loc. = Intelligent Location.

years, the change is mainly driven by evolutions in targeted regions, especially by a higher percentage of low-productivity firms in targeted regions. After the policy program begins, the gap becomes narrow for all productivity intervals. This indicates that low-productivity firms tend to relocate to targeted regions. By the relocation of these firms with widely variable productivity, the productivity distribution in targeted regions becomes closer to that of the core region. From these two findings, we can conclude that targeted regions are more likely to attract low-productivity firms after the initiation of the regional policy program. Though I cannot trace individual firms over time in my longitudinal format, this observation would be consistent with the predictions made by Baldwin and Okubo (2006) and Okubo, Picard, and Thisse (2010).

Industrial Cluster Project

As mentioned above, the Industrial Cluster project, initiated by METI in 2001, has some characteristics different from all previous policies.[15] There are two econometric analyses of the policy evaluation using microdata: Nishimura and Okamuro (2011b) and Okubo, Okazaki, and Tomiura (2016).[16]

As the industrial policy has shifted from direct to indirect intervention, the role of subsidies has declined as a policy tool. Although direct support for R&D is included as a part of the cluster policy package, public subsidies for clusters are limited to joint R&D projects of the industry-government-academia consortia. Nishimura and Okamuro (2011b) compare the impact of R&D subsidies in the Industrial Cluster project with that of indirect coordination support on firm performance; they find that the effect of indirect support is stronger than that of direct subsidies in the Japanese cluster regions. By contrast, Okubo, Okazaki, and Tomiura (2016) investigate the impact of the Industrial Cluster project on transaction networks. The focus is how indirect support rather than R&D subsidies influences the number of transaction partners as well as sales and employment.

Data
I combine two data sources: the list of member firms in the Industrial Cluster project and the transaction data compiled by Tokyo Shoko Research (TSR). The list of firms covers all firms participating in the Industrial Cluster project. While all twenty-four clusters are included in the original list, this

---

15   This subsection is based on Okubo, Okazaki, and Tomiura (2016).
16   Kodama (2008) provides a case study of TAMA, which is one of the Industrial Cluster projects.

study focuses on eleven of them by dropping those in the core region.[17] The reason for excluding these is that intensive networks were already established among many firms within geographical proximity before the cluster policy, and so it is extremely difficult to identify policy-triggered networks in these places. Among the three periods of the cluster policy, this chapter mainly investigates the impacts of cluster policy in the second period (2006–10) to examine network formation. All firms that participated in the cluster projects from 2006 to 2011 are included in my sample.

Second, the transaction data of TSR contain information on major transaction partners and cover a wide range of firms in almost all sectors. However, no information on trading value or volumes is available in the database. For each firm, up to 24 suppliers and 24 customers are reported. Not all transaction partners are covered if the firm trades with more than 24 firms. In spite of such limitations, these transaction data are unique. TSR data include basic firm characteristics such as location, number of employees, sales, and age. To analyze changes during the period, I concentrate on firms with data available for both 2006 and 2012.

Summary statistics are reported in table 6.6. Network growth is measured by the change in the number of transaction partners between 2006 and 2012. I now decompose networks by the location of their transaction partners: Tokyo, the Greater Tokyo Area, Osaka, the Greater Osaka Area, and the same prefecture (expressed as *Local* in the table).[18] Table 6.6 also reports the growth in the number of employees (*Emp*) and in *Sales* during the same period, and the initial level in 2006 for each variable, as well as for the firm's age and participation (binary dummy) in a cluster project. As shown in the table, firms expanded transaction networks on average.

Next, table 6.7 divides the sample into two subsamples, depending on the firm's participation in a cluster project. The contrasts are evident between these two groups. The growth rate of networks of participating firms is on average higher irrespective of the location of transaction partners. Participating firms expanded employment, while nonparticipants reduced the number of employees.

---

17   Excluded are (1) prefectures in the Greater Tokyo or the Kanto areas, which are Tokyo and the surrounding prefectures (Kanagawa, Saitama, Chiba, Ibaraki, Yamanashi, Tochigi, and Gunma); (2) Osaka and the surrounding prefectures (Kyoto, Hyogo, Nara, Shiga, and Mie); and (3) Aichi Prefecture, in which Nagoya City is located.

18   The Greater Tokyo Area consists of Tokyo Prefecture and surrounding prefectures in eastern Japan (Kanagawa, Saitama, Chiba, Ibaraki, Yamanashi, Tochigi, and Gunma), while I define the Greater Osaka Area as Osaka and surrounding prefectures in western Japan (Kyoto, Hyogo, Nara, Shiga, and Mie).

TABLE 6.6 Basic statistics on the growth of major metropolitan areas (2006–12)

	Mean	Sd	Min	Max	N
Network growth	0.122054	0.440698	−2.48491	3.135494	345,893
Network Tokyo growth	0.074934	0.394865	−2.83321	2.833213	345,893
Network GTokyo growth	0.099358	0.407388	−2.89037	2.944439	345,893
Network Osaka growth	0.020341	0.270065	−2.3979	2.564949	345,893
Network GOsaka growth	0.028738	0.29005	−2.3979	2.639057	345,893
Network local growth	0.131067	0.491518	−2.77259	3.258096	345,893
Emp growth	−0.04812	0.475615	−6.23048	7.438384	344,390
Sales growth	−0.19625	0.599462	−9.665	10.16579	343,388

SOURCE: Okubo, Okazaki, and Tomiura 2016.
NOTE: Emp = employment; GOsaka = Greater Osaka Area; GTokyo = Greater Tokyo Area ; Sd = standard deviation.

TABLE 6.7 Comparisons of firms in and outside of clusters (2006–12)

Cluster participation	Network growth	Network local growth	Network Tokyo growth	Network GTokyo growth	Sales growth	Emp. growth	# firms
Yes	0.173774	0.152521	0.1173	0.143907	−.05695	0.015386	1,208
No	0.1218722	0.130992	0.074786	0.099202	−.19674	−0.04835	344,685

SOURCE: Okubo, Okazaki, and Tomiura 2016.
NOTE: GTokyo = Greater Tokyo Area.

Policy Premium

To highlight the contrast between policy and nonpolicy groups, Okubo, Okazaki, and Tomiura (2016) estimate the baseline specification.

$$Growth_j = const + \alpha_1 POLICY_j + \alpha_2 x_j + \varepsilon_j. \tag{2}$$

Firms are indexed by j. The dependent variable *Growth* is the growth rate of the transaction network between 2006 and 2012, measured by the number of firms having transactions with the firm j. I compare the following measures of transaction networks by the location of the partner: the number of all transaction partners combined, those in Tokyo, and those in the same prefecture. I alternatively use networks with firms in the Greater Tokyo Area for a robustness check. As a comparison, I also estimate equation (2) with growth in sales and in employment. *POLICY* is a dummy taking the value 1 if the firm participated in a cluster project during the second period, and 0 otherwise. In my sample, all firms with data from both 2006 and 2012, and that are located outside the core region, are included in my regressions.

To focus on the impact of the policy in the second period, however, firms that participated in a cluster during the first period are excluded from my regressions. Firm characteristics before the cluster policy was initiated in 2006 are summarized by x. The error term is denoted by ε_j. Firm-level variables included in x are number of employees, sales, age of the firm, and the firm's initial level of transaction network. Prefecture dummies and industry dummies defined at the two-digit level are added to the regression.

Columns 1–4 of table 6.8 report the results from estimating the baseline specification (2). Note that robust standard errors, clustered by twelve industrial clusters to handle potential intracluster correlations, are shown in parentheses for all regressions. In all cases in the table, the cluster dummy is significantly positive, indicating that cluster firms grew faster than firms that participated in clusters. This result is after controlling for the firms' initial conditions, such as size and transaction networks observed before the cluster policy. Columns 5 and 6 of table 6.8 show that the growth rate of a network tends to be significantly higher for larger firms (in sales or employment), suggesting that larger firms are likely to have richer opportunities for contact with other firms in their transactions. On the other hand, the same table reports significantly negative coefficients on initial levels of networks in any region, indicating decreasing returns from network formation.

The effect of cluster policy may vary depending on firms' initial condition. To consider this potential variation, I add interaction terms (firm variables as of 2006 interacted with the cluster dummy) as follows.

$$Growth_j = const + \alpha_1 POLICY_j + \alpha_2 x_j + \alpha_3 POLICY_j * x_j + \varepsilon_j. \quad (3)$$

The same set of variables as in (2) is included in x here. If α_3 is significant, we can interpret that the policy effect is crucial in shaping the initial conditions of participating firms. Note that regression results that have sales or employment as the dependent variable are omitted since they are of no significant relation.

The results of such interaction terms, as reported in table 6.9 (column 2), show that the cluster policy has a significantly positive impact on the growth of transaction networks with firms located only in Tokyo. The results for overall networks and for networks with firms in the Greater Tokyo Area appear to be driven by this strong effect on networks with firms in Tokyo (column 3). Our previous finding of a significant policy effect on networks could be influenced by variations in the initial conditions of firms before their cluster participation. Since Tokyo is the dominant center of political, financial, and information functions, and contributes about 20 percent of

TABLE 6.8 Baseline regressions

	1 Network growth		2 Network Tokyo Growth		3 Network GTokyo growth		4 Network local growth		5 Employee growth		6 Sales growth	
		SD		SD		SD		SD		SD		SD
Cluster	0.07873	0.027 ***	0.0681	0.0218 ***	0.0706	0.0216 **	0.0299	0.0352 **	0.1248	0.0161 ***	0.0684	0.015 ***
Network	−0.365	−2E−04 ***	−0.0094	0.0002 ***	−0.006	0.0002 ***	−0.059	0.0005 ***	−0.006	0.0001 ***	0.0286	0.0001 ***
Network Tokyo			−0.2303	0.0002 ***								
Network GTokyo					−0.232	0.0002 ***						
Network local							−0.265	0.0004 ***				
Employees	0.02143	1E−04 ***	0.0103	8E−05 ***	0.0143	8E−05 ***	0.0187	0.0002 ***	−0.2139	0.0003 ***	0.141	0.0004 ***
Sales	0.07458	2E−04 ***	0.051	6E−05 ***	0.0512	9E−05 ***	0.0442	9E−05 ***	0.1412	0.0001 ***	−0.0968	0.0004 ***
Age	−0.0021	2E−04 ***	−0.0138	0.0002 ***	−0.014	0.0002 ***	0.019	0.0003 ***	−0.074	0.0002 ***	−0.1604	0.0002 ***
# Observations	312,840		312,840		312,840		315,429		314,639		313,190	
F	1,418.48		662.45		664.8		1,024.2		1,024.2		1,024.2	
R-sq	0.2262		0.1164		0.1233		0.1731		0.0997		0.0559	

SOURCE: Okubo, Okazaki, and Tomiura 2016.

NOTE: SD = standard deviation and is clustered-robust standard error; GTokyo = Greater Tokyo Area. Prefecture dummies and sector dummies are included in all cases. Cluster errors use 12 cluster projects (see table 6.4). Statistical significance is denoted by asterisks: *** = 1 %, ** = 5 %, * = 10 %.

TABLE 6.9 Regressions with interactions

	1 Network growth	SD	2 Network Tokyo Growth	SD	3 Network GTokyo growth	SD	4 Network local growth	SD
Cluster	0.0586285 ***	0.138089	0.2148839 ***	0.156712	0.3132481 *	0.16322	0.1977716	0.150176
Network	−0.36486 ***	4.77E−05	−0.009272 ***	5.11E−05	−0.005687 ***	6.58E−05	−0.0589461 ***	6.87E−05
Network Tokyo			−0.230175 ***	6.25E−05	0.0512 ***	9E−05	0.0442 ***	9E−05
Network GTokyo					−0.231344 ***	8.16E−05		
Network local							−0.2651691 ***	8.03E−05
Network*CLST	−0.05983 *	0.033056	−0.054624 **	0.022424	−0.053872 **	0.024411	−0.0822552 *	0.04125
Network Tokyo*CLST			−0.012125 ***	0.02731				
Network GTokyo*CLST					−0.018064	0.023547		
Network local*CLST							0.02035576 *	0.044703
Emp	0.021476 ***	6.48E−05	0.0102829 ***	2.83E−05	0.0142986 ***	3.23E−05	0.0188508 ***	0.000101
Sales	0.074781 ***	3.28E−05	0.0509699 ***	1.99E−05	0.0512361 ***	2.45E−05	0.0442725 ***	3.02E−05
Age	−0.00218 ***	6.26E−05	−0.013769 ***	4.34E−05	−0.014193 ***	4.73E−05	0.0188276 ***	0.00005
Emp*CLST	−0.00445	0.012268	0.0101539	0.022103	0.013979	0.022769	−0.0301929	0.017964
Sales*CLST	−0.0401 **	0.015373	−0.004354	0.017499	−0.015305	0.020809	−0.0133068	0.012257
Age*CLST	0.053977 ***	0.047296	0.0039488 ***	0.045674	0.0168661 ***	0.046006	0.0804313 ***	0.057651
# Observations	312,840		312,840		312,840		315,429	
F	1,418.48		662.45		664.8		1,024.22	
R-sq	0.2263		0.1164		0.1235		0.1731	

SOURCE: Okubo, Okazaki, and Tomiura 2016.

NOTE: CLST = binary dummy variable indicating participation in a cluster; SD = standard deviation; GTokyo = Greater Tokyo Area. Statistical significance is denoted by asterisks: *** = 1%, ** = 5%, * = 10%.

Japan's gross domestic product, the formation of networks with Tokyo firms should be valuable for both young and small firms, such as those that participated in clusters far from core regions.

We also see, in table 6.9, that the policy effect on networks is smaller when firms already had a large number of transaction partners before their participation in cluster projects, as indicated by the interactive terms *Network*POLICY*. This indicates decreasing returns to scale in transaction networks.

Policy Administration

Previous sections have addressed econometric evidence related to spatial sorting and network formation by Japanese cluster policies. To summarize, Japanese cluster policies have created clusters in peripheral regions but did not succeed in attracting a sizeable number of productive firms and promoting innovation and economic growth. This outcome is common to many other developed countries in recent years, as Baldwin and Okubo (2006) predict. I now consider what "innovative" cluster policy should be and how it can be fostered. To investigate this, I highlight the administrative aspects of Japanese cluster policies—i.e., how firms were selected as targets and how policies were implemented. Here, Nishimura and Okamuro (2015, 227, table 2) are intuitive. Based on interviews with cluster managers and participants, they provide a detailed comparison of the management structure of national biotechnology cluster policies in Japan, Germany, and France. In the case of Japan, the Knowledge Cluster initiative consists of R&D collaboration programs implemented by MEXT. This is different from the cluster policy developed by METI, the Industrial Cluster project, although both were carried out in the same period. In these programs, universities and public research institutes play a central role as the core of research collaboration with private companies. The total budget of the Knowledge Cluster initiative was ¥63 billion from 2002 to 2009. The annual subsidy per cluster was around ¥500 million in the first period and ¥830 million in the second period. The MEXT programs fully subsidized each research consortium through 2005. This is in a sharp contrast to German and French programs, in which each consortium was required to finance half of the budget from its own funding or other sources such as venture capital. These programs are based on a matched funding and cofunding system. Nishimura and Okamuro (2015) conclude that this "can be regarded as a typical low-incentive policy with top-down selection or limited competition with a full funding scheme despite some variations across cluster programs." Then, they conclude that "clusters may be more public-driven in Japan as compared to Germany and France, where clusters may be more private-driven."

This tendency could be at the heart of all Japanese cluster policies. Cluster policies of the early days—e.g., the Coal Mining and Industrial Relocation Subsidy policies—were perfectly driven by a strong central government initiative. The targeted regions and policy schemes were decided upon using a top-down approach, which is typical of a low-incentive policy for innovation and productivity growth. In particular, the Technopolis and Intelligent Location policies are representative of this trend. Even the Industrial Cluster project, regarded as a new policy scheme, involves the same dynamic. In spite of its application-based approach, the project does not implement the notion of competition, and is a typical low-incentive policy with top-down selection.

Conclusion

This chapter has provided an overview of Japan's long tradition of regional cluster policies. Many kinds of cluster policies are aimed at reducing the gap between peripheral, undeveloped regions and large cities. Although most of these policies increase the number of firms and establish industrial clusters, their productivity is neither high nor innovative, resulting in persistent low productivity rates in cluster regions. The Technopolis and Intelligent Location policies are perfect examples of this: the targeted regions developed clusters, but the average productivity decreased.

Recent decades in Japan have seen some new policy types—i.e., application-based and indirect ones, such as for collaboration and transaction network formation. While these policy schemes appear brand new, they still implement old management schemes that are top-down and offer little incentive. Japanese cluster policies should be immediately reformed in terms of their approach to management, and incentive schemes similar to those in other developed countries should be applied. In particular, incentive schemes implemented by German and French cluster funding systems might be a solution to the current problems of industrial cluster policies in Japan. As mentioned above, these other systems adopt a matched funding system (e.g., 50 percent of funding is subsidized by the government). This is in sharp contrast to the full funding schemes used in Japanese regional cluster policies. The matched funding scheme has been theoretically known as an incentive scheme, and the Japanese government has already applied it in many policies, such as for R&D subsidies. It might prove useful to improve cluster policies in Japan as well.

References

Baldwin, Richard, and Toshihiro Okubo. 2006. "Heterogeneous Firms, Agglomeration and Economic Geography: Spatial Selection and Sorting." *Journal of Economic Geography* 6, no. 3: 323–46.

Bondonio, Daniele, and John Engberg. 2000. "Enterprise Zones and Local Employment: Evidence from the States' Programs." *Regional Science and Urban Economics* 30, no. 5: 519–49.

Devereux, Michael, Rachel Griffith, and Helen Simpson. 2007. "Firm Location Decisions, Regional Grants and Agglomeration Externalities." *Journal of Public Economics* 91, nos. 3–4: 413–35.

Dupont, Vincent, and Philippe Martin. 2006. "Subsidies to Poor Regions and Inequalities: Some Unpleasant Arithmetic." *Journal of Economic Geography* 6, no. 2: 223–40.

Duranton, Gilles, Philippe Martin, Thierry Mayer, and Florian Mayneris. 2010. *The Economics of Clusters: Lessons from the French Experience.* Oxford: Oxford University Press.

Falck, Oliver, Stephan Heblich, and Stefan Kipar. 2010. "Industrial Innovation: Direct Evidence from a Cluster-Oriented Policy." *Regional Science and Urban Economics* 40, no. 6: 574–82.

Fontagné, Lionel, Pamina Koenig, Florian Mayneris, and Sandra Poncet. 2013. "Cluster Policies and Firm Selection: Evidence from France." *Journal of Regional Science* 53, no. 5: 897–922.

Forslid, Rikard, and Toshihiro Okubo. 2014. "Spatial Sorting with Heterogeneous Firms and Heterogeneous Sectors." *Regional Science and Urban Economics* 46: 42–56.

Fujita, Masahisa, and Takatoshi Tabuchi. 1997. "Regional Growth in Postwar Japan." *Regional Science and Urban Economics* 27, no. 6: 643–70.

Kodama, Toshihiro. 2008. "The Role of Intermediation and Absorptive Capacity in Facilitating University-Industry Linkages—An Empirical Study of TAMA in Japan." *Research Policy* 37, no. 8: 1224–40.

Martin, Philippe, and Carol Ann Rogers. 1995. "Industrial Location and Public Infrastructure." *Journal of International Economics* 39, nos. 3–4: 335–51.

Martin, Philippe, Thierry Mayer, and Florian Mayneris. 2011. "Public Support to Clusters: A Firm Level Study of French 'Local Productive Systems'." *Regional Science and Urban Economics* 41, no. 2: 108–23.

Matsuura, Toshiyuki. 2012. "Nihon kigyō no honsha bumon no ritchi ni tsuite: Honsha iten no kettei yōin to shōsansei ni yoru senbetsu"

[Location of the head office division of Japanese companies: Determinants of head office relocation and selection by productivity]. RIETI Discussion Paper Series 12-J-022, Research Institute of Economy, Trade and Industry, Tokyo.

Melitz, Marc J. 2003. "The Impact of Trade on Intra-Industry Reallocations and Aggregate Industry Productivity." *Econometrica* 71, no. 6: 1695–725.

Midelfart-Knarvik, Karen Helene, Henry G. Overman, Philip R. Lane, and Jean-Marie Viaene. 2002. "Delocation and European Integration: Is Structural Spending Justified?" *Economic Policy* 17, no. 35: 321–59.

Nishimura, Junichi, and Hiroyuki Okamuro. 2011a. "R&D Productivity and the Organization of Cluster Policy: An Empirical Evaluation of the Industrial Cluster Project in Japan." *Journal of Technology Transfer* 36, no. 2: 117–44.

———. 2011b. "Subsidy and Networking: The Effects of Direct and Indirect Support Programs of the Cluster Policy." *Research Policy* 40, no. 5: 714–27.

———. 2015. "Local Management of National Cluster Policies: Comparative Case Studies of Japanese, German, and French Biotechnology Clusters." *Administrative Sciences* 5: 213–39.

———. 2018. "Internal and External Discipline: The Effect of Project Leadership and Government Monitoring on the Performance of Publicly Funded R&D Consortia." *Research Policy* 47, no. 5: 840–53.

Okubo, Toshihiro. 2012. "Anti-Agglomeration Subsidies with Heterogeneous Firms." *Journal of Regional Science* 52, no. 2: 285–99.

———. 2016. "Sangyou shuuseki no koudoka niyoru keizaikas-seika" [Economic development by innovative clusters]. Chapter 2 in *Konpakuto na Sangyou Shuuseki he—Juunanna nettowa-ku de sasaeru* [Toward compact industrial clusters—supported by flexible networks]. NIRA Research Report. Tokyo: NIRA.

Okubo, Toshihiro, and Eiichi Tomiura. 2010. "Industrial Relocation Policy and Heterogeneous Plants Sorted by Productivity: Evidence from Japan." RIETI Discussion Papers 10016, Research Institute of Economy, Trade and Industry, Tokyo.

———. 2012. "Industrial Relocation Policy, Productivity, and Heterogeneous Plants: Evidence from Japan." *Regional Science and Urban Economics* 42, nos. 1–2: 230–39.

———. 2014. "Skew Productivity Distributions and Agglomeration: Evidence from Plant-Level Data." *Regional Studies* 48, no. 9: 1514–28.

———. 2016. "Multi-Plant Operation and Headquarters Separation: Evidence from Japanese Plant-Level Panel Data." *Japan and the World Economy* 39: 12–22.

Okubo, Toshihiro, Pierre M. Picard, and Jacques-François Thisse. 2010. "The Spatial Selection of Heterogeneous Firms." *Journal of International Economics* 82, no. 2: 230–37.

Okubo, Toshihiro, Tetsuji Okazaki, and Eiichi Tomiura. 2016. "Industrial Cluster Policy and Transaction Networks: Evidence from Firm-Level Data in Japan." Keio-IES Discussion Paper Series 2016-019, Institute for Economics Studies, Keio University, Tokyo.

Porter, Michael E. 2000. "Location, Competition, and Economic Development: Local Clusters in a Global Economy." *Economic Development Quarterly* 14, no. 1: 15–34.

Viladecans-Màrsal, Elisabet, and Josep Maria Arauzo-Carod. 2012. "Can a Knowledge-Based Cluster Be Created? The Case of the Barcelona 22@ District." *Papers in Regional Science* 91, no. 2: 377–400.

CHAPTER 7

A Comparative Study of Two Innovation Clusters

Using the Triple Helix Model to Observe the Economic Contributions of Industry vs. Research Entities

Injeong Lee and Wonjoon Kim

Innovation has become increasingly contingent on how scientific and technological communities and the industrial sector interact with one another. This means that innovative capacity relies on not only the output of individual actors (universities, research institutes, businesses) but also effective communication and collaboration at the regional and national level (OECD 1999). In this regard, characteristics underlying the linkages among heterogeneous actors and the channels for knowledge diffusion within a geographic area are central to notions such as regional innovation systems and innovative clusters.

The triple helix model can help us to delineate top innovating regions like Silicon Valley and Hsinchu Science Park. It zooms in on university-industry-government relations and focuses on how their roles have evolved through interplay. The model presumes that the driving force of economic growth is collectively organized knowledge (Ivanova and Leydesdorff 2014). During the construction of this knowledge, institutional spheres overlap, with each

This work was supported by the National Research Foundation of Korea through a grant funded by the Korean Government (NRF-2018S1A3A2075175).

taking on some of the tasks of the others, and where these spheres make contact, blended organizations arise (Etzkowitz and Leydesdorff 2000). Since the introduction of this theoretical model, it has been used to examine various regions (Park, Hong, and Leydesdorff 2005; Leydesdorff and Fritsch 2006; Etzkowitz, de Mello, and Almeida 2005) and industries (Petersen, Rotolo, and Leydesdorff 2016; Leydesdorff and Deakin 2011; Zhang et al. 2014).

In this chapter, we use the triple helix model, with the aid of social network analysis, to compare two innovation clusters: South Korea's Daedeok Innopolis and Germany's Silicon Saxony. The clusters are examined in terms of the strength of the connections among the universities, industries, and other government research institutions (GRIs) in each cluster, and the roles of these entities within their networks. Through this comparison we aim to discover the structural factors behind the distinct industrial outputs of two clusters developed with strong government support.

We believe comparing these two clusters from this perspective can help answer a key question: How can universities, industries, and GRIs best interact within an innovation cluster to strengthen its industrial functions and activities, in order to maximize its contributions to the regional and national economy? Previous studies have underscored the importance of this question. The answers will have important implications for policymakers and regional developers.

Theoretical Background

Defining Innovation Clusters

Innovation clusters aim to help transform scientific knowledge and expertise into commercialized products through cooperative interaction between the academic and industrial sectors. At the core of the concept is the underlying assumption, supported by the linear model of innovation, that value is created from technology, which derives from scientific research. Therefore, the role of the innovation cluster is to foster a "catalytic incubator environment," which is essential for basic science at academic institutions to be converted into commercially feasible innovations (Westhead 1997; Hansson, Husted, and Vestergaard 2005).

Among the various types of innovation clusters, research parks are primarily composed of residents heavily engaged in basic and applied research (Link and Scott 2003). A research park is usually established on or near a university campus, to benefit from the university's ongoing research and base of scientific knowledge. Universities not only deliver scientific information but also elaborate on this knowledge, in consideration of their connection to other entities in the research park (Grassler and Glinnikov 2008; Link and Scott 2003).

A key feature of research parks is the high frequency of research collaboration (Dahlstrand and Smith 2003). University research usually results in publications, which are widely disseminated, and in reproducible experiments (Pavitt 1989). This kind of research is not as specific as the research and development (R&D) typically conducted by companies and is easily proliferated and exchanged within research parks. Human resources are widely exchanged as well: contacts are maintained between research institutions and firms in research parks, students are involved in businesses, issue-oriented discussions occur regularly, and so on (Grassler and Glinnikov 2008). We can thus expect that cooperation occurs quite frequently within research parks. However, the probability of such cooperation to evolve into product or service development that requires intense knowledge concentration for a specific technology is relatively low.

In contrast, industrial parks are not necessarily affiliated with academic institutions, but need to be attractive to actors in manufacturing, sales, support, and professional service functions (Taylor 1983). Business R&D activities result in knowledge that is not only specific, but partly tacit and therefore difficult and costly to reproduce (Pavitt 1989). A previous study found that scientific or technological information is not "something in the air," and thus more frequent interaction within a cluster is not closely related to the higher innovative performance of an individual enterprise (Cantner, Conti, and Meder 2010). Knowledge transfer in industrial parks is more complicated than in research parks, because tacit knowledge does not spread freely within an area (Cantner, Conti, and Meder 2010).

Using the Triple Helix Model to Assess Innovation

Leydesdorff and Etzkowitz (1998a) introduced the triple helix model to explain the complex connections among universities, industries, and governments in an innovation cluster. In the model, a government can stimulate interaction among institutions and network development across institutional boundaries (Leydesdorff and Etzkowitz 1998b). The model describes the process by which three types of entities (university, industry, and government) evolve while being intertwined with one another, similar to the double helix of DNA. In the evolutionary process, innovative knowledge can be produced as points of contact are formed between the spirals and new roles and new organizations are created at the interfaces. These intermediate organizations and their networks are not reliant on the primary roles of the three entities, but rather are motivated to solve problems that arise depending on the circumstances (Etzkowitz 2003; Leydesdorff and Meyer 2006).

To examine the roles of these entities in fostering innovation, we need to understand that triple helix models can be categorized into three types. In type I, interaction across entities is facilitated by agencies such as technology transfer offices and industry liaisons. In type II, each helix functions as a distinct communication system that includes the functions of technological innovation, market operation, as well as independent control at the interfaces (Nelson and Winter 1982). In type III, universities, industries, and governments perform their traditional functions, but each entity is also expected to function in ways similar to the other entities. For example, universities create technology holding companies and perform a quasi-governmental role as innovation organizers (Leydesdorff and Etzkowitz 1998b).

In this chapter, we concentrate on the characteristics of model type III, where the roles of academia and industry are extended by the demand of the other participants and are no longer limited to their conventional functions. They perform roles in combination with other entities, and sometimes an intermediate organization is required to bridge different entities. Correspondingly, it is expected that the role of each entity in the innovation cluster differs depending on the major functional characteristics of the cluster. That is, the role of a university could differ depending on whether the cluster is a research park or an industrial park.

Innovation Clusters as Social Capital

Numerous researchers have pointed out the function of innovation clusters as places for intercommunication. According to Porter's definition of an innovation cluster, "a regional cluster is a form of network that occurs within a geographic location, in which the proximity of firms and institutions ensures certain forms of commonality and increases the frequency and impact of interactions" (Porter 2008). Here, what determines the cluster outwardly is the geographical proximity of entities such as universities, institutes, and companies, and what determines the cluster inwardly are the interactions among these entities such as cooperation, joint R&D, learning know-how, and so on. From this perspective, the crucial function in the process of achieving economic growth is the circulation of knowledge or information among the entities, such as universities and industries. For example, universities provide new knowledge or related human resources in general (Bercovitz and Feldman 2006; Rosenberg and Nelson 1994), and industries realize this knowledge by developing new technologies or products that secure economic growth.

Accordingly, many innovation studies investigate clusters from the perspective of social capital. Here, social capital denotes "the information, trust, and norms of reciprocity inherent in one's social networks" (Woolcock 1998). Gordon and McCann (2000) distinguish clusters from agglomerations, because clusters demonstrate not merely economic feedback on possibilities and complementarities, but also indicate a particular level of social combining. In addition, according to Steiner and Hartmann (2006) clusters are "social technologies" that empower and assist knowledge interactions between individual economic actors.

Social capital in innovation clusters presents a number of advantages. First, social capital impacts the productivity of a network by diminishing common uncertainties regarding the specialization of labor. Second, it lowers transaction costs due to stable interactions inside clusters. Third, from an institutional perspective, it influences the costs of coordination. Fourth, it has a synergistic effect on the innovation process since, through networking, actors can enhance the quality and variety of their knowledge (Ramhorst-Vejzagic, Huggins, and Ketikidis 2009; Woolcock and Narayan 2000).

Previous studies have suggested how innovation clusters function in the development of technology and economic growth from a social capital perspective. Those players that contribute to forming social capital that in turn promotes the creation of knowledge and technology, the sharing of that knowledge, and endogenous regional development, are located where networking between organizations is constructed and operated most successfully (Cooke 2001).

How an innovation cluster can be most efficiently managed as an item of social capital itself has also been discussed. Burt (2009) introduced the term "structural hole," an important concept that illustrates how a network can be maintained and administered as social capital. This concept refers to the detached state of a network; distinct nodes belonging to the various groups in a network are not redundantly connected. Nodes can be joined to either side of a network via structural holes. In other words, an agent who acts as a mediator between connected groups can acquire comparative advantages. The agent can function as a gatekeeper for valuable information. The key aspect of this concept is that structural holes function as a buffer, delivering benefits that are supplemental rather than redundant (Burt 2009).

In general, entering the center of a network is difficult, requiring significant time and effort. However, a network can be controlled effectively and easily through filling the structural holes. The competitive power of a network is determined by the entities at the connection nodes, not by the number of connections. An advantageous position is determined by nonredundancy and low constraints (Burt 2009).

Therefore, if we divide networks by category, as integrated or balkanized (Merluzzi and Burt 2013; Putnam, Leonardi, and Nanetti 1994), balkanized networks are the most effective. Figure 7.1 illustrates the formation of an integrated network with dense linkage among the entities. In this type of network, frequent interactions among the entities occur, but these are routine and overlapped, and in some cases institutionalized (Putnam, Leonardi, and Nanetti 1994). In comparison, the connections in the balkanized network are loose, and most entities are linked indirectly via a few actors (Burt 2005). Burt (1992) calls these blanks in the network structural holes, which can be filled by being connected via one or two more links with a strategic purpose (Burt 2009). The structural hole can increase information flows and regulate knowledge flows.

FIGURE 7.1 Integrated and balkanized networks: A comparison

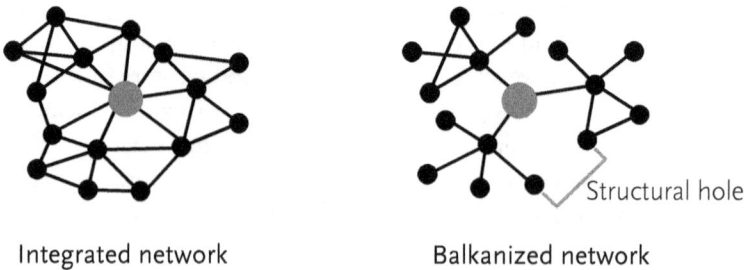

Integrated network   Balkanized network

SOURCE: Authors.

At first glance, it might seem that integrated networks are better connected and thus appropriate for the circulation of information, while balkanized networks are partially broken, so knowledge flows would be blocked. However, according to the arguments of Granovetter (1973), strongly tied networks (i.e., integrated networks) do not provide opportunities for social capital, but rather they might actually become constraints, while new opportunities can be obtained through weak ties, such as in a balkanized network. For example, a person planning to start a new business can obtain more useful information from a group the person encounters occasionally than from a group the person interacts with frequently or continuously (Granovetter 1973). In line with this, Burt (1992) also notes the weakness of strong ties. Strongly tied/integrated networks are generally inefficient due to their dense and overlapped linkage. However, weakly tied/balkanized networks are more efficient, interacting relatively loosely. Moreover, weak ties function as intermediation, fostering more efficient use of resources in the network (Burt 2009).

Based on these arguments, we can assume that industrial parks are more likely to have structural holes and therefore more efficient networking. This is partly because the entities composing research parks appear to be relatively more homogeneous, creating more integrated networks than those of industrial parks (Löwegren 2000; Löfsten and Lindelöf 2005). In research parks, there tend to be larger numbers of entities (i.e., universities and government institutions) that function as knowledge creators, while other entities (i.e., industries) appear to be smaller in number and function with different aims to create greater economic value. In contrast, the composition of industrial parks tends to be more heterogenous and complex, since members take charge of all the processes in the linear model of innovation from basic research to mass production. Thus, there is greater potential to build balkanized networks with more significant roles for industries, which results in more structural holes.

An Overview of Exemplary Innovation Clusters

The primary purpose of our study is to identify the structural differences between an industry-oriented innovation cluster (i.e., Silicon Saxony) and a research-based cluster (i.e., Daedeok Innopolis). This study also aims to provide valuable policy recommendations for the development of innovation clusters with more industrial outcomes. It is important to first validate that these two clusters have similar and comparable characteristics.

Silicon Saxony in Dresden seems in many ways a comparable cluster to Daedeok Innopolis in Daejeon. Dresden, since the reunification of Germany, is emblematic of the former East Germany's remarkable economic growth; in fact, the entire state has benefited from the successful management of innovation clusters (Broll and Roldán-Ponce 2011; Röhl 2000). Similarly, Daedeok Innopolis is an exemplar of South Korea's rapid national development. In addition, both clusters have a similar focus, specializing in information and communication technology and nanotechnology.

The two clusters have distinct differences, too, in terms of their innovation performance and industrial structures, that make comparing them a valuable exercise. Silicon Saxony is an industrial park that has, in a relatively short period of time, delivered outstanding results in the industrial sector, and reached the final phase of the linear model of innovation: mass production. On the other hand, Daedeok Innopolis was initially established as a research-focused cluster. Strictly speaking, it remains a research park that is oriented toward research and education, although it is currently intensifying efforts to produce desired industrial outcomes.

TABLE 7.1 Comparison of Daedeok Innopolis and Silicon Saxony

	Daedeok Innopolis	Silicon Saxony
Area	540.1 km²	328.8 km²
Population (2014)	1,531,809	536,308
Universities (2014)	7	4
Institutes (2014)	27	14
Companies (2014)	1,516	2,100
GRDP (2013)	US$39,832 million*	US$26,969 million[†]
Ratio of exports to GRDP	10% (US$4,029, 2013)	50.9% (2012)
GDP per capita (2013)	US$24,215*	US$32,023[†]

SOURCE: Authors.
NOTE: *Daejeon; [†]Dresden; GDP = gross domestic product; GRDP = gross regional domestic product.

There are more firms in Silicon Saxony than in Daedeok Innopolis (see table 7.1) and several of them (e.g., Global Foundries and Infineon) are so-called hidden champions, meaning that they are the number one or two company in their field in the global market and have revenue below US$4 billion and a low level of public awareness (Simon 2009); there are no such hidden champions in Daedeok. Silicon Saxony's gross domestic product per capita is nearly 1.3 times more than that of Daedeok Innopolis, and the ratio of its exports to gross regional domestic product is also much higher than Daedeok's.

Research Methods and Data

Social Network Analysis

Social network analysis (SNA) views social relationships with regard to network theory, as composed of nodes (single individuals) and ties (the relationships between individuals). This is captured in a social network diagram, in which nodes are expressed as circles and ties are expressed as lines. From the perspective of SNA, regular patterns in the relationships among interacting actors can be visualized as structures (Wasserman and Faust 1994). This methodology can facilitate insights into specific connections by examining not only the degree and frequency of cooperation, but also looking at which nodes cooperate the most and the effectiveness of that cooperation.

Centrality Indices

Centrality indices, such as those that focus on the degree and closeness of centrality, may be used to investigate the characteristics of network structures. The degree of centrality identifies how much and how often entities are connected within a cluster (Freeman 1978). Referring to table 7.2, the degree of centrality (C_D) initially measures a node's quantity of linkages inside a network. However, we implement Freeman's general formula for centralization when calculating the degree of centrality in order to consider the degree to which nodes' centrality scores vary. In formula (1), i indicates the node of interest and g denotes the total amount of nodes. C_D (n^*) refers to a node's maximum value in a network (Freeman 1978).

TABLE 7.2 Descriptions of normalized centrality indices and Network Concentration Index

Index	Formula	Constraint
Degree centrality (1)	$C_D = \sum_{i=1}^{g} [\, C_D\,(n^*) - C_D(n_i)](g-1)(g-2)]$	$0 \leq C_i \leq 1$
Closeness centrality (2)	$C_c\,(n_i) = \dfrac{g-1}{\sum_{j=1}^{g} d(n_{i,}\,n_j)}$	$i < j, i \neq j$ $0 \leq C_i \leq 1$
Network Concentration Index	$NCI_i = \sum_{j=1}^{n} \left(\dfrac{Link_j}{total\ Link_i}\right)^2$	$0 \leq NCI_i \leq 1$

SOURCE: Authors.

To measure closeness, the time required to move from one node to another, using optimal pathways, is used (Freeman 1978). This builds on the average shortest path length in formula (2) in order to calculate the normalized closeness of centrality, where $d(n_i, n_j)$ indicates the distance between two nodes (n_i, n_j) (Freeman 1978; Valente and Foreman 1998).

Although these indices describe some of the complexity of network structures, they do not indicate the intensity of the connections within a network (Lee and Kim 2017). Therefore, besides the centrality indices, an invented network index is applied here to estimate the knowledge concentration rates inside a network. This is called the Network Concentration Index (NCI) and is derived from the Herfindahl-Hirschman Index (HHI). The HHI calculates the degree of competition and market concentration among industries. Using formula (3) to measure the NCI, $Link_j$ is the number of connections from node i to node j, and $Total\ Link_i$ is the total amount of connections of node i. This helps explain, for example, how the links of node i are focused on particular nodes (Lee and Kim 2017). Accordingly, the network structure is analyzed in terms of the complexity as well as the intensity of the connections, using both centrality indices and NCI.

Data: Joint Patent Applications

To illustrate the networking situation within each innovation cluster, we collected information about the joint patent applications of universities, GRIs, and companies (with more than five patent applications) located in it. Following Balconi, Breschi, and Lissoni (2004), we assumed that applicants listed on the same patent are mutually acquainted and have interchanged scientific or technological knowledge (Cantner and Graf 2006; Balconi, Breschi, and Lissoni 2004). Therefore, for patents with more than one applicant within the same cluster, we presumed that there had been interaction and research cooperation and connected these joint applicants in the network diagram using a line.

There were 4 universities, 20 institutes, and 32 industries in Daedeok Innopolis between 1984 and 2013. Therefore, the sum of the nodes created for patent applications is 65,694. In the same period, Silicon Saxony had 2 universities, 16 institutes, and 79 industries with a sum of 4,562 nodes. GRIs had a significantly larger number of patents in Daedeok Innopolis than did universities or industry. In Silicon Saxony, by contrast, industry had a significantly larger number of patents than did universities or GRIs, which indicates that it is more of an industrial park than a research park.

Analysis Results

Figures 7.2 and 7.3 present dynamic changes in the network structures of Daedeok Innopolis and Silicon Saxony based on our analysis of joint patent applications. They exhibit an evolution in the strength of connections in both clusters over a ten-year period, from 1992 to 2013 (data from the 1980s were set aside because the early stages of the clusters' establishment lacked any remarkable events). Looking at figure 7.4, while Daedeok Innopolis's nodes are well connected and have no clear disconnections, the network structure of Silicon Saxony is broken, with some disconnections. A major university is the key entity in each network—the Korea Advanced Institute of Science and Technology (KAIST) in Daedeok Innopolis and Dresden University of Technology (TU Dresden) in Silicon Saxony. These are located at the center of the networks, because, as educational institutions where all types of basic science and applied science are undertaken, they are involved in diverse technologies.

FIGURE 7.2 Daedeok Innopolis's network structure: A comparison of two decades

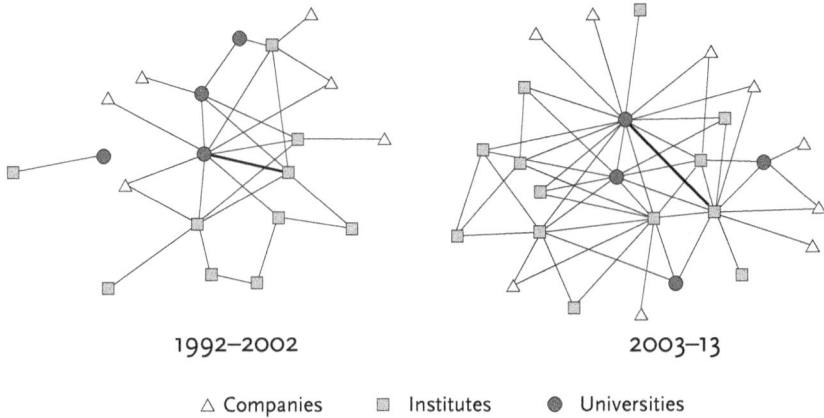

1992–2002   2003–13

△ Companies   ⊡ Institutes   ● Universities

SOURCE: Authors.

FIGURE 7.3 Silicon Saxony's network structure: A comparison of two decades

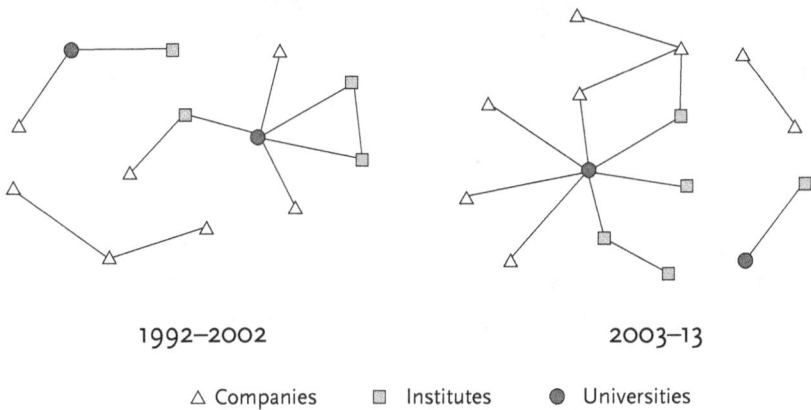

1992–2002   2003–13

△ Companies   ⊡ Institutes   ● Universities

SOURCE: Authors.

Characteristics of the Network Structure

A network's degree of centralization and the degree to which its linkages focus on particular entities (i.e., the intensity of concentration) depends on the type of cluster. To determine these characteristics, we calculated the average centrality indices, such as for the degree of centrality and closeness, and the average NCI for each entity in each cluster; these data are summarized in tables 7.3 and 7.4. In the process, all indices were normalized and examined to ensure statistically meaningful differences between the indices in tables 7.3 and 7.4 using t-tests at the 95 percent significance level.

FIGURE 7.4 The Daedeok Innopolis and Silicon Saxony networks compared, 1984–2013

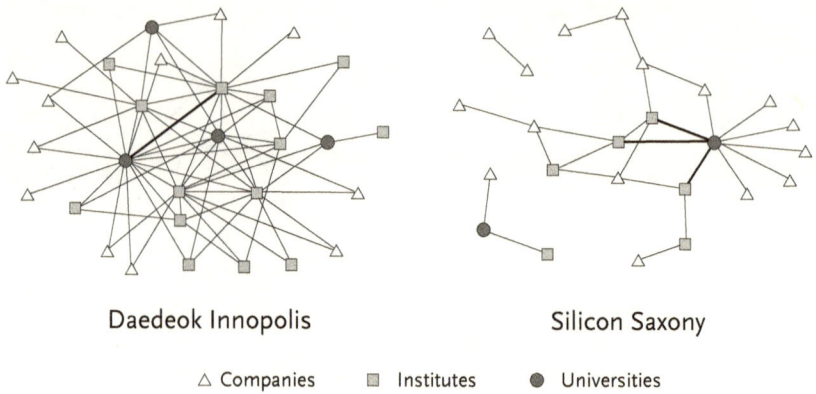

Daedeok Innopolis   Silicon Saxony

△ Companies   ▢ Institutes   ● Universities

SOURCE: Authors.

Daedeok Innopolis has a greater degree of both centrality (the quantity of direct linkages) and closeness (the amount of indirect linkages) than Silicon Saxony (cf. table 7.3 and 7.4). This indicates that organizations in Daedeok Innopolis interact with one another both directly and indirectly much more than those of Silicon Saxony from the perspective of knowledge flows. This aligns with our finding that Daedeok Innopolis (a research park) has a significantly more connected network structure than does Silicon Saxony (an industrial park). Meanwhile, the average NCI results demonstrate that in Silicon Saxony an entity's linkages tend to be with fewer other entities (and are thus more concentrated) than in Daedeok Innopolis. This supports the hypothesis that industrial parks have more concentrated linkages than do research parks.

TABLE 7.3 Types of entities in Daedeok Innopolis, characterized using normalized centrality indices and Network Concentration Index

	Degree	Closeness	Network Concentration Index
University	0.168	0.302	0.150
Institute	0.070	0.263	0.319
Industry	0.011	0.228	0.667
Sum	0.043	0.246	0.436

SOURCE: Authors.
NOTE: All indices were normalized and examined to ensure a statistically meaningful difference between the indices in tables 7.3 and 7.4 using t-tests at the 95 percent significance level.

TABLE 7.4 Types of entities in Silicon Saxony, characterized using normalized centrality indices and Network Concentration Index

	Degree	Closeness	Network Concentration Index
University	0.058	0.137	0.306
Institute	0.011	0.131	0.444
Industry	0.003	0.128	0.802
Sum	0.006	0.128	0.671

SOURCE: Authors.
NOTE: All indices were normalized and examined to ensure a statistically meaningful difference between the indices in tables 7.3 and 7.4 using t-tests at the 95 percent significance level.

Figure 7.5 shows that the average degree of centrality increased over time in both clusters, but at a significantly faster rate in Daedeok Innopolis than in Silicon Saxony. This is true even though these indices were normalized because of the significant differences between their total values in each of the two clusters. In particular, the degree of centrality increased more rapidly for universities. This is likely because universities participate in almost all fields of science and technology, while individual companies make use of only a few specific technologies. It follows that the knowledge concentration of universities is lower than that of industries. Further, this demonstrates the important role of universities in the knowledge flows of both clusters.

By contrast, the NCI trends of both clusters (figure 7.6) exhibit somewhat different patterns. In Daedeok Innopolis, the NCI decreased consistently over time for all entities. This pattern indicates that collaboration among organizations was evolving to be more even, and less concentrated in a few specific organizations. This could be because capacity to create and disseminate technological knowledge had become more equalized among organizations, or because there were no lead organizations directing the collaborative creation of technological knowledge within the network. Such a network has been designated as relatively inefficient—a topic will be further explored in the next section, alongside a discussion of structural holes.

Silicon Saxony's NCI exhibited interesting patterns. The NCIs of the various entities fluctuated over time, although all eventually decreased. A more interesting pattern is the mirror image of the university and industry NCIs: when the university NCI increases, the industry NCI decreases, and vice versa. This indicates either that these two types of entities are in close collaboration, such that one affects the knowledge flow of the other, or that their knowledge flows are complementary, a situation not found in Daedeok Innopolis. Consequently, these heterogeneous NCI patterns indicate clear differences in the two clusters' network characteristics.

FIGURE 7.5 Trends in the degree of centrality: Daedeok Innopolis vs. Silicon Saxony, 1989–2009

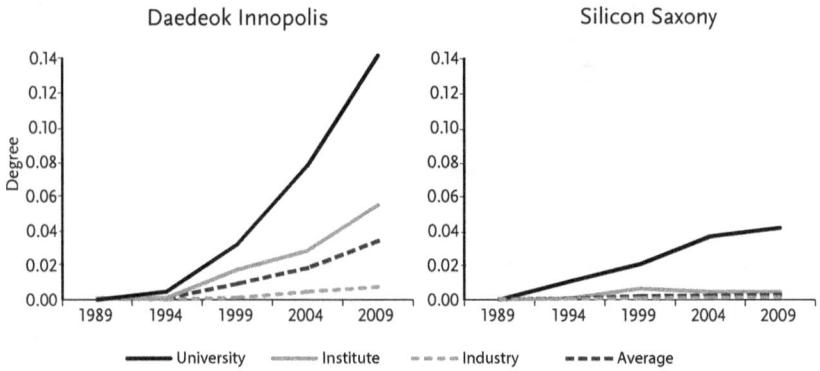

SOURCE: Authors.

FIGURE 7.6 Average NCI trends: Daedeok Innopolis vs. Silicon Saxony, 1989–2009

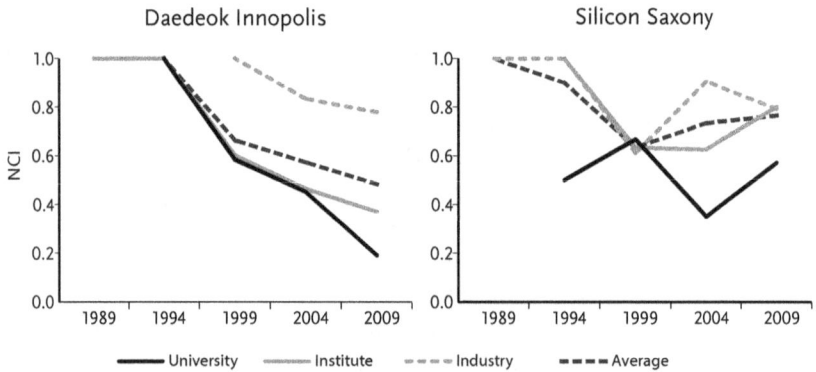

SOURCE: Authors.
NOTE: NCI = Network Concentration Index.

Efficiency of the Network in a Cluster

To determine how effectively a network is maintained and administered for the creation of technological knowledge, the network's efficiency is measured using the concept of structural holes. Silicon Saxony is more efficient overall (see table 7.5), which indicates that networking within Daedeok Innopolis is more redundant and constrained than in Silicon Saxony. One possible reason for this is that the positioning of nodes in Silicon Saxony is more suitable for creating technological knowledge.

As seen from figure 7.4, the Daedeok Innopolis network has fewer structural holes and may be defined as an integrated network, while Silicon Saxony's is a balkanized network with more structural holes. Silicon Saxony is more efficient in its dissemination of information and regulation of technological knowledge flows, and these network benefits could serve as social capital to fill the structural holes.

TABLE 7.5 Types of entities in Daedeok Innopolis and Silicon Saxony, characterized by efficiency index

	Daedeok Innopolis	Silicon Saxony
University	0.818	0.995
Institute	0.769	0.920
Industry	0.773	0.997
Sum	0.777	0.978

SOURCE: Authors.
NOTE: All indices were normalized and examined to ensure a statistically meaningful difference between the indices in tables 7.3 and 7.4 using t-tests at the 95 percent significance level.

Implications and Conclusions

Using the triple helix model, this chapter zooms in on the relationship among universities, companies, and GRIs—the main actors in an innovation cluster. We examine a Korean cluster that was initially established to be research oriented but that is now trying to increase its economic results. We compare this to a German innovation cluster that has developed important market technologies and fostered small- and medium-sized enterprises through effective interactions among universities, firms, and GRIs.

For this analysis, we considered joint patent applications from entities in each of the two clusters. When more than one applicant applied for the same patent, these joint applicants were connected using a line in the network diagram, and these interactions formed the network structures in our analysis. The results and implications drawn from the analysis are as follows.

First, the absolute quantity of interactions (degree of centrality) among organizations within Daedeok Innopolis was greater but the concentration of these interactions (NCI) was less than in Silicon Saxony. That is, the collaborations and interactions among entities were significantly more active and dispersed in Daedeok Innopolis than in Silicon Saxony. This finding indicates that more focused and intensive collaborations involving a few leading entities have greater economic impact.

This is somewhat contrary to expectations but can be explained from the perspective of social capital. Rather than the variety or number of collaborative research outputs, intensive collaborations among a few important entities do the most to boost an innovation cluster's economic contributions. Hence, a central or local government that manages and supports innovation clusters should be careful when promoting joint R&D activities among cluster entities. Rather than promoting the number and diversity of R&D collaborations across the board, as often occurs in public-driven clusters, the policy focus needs to be on strengthening and deepening meaningful collaborations.

Second, we determined that networking within Daedeok Innopolis is characterized by more overlaps and constraints than in Silicon Saxony. That is, Daedeok Innopolis is less efficiently structured from the perspective of social capital. In addition, Silicon Saxony's universities were considerably reliant on industries. To capitalize on structural holes, the unnecessary and redundant networking in Daedeok Innopolis should be prevented. One way to achieve this is to change the indicator for measuring the technological knowledge output of universities and GRIs from the number of patent applications they generate. As public institutions, these entities have been encouraged to introduce as many patents as possible with the expectation that a larger number of patents has more economic benefits—plus it is an indicator of performance that is easy to measure. However, our findings demonstrate that this type of quantity-oriented policy is less effective and potentially decreases the efficiency of a network in fostering technical knowledge.

Broadly speaking, there are two types of clusters: those driven by research institutes and those driven by industry. Our results emphasize the important role of companies in innovation clusters. As the global innovation paradigm has shifted toward an entrepreneurial economy, expectations that universities be the major sources of innovation and firm creation have grown. However, based on our results, a university's potential economic benefits within a cluster are difficult to realize without close collaboration from the industry side.

In Silicon Saxony, as in Silicon Valley, the role of industry is significant. This is an important clue in answering the question of how to best replicate the Silicon Valley model. Many researchers and policymakers have searched for the core of the Silicon Valley model in order to benchmark it and to embed it in their own clusters. Based on our results, the core seems to be industry-driven innovation. While universities provide frontier innovations, as well as human resources for those innovations, companies that transform and scale up the innovations into products and take the risk of introducing them into markets have the greatest economic impact in a cluster. And to transform and scale up frontier innovations, it seems that "deep ties" are needed. In other words, a few very close collaborations do more than numerous light connections to internalize companies' innovation knowledge. Therefore, an important aspect of the industry-driven innovation model is the presence of companies that can lead, transform, and scale up the innovations and bring them into markets. Policymakers need to pay attention to this point.

As to be expected, there are limitations to this study. First, due to the limitations of the central patent management systems in South Korea and Germany, information on patent citations was unavailable. Further, attempts to generalize these findings should be undertaken with caution, since there are some characteristics that are unique to Daedeok Innopolis and Silicon Saxony, as well as to South Korea and Germany. Future studies that compare other innovation clusters with similar research frameworks could strengthen this discussion and generate other important findings.

References

Balconi, Margherita, Stefano Breschi, and Francesco Lissoni. 2004. "Networks of Inventors and the Role of Academia: An Exploration of Italian Patent Data." *Research Policy* 33, no. 1: 127–45. https://doi .org/10.1016/S0048-7333(03)00108-2.

Bercovitz, Janet, and Maryann Feldman. 2006. "Entrepreneurial Universities and Technology Transfer: A Conceptual Framework for Understanding Knowledge-Based Economic Development." *The Journal of Technology Transfer* 31, no. 1: 175–88. https://doi.org/10 .1007/s10961-005-5029-z.

Broll, Udo, and Antonio Roldán-Ponce. 2011. "Clustering in Dresden." *European Planning Studies* 19, no. 6: 949–65. https://doi.org/10.1080/o 9654313.2011.568806.

Burt, Ronald S. 1992. *Structural Holes. The Social Structure of Competition.* Cambridge, MA: Harvard University Press.

———. 2005. *Brokerage and Closure: An Introduction to Social Capital.* Oxford: Oxford University Press.

———. 2009. *Structural Holes: The Social Structure of Competition.* Cambridge, MA: Harvard University Press.

Cantner, Uwe, and Holger Graf. 2006. "The Network of Innovators in Jena: An Application of Social Network Analysis." *Research Policy* 35, no. 4: 463–80. https://doi.org/10.1016/j.respol.2006.01.002.

Cantner, Uwe, Elisa Conti, and Andreas Meder. 2010. "Networks and Innovation: The Role of Social Assets in Explaining Firms' Innovative Capacity." *European Planning Studies* 18, no. 12: 1937–56. https://doi .org/10.1080/09654313.2010.515795.

Cooke, Philip. 2001. *Knowledge Economies: Clusters, Learning and Cooperative Advantage.* London: Routledge.

Daedeok Innopolis. N.d. "Statistical Overview of Daedeok Innopolis." Accessed 2015. https://www.innopolis.or.kr/board;jsessionid=EC7 EF5D97FFEB91C5D9C22DC3368D57C?menuId=MENU00669 &siteId=null.

Dahlstrand, Åsa Lindholm, and Helen Lawton Smith. 2003. "Science Parks and Economic Development." In *Globalization of Technology*, edited by Prasada Reddy. Paris: United Nations Educational, Scientific and Cultural Organization and Encyclopedia of Life Support Systems (UNESCO-EOLSS).

Etzkowitz, Henry. 2003. "Innovation in Innovation: The Triple Helix of University-Industry-Government Relations." *Social Science Information* 42, no. 3: 293–337. https://doi.org/10.1177/05390184030423002.

Etzkowitz, Henry, and Loet Leydesdorff. 2000. "The Dynamics of Innovation: From National Systems and 'Mode 2' to a Triple Helix of University–Industry–Government Relations." *Research Policy* 29, no. 2: 109–23. https://doi.org/10.1016/S0048-7333(99)00055-4.

Etzkowitz, Henry, José Manoel Carvalho de Mello, and Mariza Almeida. 2005. "Towards 'Meta-Innovation' in Brazil: The Evolution of the Incubator and the Emergence of a Triple Helix." *Research Policy* 34, no. 4: 411–24. https://doi.org/10.1016/j.respol.2005.01.011.

Freeman, Linton C. 1978. "Centrality in Social Networks Conceptual Clarification." *Social Networks* 1, no. 3: 215–39. https://doi.org /10.1016/0378-8733(78)90021-7.

Gordon, Ian R., and Philip McCann. 2000. "Industrial Clusters: Complexes, Agglomeration and/or Social Networks?" *Urban Studies* 37, no. 3: 513–32. https://doi.org/10.1080/0042098002096.

Granovetter, Mark S. 1973. "The Strength of Weak Ties." *American Journal of Sociology* 78, no. 6: 1360–80. https://doi.org/10.1086/225 469.

Grassler, Andreas, and Roman Glinnikov. 2008. "Knowledge Transfer in Science Parks." Baltic Business School, University of Kalmar, Sweden.

Hansson, Finn, Kenneth Husted, and Jakob Vestergaard. 2005. "Second Generation Science Parks: From Structural Holes Jockeys to Social Capital Catalysts of the Knowledge Society." *Technovation* 25, no. 9: 1039–49. https://doi.org/10.1016/j.technovation.2004.03.003.

Ivanova, Inga A., and Loet Leydesdorff. 2014. "Rotational Symmetry and the Transformation of Innovation Systems in a Triple Helix of University–Industry–Government Relations." *Technological Forecasting and Social Change* 86 (July): 143–56. https://doi.org/10 .1016/j.techfore.2013.08.022.

Lee, Sanghoon, and Wonjoon Kim. 2017. "The Knowledge Network Dynamics in a Mobile Ecosystem: A Patent Citation Analysis." *Scientometrics* 111, no. 2: 717–42.

Leydesdorff, Loet, and Henry Etzkowitz. 1998a. "The Triple Helix as a Model for Innovation Studies." *Science and Public Policy* 25, no. 3: 195–203. https://doi.org/10.1093/spp/25.3.195.

———. 1998b. "Triple Helix of Innovation: Introduction." *Science and Public Policy* 25, no. 6: 358–64. https://doi.org/10.1093/spp/25.6.358.

Leydesdorff, Loet, and Mark Deakin. 2011. "The Triple-Helix Model of Smart Cities: A Neo-Evolutionary Perspective." *Journal of Urban Technology* 18, no. 2: 53–63. https://doi.org/10.1080/10630732.2011.60 1111.

Leydesdorff, Loet, and Martin Meyer. 2006. "Triple Helix Indicators of Knowledge-Based Innovation Systems." *Research Policy* 35, no. 10: 1441–49. https://doi.org/10.1016/j.respol.2006.09.016.

Leydesdorff, Loet, and Michael Fritsch. 2006. "Measuring the Knowledge Base of Regional Innovation Systems in Germany in Terms of a Triple Helix Dynamics." *Research Policy* 35, no. 10: 1538–53. https://doi.org /10.1016/j.respol.2006.09.027.

Link, Albert N., and John T. Scott. 2003. "U.S. Science Parks: The Diffusion of an Innovation and Its Effects on the Academic Missions of Universities." *International Journal of Industrial Organization* 21, no. 9: 1323–56. https://doi.org/10.1016/S0167-7187(03)00085-7.

Löfsten, Hans, and Peter Lindelöf. 2005. "R&D Networks and Product Innovation Patterns—Academic and Non-Academic New Technology-Based Firms on Science Parks." *Technovation* 25, no. 9: 1025–37. https://doi.org/10.1016/j.technovation.2004.02.007.

Löwegren, Marie. 2000. "Advantages of a Science Park Location: Case Studies from the Ideon Science Park." Thesis, Department of Business Administration, Lund University, Sweden.

Merluzzi, Jennifer, and Ronald S. Burt. 2013. "How Many Names Are Enough? Identifying Network Effects with the Least Set of Listed Contacts." *Social Networks* 35, no. 3: 331–37. https://doi.org/10.1016 /j.socnet.2013.03.004.

Nelson, Richard R., and Sidney G. Winter. 1982. *An Evolutionary Theory of Economic Change.* Cambridge, MA: The Belknap Press of Harvard University Press.

Organisation for Economic Co-operation and Development (OECD). 1999. *Managing National Innovation Systems.* Paris: OECD.

Park, Han Woo, Heung Deug Hong, and Loet Leydesdorff. 2005. "A Comparison of the Knowledge-Based Innovation Systems in the Economies of South Korea and the Netherlands Using Triple Helix Indicators." *Scientometrics* 65, no. 1: 3–27. https://doi.org/10.1007 /s11192-005-0257-4.

Pavitt, Keith. 1989. "What We Know about the Usefulness of Science: The Case for Diversity." Science Policy Research Unit Discussion Paper no. 65, University of Sussex, London.

Petersen, Alexander M., Daniele Rotolo, and Loet Leydesdorff. 2016. "A Triple Helix Model of Medical Innovation: Supply, Demand, and Technological Capabilities in Terms of Medical Subject Headings." *Research Policy* 45, no. 3: 666–81. https://doi.org/10.1016/j.respol .2015.12.004.

Porter, Michael E. 2008. *On Competition.* Boston, MA: Harvard Business School Publishing.

Putnam, Robert D., Robert Leonardi, and Raffaella Nanetti. 1994. *Making Democracy Work: Civic Traditions in Modern Italy.* Princeton, NJ: Princeton University Press.

Ramhorst-Vejzagic, Amira, Robert Huggins, and Panayiotis H. Ketikidis. 2009. "Social Capital and Clusters—Literature Review." In Proceedings on the 2nd International Conference on Entrepreneurship, Innovation and Regional Development, Thessaloniki, Greece, April 24–25.

Röhl, Klaus-Heiner. 2000. "Saxony's Capital Dresden: On the Way to Become Eastern Germany's First Innovative Milieu?" Discussion Paper 5/2000, Technische Universität Dresden, "Friedrich List" Faculty of Transport and Traffic Sciences, Institute of Transport and Economics, Dresden, Germany.

Rosenberg, Nathan, and Richard R. Nelson. 1994. "American Universities and Technical Advance in Industry." *Research Policy* 23, no. 3: 323–48. https://doi.org/10.1016/0048-7333(94)90042-6.

Simon, Hermann. 2009. *Hidden Champions of the Twenty-First Century: Success Strategies of Unknown World Market Leaders.* Dordrecht: Springer.

Steiner, Michael, and Christian Hartmann. 2006. "Organizational Learning in Clusters: A Case Study on Material and Immaterial Dimensions of Cooperation." *Regional Studies* 40, no. 5: 493–506. https://doi.org/10.1080/00343400600757494.

Taylor, Tony. 1983. "High-Technology Industry and the Development of Science Parks." *Built Environment* 9, no. 1: 72–78.

Valente, Thomas W., and Robert K. Foreman. 1998. "Integration and Radiality: Measuring the Extent of an Individual's Connectedness and Reachability in a Network." *Social Networks* 20, no. 1: 89–105. https://doi.org/10.1016/S0378-8733(97)00007-5.

Wasserman, Stanley, and Katherine Faust. 1994. *Social Network Analysis: Methods and Applications.* Cambridge, UK: Cambridge University Press.

Westhead, Paul. 1997. "R&D 'Inputs' and 'Outputs' of Technology-Based Firms Located on and off Science Parks." *R and D Management* 27, no. 1: 45–62. https://doi.org/10.1111/1467-9310.00041.

Woolcock, Michael. 1998. "Social Capital and Economic Development: Toward a Theoretical Synthesis and Policy Framework." *Theory and Society* 27, no. 2: 151–208.

Woolcock, Michael, and Deepa Narayan. 2000. "Social Capital: Implications for Development Theory, Research, and Policy." *The World Bank Research Observer* 15, no. 2: 225–49. https://doi.org/10 .1093/wbro/15.2.225.

Zhang, Yi, Xiao Zhou, Alan L. Porter, Jose M. Vicente Gomila, and An Yan. 2014. "Triple Helix Innovation in China's Dye-Sensitized Solar Cell Industry: Hybrid Methods with Semantic TRIZ and Technology Roadmapping." *Scientometrics* 99, no. 1: 55–75. https:// doi.org/10.1007/s11192-013-1090-9.

Decentralization and Distributed Innovation
Catch-Up and Leapfrog
David Lee Kuo Chuen

The catch-up of developing economies to advanced economies has been slower than some people predicted. This chapter argues that decentralized technology and distributed innovation may be able to narrow the gap. If member governments of the Association of Southeast Asian Nations (ASEAN) allow decentralization and distributed innovation to take place, this may give their developing economies the best chance to leapfrog more advanced economies.

According to the catch-up hypothesis, all economies will eventually converge in terms of per capita income since poorer economies tend to grow more rapidly than wealthier economies. In other words, low-income economies will catch up to more robust ones (Abramovitz 1986). Poorer countries tend to replicate the production methods, technologies, and institutions of developed countries. Since the decay in marginal returns to capital is much slower in these poorer countries, they will eventually catch up to capital-rich ones. These ideas have dominated development thinking for more than thirty years.

Yet the forecasted catch-up hypothesized by Abramovitz has not transpired, in particular where there are no social capabilities—i.e., in those developing countries that fail to adapt new technology, attract capital, and participate in the global market. Failure to adopt new technology results in an inability to generate more capital. Inability to access or attract capital in turn mitigates the catch-up effect. The key to catching up may be that technology and capital must be traded freely and be affordable to low-income economies. Expensive or unavailable technology or capital will prevent the effect from occurring. The democratization of technology, capital, and information are prerequisites to the smooth functioning of the catch-up effect. However, even in the absence of such democratization, some economies have made tremendous progress. The East Asian Tigers (Singapore, Hong Kong, South Korea, and Taiwan) rapidly converged with developed economies between 1960 and 1980. Post-1980, the Asian Miracle, by which Asian nations with initially low industrialization and development levels, such as China, transformed into developed and sophisticated societies, is even more phenomenal. From 2008 on, China's growth surprised many, and with innovations such as internet finance, China has leapfrogged many financial centers. Yet apart from these East Asian economies, no other developing economies in the world have converged with developed ones.

In the literature on industrial organization and economic growth, Fudenberg et al. (1983) outline the conditions under which a new entrant can leapfrog an established firm. These conditions are not only relevant to firms but can apply to countries, too. Monopolists have less incentive to innovate as they are comfortably earning rents from old technologies (Tirole 1988, 391–92). Incumbent technologies eventually lose their leadership when start-ups are more prepared to take risks and adopt new, radical technological innovations. Finally, radical innovations become the new paradigm, and the newcomers leapfrog ahead of the once-leading firms (or countries). Schumpeter derived a new theory from the work of Karl Marx, which he called the gales of creative destruction (Schumpeter 1942). By this force, newcomers take the place of their predecessors. These and related analyses preceded the invention of digital handsets and the internet. The availability and high penetration of information and communication technologies have led to unprecedented rapid growth in some countries like China, lending a fresh perspective to the catch-up hypothesis.

There is evidence to suggest that digital finance via the use of mobile phones has played a part in transforming China and has lifted 600 million people out of poverty. The innovation in China is technologically centralized, a term that we shall define below. However, there is also evidence to suggest that in 2017 China's economy reached a plateau, and a new form of decentralized technology, such as blockchain, may propel the next industrial revolution.[1]

1   Nakamoto (2008) wrote a white paper that revolutionized digital innovation, articulating a peer-to-peer decentralized payment network. Decentralized technology and

In chapter 4 of this volume, Wong states that, while a significant portion of the growth of technology start-ups in Singapore has been driven by new top-down public policies, it is based primarily on internet/mobile/e-commerce services, with relatively few "deep-technology"-based start-ups. But recently, we are seeing signs that bottom-up community-driven blockchain ICO projects in Singapore (Greene and Lee 2019) with deep technology are growing in large numbers there.

Similarly, in chapter 9, Moon and Lee, in their study of six Asian countries, argue that top-down incentives promoting small- and medium-sized enterprises (SMEs) may not necessarily be beneficial and that innovation-led "smart" growth mainly occurs under conditions where medium-to-large firms spin off SMEs. They suggest that the critical element of competitiveness, and not necessarily entrepreneurial innovation, stems from an efficient bottom-up integration of different elements throughout an ecosystem rather than from the top down. Both these chapters point to the importance of decentralization in policy governance and distributed innovation.

Hsieh, in chapter 5, concludes that the key lesson to be gained from the success of Taiwan's machinery industry is not the size of its firms, but the specific ways in which its network of firms and public research institutes are linked in a decentralized system. Collaborative learning and the ability of firms to tap into decentralized networks for production and innovation are keys to innovative growth.

In chapter 2, Tse, discussing China, argues that the exponential part of that economy's phenomenal growth is not due to a detailed top-down plan supported by profound economic analysis, but by incremental and disruptive innovation. Firms can increase value by improving a product, reducing its cost, improving the efficiency of a supply chain, or improving distribution channels, all of which fall under incremental innovation. Incremental innovation will only increase a firm's competitiveness in a free-market economy. However, it is the supporting infrastructure that propels exponential growth through disruption. Activities that lead to the creation of a supporting infrastructure needed to realize the intended value proposition constitute what is called "disruptive innovation." These activities are essentially unplanned, bottom up, and mission based. Again, a certain degree of decentralization in policy governance and bottom-up, user-driven distributed innovation play a major role in producing positive outcomes.

---

distributed innovation have several powerful features, including the possibility of autonomous organization with blockchain technology. Under certain circumstances, autonomous organizations may be more efficient than centralized governments and enterprises. See Lee and Low (2018) for more on decentralized yet inclusive financial technology, and Lee and Deng (2017) for more on distributed ledger technology.

The evidence from these chapters seems to suggest that while top-down policies are important to consider, some degree of decentralization (more in policy governance than in government itself) and distributed innovation may work well. Disruptive innovative growth stems from the ecosystem underlying those bottom-up, decentralized, user-driven activities. However, we need to more precisely define decentralization and distributed innovation to hold a meaningful discussion of the catch-up (and leapfrog) process.

Innovation Defined

Here we shall focus on Schumpeter's definition of innovation. Innovation is broader than invention. While it includes the invention of new technologies and disruptive business models, it also includes the commercialization of new technology, materials, methods, or processes. It also encompasses the accumulation of knowledge and the applications of new ideas in different ways, through collaboration with others, or by participating in global value transfer or international markets. Innovation is not what is being produced, but rather how (Lederman and Maloney 2012; Maloney and Caicedo 2017).

Why the Slow Catch-Up? Production, Technological Adoption, and Invention Capabilities

The three primary reasons that developing economies are not catching up, according to Cirera and Maloney (2017), are barriers to accumulating physical and human capital, low firm capabilities, and weak government capacities.

These factors have resulted in a low level of technological adoption in developing countries. A simple policy response of merely providing additional incentives for research and development is inadequate in tackling the multiple constraints to technological adoption. The purpose of this chapter is to determine if decentralization or distributed innovation can provide a different angle in rethinking and addressing the innovation paradox.

In the innovation paradox, returns on technological adoption are thought to be extremely high, yet developing countries appear to invest very little in innovation. While evidence seems to suggest that firms from developing economies are undertaking innovation—across the income spectrum and in all sectors—this too often consists of marginal improvements in processes or products. Only on rare occasions do the data suggest significant technology adoption or new product imitation; even rarer do we observe frontier research being conducted.

Cirera and Maloney (2017), drawing heavily on neoclassical economics and the literature on national innovation systems, focus on the complements to innovation investment that are critical in achieving high potential returns, the range of firm capabilities needed to undertake innovation and take it to market, and the range of government capabilities required to implement effective innovation policies.

In contrast with the neoclassical model's focus on the role of the firm, considering the national innovation system encompasses the nonlinear nature of knowledge creation. There are three layers of capabilities: production, technological adoption, and invention. Maloney (2017) has also described the innovation system by articulating three pillars (see table 8.1).

TABLE 8.1 Three pillars of a national innovation system

Supply	Accumulation/Allocation	Demand
Universities/think tanks/ technology extension centers	Physical capital/human capital/knowledge	The firm

1. Human capital
2. Support in upgrading capability
  a. Productivity/quality extension services
  b. Process/best practice dissemination
  c. Advanced consulting services
3. Domestic science and technology
4. International/national innovation system (government research institutes, universities, etc.)
	1. Barriers to all accumumation
	  a. Credit
	  b. Entry/exit barriers
	  c. Business/regulatory climate
	  d. Rule of law
	2. Barriers to knowledge accumulation
	  a. Rigidities (labor, etc.)
	  b. Seed/venture capital
	  c. Innovation externalities
		1. Incentives to accumulate
		  a. Macro context
		  b. Competitive structure
		  c. Trade regime and international network
		2. Firm capabilities
		  a. Core competencies (management)
		  b. Production systems
		  c. Technological absorption and production

SOURCE: Author's elaboration of Maloney (2017).

Overall, the Maloney model provides a framework for understanding the environment within which firms' innovation occurs. It highlights how demand and supply for innovation interact and the barriers to accumulation and allocation. The government oversees this evolution and the overall functioning of the system, and is tasked with monitoring, conflict resolution, and coordination of the various actors.

The evidence from Cirera and Maloney (2017) suggests that while the returns to innovation are often high, they can nonetheless be negative as well. Negative returns occur when there is a very low level of development, especially if there is a lack of physical and human capital. If a firm cannot import the necessary machines and labor, or utilize new organizational techniques, there will be no production or technological adoption. The resulting returns to innovation can be low. The main impediments are usually the costs of doing business, trade regimes, competitiveness frameworks, capital markets, or disincentives to accumulate knowledge. All these impediments lead to high costs, low returns, and therefore low investment.

Meanwhile, critical factors complementing innovation capability are managerial and organizational practices. A range of capabilities must be acquired before one can effectively innovate and manage projects. In particular, capabilities to respond to market conditions, identify new technological opportunities, develop a plan to exploit them, and cultivate the necessary human resources are both crucial and lacking in many developing economies. These are fundamental to productivity and quality upgrading. Without good managerial capabilities and good practices, the result will be low returns and therefore low investment.

In turn, what drives managerial capabilities is an environment that will accelerate the exit of poorly run firms and allow the upgrading of the best firms. Allowing inefficient firms to survive or failing to provide adequate incentives for firms to upgrade, according to evidence, negatively impacts managerial capabilities. Firms with diffuse ownership tend to perform better than those whose ownership is concentrated in the government or one family. Companies with foreign investment and ownership have better-managed research and development and are more able to achieve innovation. Openness helps with upgrading and exposure to new ideas. The importing of new technology and access to international markets also assist innovation. In many cases, spillovers do not occur because these complementary capabilities are missing in domestic firms. Accumulation of knowledge is therefore impeded.

The governments of many developing countries lack the human resources and organizational efficiency necessary to design and implement policies that foment innovation. Policy design, the efficacy of policy implementation, the coherence of polices across sectors and time periods, and predictability are all key to catching up.

When export-led growth slowed in the 1990s, governments in Asia encouraged businesses to go regional. Many enterprises were acquiring factories and land in neighboring countries to provide services nearer to major customers that had moved due to lower business costs. However, owing to barriers to accumulating physical and human capital, low firm capabilities, and weak government capacities in those developing countries, most of these investments had huge negative returns. Foreign investments bring foreign debts in the short term; plus, lack of foreign reserves in these countries made them vulnerable to currency attacks. The 1997 Asian financial crisis and the 2008 global financial crisis produced many examples of low returns or failed investments that help explain why the convergence predicted by the catch-up hypothesis has not materialized.

Decentralized Regimes

There are various types of decentralization, touching on policy governance and political, administrative, fiscal, economic/market, and environmental practices, as well as libertarian, socialist, and free markets. It is important to make a distinction between decentralization in policy governance and in technology. We have described why policy governance may be important for innovative growth, as described in previous chapters. However, here we will focus on technological decentralization and especially in regard to information technology and networks.

The term "decentralization" has been used extensively in discussions of government organization, especially in determining whether centralized and decentralized models will lead to a more equitable society. While decentralization may increase productive efficiency, it may undermine allocative efficiency by making the redistribution of wealth more difficult if there is a lack of transparency. Without transparency and centralization, there may be larger disparities between rich and poor regions, especially during times of crisis, when the national government may not be able to assist regions needing help (Prud'homme 1994).

Network theory uses the same terms for system structures. A centralized network is often referred to as a network of different nodes connected to a single server or computer, with a single point of failure. At the other extreme, a distributed network usually refers to different peer-to-peer nodes connected to one another without a single point of failure. What lies in between is a whole range of decentralized networks with some peer-to-peer nodes gravitating to the better-endowed nodes, which act as miniature centers.

Centralized and Decentralized Systems: Definitions

Decentralization is a dynamic process in which powers, functions, etc., are distributed away from a central location or authority so that there are fewer points of control or there is eventually no single point of failure or control. This is in contrast to a centralized system, in which a centralized authority exerts control over other components directly or through a hierarchical system. Such a hierarchical system can instruct middle-level nodes or components to perform certain functions. The particular view of a centralized system in a robotic system was mentioned in Bekey (2005).

In cloud computing, for example, both the governance and system are centralized. Anyone who wishes to enter the system needs central authority approval. More important, there is a single point of failure or attack, such as the server or the administrator.

While any system that is not centralized may be considered decentralized, Rohit Khare puts forward a formal definition of a decentralized system, characterized by decentralized governance and decentralized technology: "A decentralized system is one which requires multiple parties to make their own independent decisions" (quoted in Pace Project [n.d.]).

In such a system, no single authority makes decisions for others. All parties have system access without being subject to a central authority. Parties (e.g., peers, nodes, etc.) freely interact with one another and can make their own decisions, regardless of peer decisions.

Distributed Innovation

Distributed innovation is not to be confused with a distributed system. Distributed innovation models are characterized by transparent communications, collective decision-making processes, distributed actions, and voluntary involvement. There is a particular category of these models, known as user innovation models, that empower people in social programs and transform them into active co-creators who innovate. These offer an alternative strategy to reframe scaling issues and expand the impact of innovative solutions to societal challenges. User innovation models operate in an open environment that facilitates the sharing of experiences, rapidly replicates and adopts new ideas, and enhances the final impact of new social innovations. Users and beneficiaries participate voluntarily and develop ad hoc solutions with a higher probability of success. This co-creation process reinforces communal recognition of people's value, increases motivation and bottom-up contributions, and results in the development of increasingly innovative practices.

The user innovation model, as a relatively stable category of systematic innovation, is best described by Gabison and Pesole (2014) as a bottom-up innovation that exploits and leverages new technology capabilities through open distributed infrastructure such as the internet.

> The full exploitation of new technology capabilities and future internet requires an open distributed infrastructure able to leverage the potential of bottom-up social innovations. There are several examples of social innovation collaborative initiatives in an open context: Smart Cities, Open Data, Living Labs, time banks and digital currencies, new models of urban mobility, new models of collaborative consumption and also collaborative events such as BarCamps, Open festival, competitions etc. (Gabison and Pesole 2014, 22)

The key concepts are open, distributed, user driven, and social. These are not mutually exclusive concepts, though they might have different focal points. Specifically, open innovation focuses on profits, distributed innovation focuses on grassroots cooperation, user innovation focuses on well-being, and social innovation on societal improvement. While open innovation is profit driven, distributed innovation facilitates and intensifies the emergence of creativity and grassroots civic innovations. User innovation, on the other hand, leads to systematic innovation via an accumulation of gradual innovation or disruptive innovation. Social innovation allows for less compliance with regulation and increases sustainability. West and Gallagher (2006) interpret open innovation more broadly to include the change in use, management, and employment of intellectual property internal to an organization, beyond single-channel innovations (that simply involve using external resources from customers, rival companies, and academic institutions).

Decentralized Technology and Centralization

Let us define more specifically what we mean by centralized and decentralized technology. Centralized technology, which includes centralized computing, is technology that has a central point of control. Centralized computing is computing done at a central location, with a centralized server, or by using terminals attached to a central computer. The central computer performs the computing function and controls the remote terminals. The main weakness of centralized technology is that there is a single point of attack that can affect the entire functioning of that technology.

In the design of decentralized technology, offline governance and the system itself are both decentralized. (It is possible for a decentralized system to have a degree of offline, centralized governance.) A distributed ledger such as a permissioned blockchain is not a decentralized system and therefore not decentralized technology.

Without digitalization and transparency, decentralized governance can have many well-documented complexities:

- It may make national policy coordination too complex.
- It may allow local elites to capture functions.
- Local cooperation may be undermined by any distrust between the private and public sectors.
- It may result in higher enforcement costs and conflict for resources if there is no higher level of authority (FAO 2002).
- It may not be as efficient for standardized, routine, network-based services, as opposed to those that need more complicated inputs.
- There may be a loss of economies of scale in the procurement of labor or resources, and the expense of decentralization can rise, even as central governments lose control over financial resources (CIESIN n.d.).

All the above, however, are solvable with the distributed ledger technology (DLT); we shall discuss how Singapore is taking advantage of this new technology.[2]

With the advancement of information and communication technology comes the mass adoption of open innovation—i.e., innovation that is collaborative and openly shared by both producers and users. It is "open" in the sense of involving a diverse network of partners, customers, and other stakeholders that collaborate. User innovation (von Hippel 2005), cumulative innovation (Scotchmer 2004; Murray and O'Mahony 2007), and open innovation (Chesbrough 2003, 2006) are all streams of research relevant to the distributed innovation model.

In the following sections, we discuss the different types of innovation that led to the rise of Asian economies, from China's use of centralized financial technology (fintech) to Singapore's use of DLT. We hope to stimulate future debates on how user innovation can assist developing economies in catching up in a systematic and nonchaotic way.

This chapter argues that systems featuring decentralization and distributed innovation have many characteristics that will overcome the three main obstacles to convergence. Decentralized systems and new technology are going to accelerate convergence and allow developing ASEAN economies to leapfrog. We will present two cases with different degrees of distributed innovation, starting with a centralized case. Case I, Ant Financial, demonstrates that Chinese fintech has moved ahead of many global financial centers. Case II, Project Ubin, demonstrates Singapore's willingness to experiment with a decentralized system in many areas, including the trade and supply chain.

Case I: Ant Financial and Chinese Fintech

Creation is the action or process of bringing something into existence. Invention is the action of creating something new, typically a process or a device. Evolution is the gradual development of something. In the past fifteen years, we have seen the creation, invention, and the evolution of the Chinese internet finance industry. Perhaps it is ironic to see capitalism at its best in a transitioning socialist economy. In China we have witnessed Schumpeter's creative destruction, what he termed "the essential fact about capitalism"—the incessant product and process innovation mechanism by which new production units replace outdated ones.

---

2   Blockchain is a special type of DLT.

Ant Financial is an excellent example of creative destruction. The concept underlying Ant Financial was born out of necessity; Alibaba, an e-commerce firm, required a trusted intermediary to act as an escrow. That simple need, along with an imperfect money market that capped deposit rates, and a push toward the socialist objective of financial inclusion, became the catalyst for the birth of a capitalist internet finance system in China. Bank deposit rates were capped for depositors, and banks were not lending to producers or micro, small, and medium enterprises. With regulations not in place and imperfect markets decentralized, there were abundant opportunities to experiment with new ideas.

The Chinese term *dianfu* (revolution) does not signify the overthrow or repudiation and the complete replacement of an established government or political system by the people; it describes a sudden, complete, or marked change in the business world. In the three years from 2014 to 2017, China saw the rapid digitization and digitalization of its economy, especially in finance.

The American physicist and inventor John Vincent Atanasoff invented the first electronic digital computer in the 1930s at Iowa State College, but it took a long time to diffuse. The digital revolution is the change from mechanical and analog electronic technology to digital electronics from the 1950s, with the adoption and proliferation of digital computers and digital record keeping that continues to the present day. We have seen the democratization of information in this digital era, characterized by an increase in the speed and breadth of knowledge diffusion across the economy and society.

Weak Coordinated Governance

Even though the digital economy was perceived to be centrally governed, the government's capabilities were in reality weak. Issues regarding the complexity of financial products, deleveraging of the financial system, and liquidity flow to speculative activities especially in the real estate sector have challenged policymakers. Until recently, policymakers were unable to identify market failures of traditional banks and to design appropriate policies to redress these failures. Quantitative easing and prudential policies were tools used substantially in response to the global financial crisis. At that time, there were no strong practices of public management or the oversight of implementation efficacy, nor were there processes for evaluating, adapting, and modifying or terminating policies when needed. Policy governance was decentralized such that there was hardly any coherent policy across countries; indeed, within China there was no active coordination across ministries and agencies. Beyond indiscriminate lending and borrowing, the emergence of peer-to-peer lending, fintech, and DLT had all complicated matters even further. There was no single centralized policy and therefore no centralized governance.

Before the September 4, 2017, crackdown on initial crypto-token offerings (ICOs)[3] that saw seven ministries and agencies working together to enact a total ban, the internet finance market was a jungle. The digital payment and peer-to-peer (P2P) lending market had been for years similarly unregulated. The appropriate Chinese phrase to describe this was *yecao congsheng, yeman shengzhang* (weeds were permitted to grow as wildly and as quickly as they could). These internet finance firms, viewed as insignificant and unable to destabilize the financial system, were for a long time left alone and loosely monitored. Long-term money market instruments were packaged into short-term deposits with daily withdrawal facilities. These facilities, made possible by the internet, cell phones, apps, and QR codes, are what led to the mass adoption of Alipay and the exponential growth of deposits into Yu'e Bao.[4] There was no policy consistency or predictability, nor any guarantee of a predictable environment for long-run innovation investing. In such an unpredictable regulatory environment, where long-time unregulated activities can be declared illegal overnight, it was utterly risky and only made possible because there was an infrastructure for digital communication using a smartphone, and secure QR code technology was available (People's Bank of China 2017). While China's financial market is enormous—a positive for innovation and business models to scale exponentially—it is also sprawling and difficult to control. It is conceivable, in a market that is speculative, that the rapid growth of innovation and reach can give rise to bubbles in a wide range of asset classes, some more shadowy than others (E. Lee 2017; Acheson 2017).

It was in this decentralized and yet top-down environment that the world's largest internet finance company was born. In China, being opportunistic is an essential factor in reaping the supernormal returns from the success of innovation, but it is also a significant factor in speculation that attracts heavy regulatory intervention. While some may argue that success is merely a matter of pure grit and a sense of mission, the author has identified some of the characteristics of companies that are successful in this initial stage

---

3   ICO stands for initial coin offering or initial crypto-token offering. It is a method for blockchain projects or experiments to gain funding access using a swap of some common cryptocurrencies such as bitcoin, Ether, Zcash, or other heavily traded cryptocurrency for the project's newly created token.

4   Yu'E Bao (Chinese for "leftover treasure") is an interest-paying money market fund made available through Ant Financial's Alipay platform; it has no minimum investment or time frame and can be used to make credit card payments, buy products, and more. Its interest rate was initially much higher than bank deposit rates.

of transformation, identified by the acronym LASIC: low profit margin, asset light, scalable, innovative, and compliance easy (Lee and Teo 2015).

Digitization, Digitalization, Disintermediation, and Democratization

With the payment infrastructure in place, conditions were ripe for the four *d*'s: digitization, digitalization, disintermediation, and democratization. Moreover, the economy was ready for a digital revolution and more importantly, for an information revolution, which is characterized by a shift from traditional industry to an economy based on information computerization. This information age, also known as the computer age, digital age, or new media age, relies on digital means. However, the definition of "digital" continues to evolve with the emergence of new technologies, modern user devices, and novel methods of interaction with other humans and devices. China created a knowledge-based economy with the use of the smartphone, since telecommunication networks were made available to the most remote areas. It was the neutrality of the socialist connectivity-inclusion mindset that prepared the ground for innovations in digital finance. However, China's ingenuity was the ability of its technology entrepreneurs to come up with new business models beyond the imagination of even Silicon Valley. Gradual innovation is a term to describe innovation due to marginal improvements in processes or products. However, it must eventually lead to mass technology adoption or new product imitation. Having existing infrastructure is essential, but without the capabilities, skills, and more importantly, the culture, generic services cannot scale. China has a strong culture of commercializing emerging technology. The information industry can cater to the personalized needs of individuals, simplifying the procedure of decision making, and significantly lower the costs for both providers and buyers. Economic incentives were inclusive and accepted overwhelmingly by participants from every party in the ecosystem. Underlying this information age, formed by capitalizing on the digital micro-miniaturization of computers, is a social revolution. The modernizing of information and communication processes has become the driving force for this revolution. But in a socialist and commercial sense, the mission is about helping the small and underserved use technology, and then consequently benefitting businesses.

Low Profit Margin, Asset Light, Scalable, Innovative, and Compliance Easy

The focus of the internet finance companies involved in this revolution was to scale and serve the entire pyramid rather than just the bottom of the pyramid, and to promote sustainability with innovation, low costs, and low profit margins. Of course, one key to the success of financial innovations in China is the government's inability to coordinate control of, or its hands-off approach to, any projects that help its social objectives. Examples include JD.com, Tencent, PingAn, Lufax, and many other internet finance companies. China's internet finance innovation is also an excellent example of the diffusion of innovation theory (Rogers 2003). Rogers (2003) argues that diffusion is the process by which an innovation is communicated over time among the participants in a social system. The entire internet finance innovation cycle can be explained with this theory, showing how an idea and product gained momentum and spread through the entire population and social system in a period of four years. The catch-up hypothesis was also clearly demonstrated in the proliferation of P2P lending in China, with the urban growth of platforms spilling over to poorer rural areas from 2014 to 2017. The sector's employment numbers grew exponentially. Follower organizations and regions arose thanks to the radiation of ideas, products, and technologies. Rural areas invested far less than cities. Many local firms and local governments appeared to miss opportunities for productivity growth and lost competitiveness. Unlike the more successful P2P companies such as Lufax and CreditEase that relied on a financial inclusion strategy and technology to expand from cities to rural areas, many of the P2P companies had no real strategy or technology. Many of them were scams as they were utilizing neither wealth management techniques, big data, nor technology to reduce risks. Eventually, very tight regulations had to be imposed on the sector, thus stifling or even destroying the innovation.

Despite the challenges, many of these fintech companies continued to grow in the range of their services and beyond China, with both LuFax and CreditEase expanding to Singapore in 2017. Lu International, the international arm of Lufax, was granted a capital market license for digital wealth management in Singapore in 2017. CreditEase has since expanded into Silicon Valley and diversified its services to include marketplace lending, crowdfunding, robo-advisory services, insurance technology, and blockchain. In 2018, Lufax raised US$1.33 billion in its private equity round with a valuation of US$38 billion. CreditEase FinTech Investment Fund had an equivalent of US$1 billion in total committed capital and was ranked the third-most active fintech venture capitalist by CB Insights in 2018.

China's Innovation Paradox

Yes, the Chinese government's social mission of serving the entire pyramid is important. However, without the business sense and the desire to amass wealth in the shortest possible time, the business model cannot scale as fast. However, this strong desire to accumulate wealth also brings with it a paradox: the factors that drove innovation may become the very same ones that will destroy it. Success will lead to its own failure, and that is the most prominent innovation paradox in China. The diffusion process is more than exponential—it is explosive, as seen in P2P lending and ICOs. Despite its stable central government, China's vastness means that the execution of governance is decentralized, a fact that has earned China the title of "the largest sandbox in the world." Perhaps that should be amended to "sand space," as no box can contain the business ideas that are flourishing in China. Despite the paradox, the results have been fairly amazing and are the envy of many other developing countries. Many Chinese internet tech companies have grown to become giants; in fact, of the top ten global fintech companies, half are from China (see table 8.2), and we can make some interesting observations about them.

TABLE 8.2 Global top ten fintech companies by innovation (2016)

Rank	Fintech company	Nature of business
1	**Ant Financial**	Digital banking
2	**Qudian**	Student microloans
3	Oscar	Health insurance
4	**Lufax**	P2P loan and financial services
5	**ZhongAn**	Online insurance
6	Atom Bank	Digital banking
7	Kredictech	Credit for the underbanked
8	Avant	Microloans to the underserved
9	Sofi	Student and personal loans
10	**JD Finance**	Supply chain financing

SOURCE: KPMG, H2 Ventures, and author.
NOTE: Chinese companies are in bold. Ranking was based on total capital raised, rate of capital raising, geographical diversity, sectorial diversity, and others (degree of product, service, and business model innovation). P2P = peer-to-peer.

Market value
The market valuation of fintech companies is larger than that of most banks. For example, Ant Financial had a market capitalization of US$60 billion in

2016 (US$150 billion in 2020) and is larger than American Express Bank, Morgan Stanley, PNC Financial, or the Bank of New York.

Investment demand

There is great investment demand in the Chinese fintech companies. In 2016, Ant Financial raised US$4.5 billion in one of the largest funding rounds for a private internet company; P2P lending and online wealth management company Lufax raised US$1.2 billion; online direct sales JD.com's subsidiary JD Finance raised US$1 billion; and installment e-commerce firm Qudian[5] (known as Qufenqi before this exercise) raised US$449 million. In September 2017, China's first internet-only insurer, ZhongAn Online Property and Casualty Insurance Co. Ltd., raised US$1.5 billion in Hong Kong's biggest ever fintech initial public offering (IPO). ZhongAn was formed in November 2013 by Alibaba's executive chairman, Jack Ma; Tencent's chairman, Pony Ma: and PingAn Insurance Group Co. of China Ltd.'s chairman, Peter Ma. The appetite for fintech from the investment community, especially for inclusive fintech, has been enormous and there are good reasons for this.

Soaring profits

The profits of Chinese fintech companies are growing faster than those of global banks. For example, Ant Financial's revenue jumped 92 percent to ¥10.2 billion in 2014 with ¥2.6 billion in net profits, resulting in a profit margin of 26 percent. What is more interesting is that it was expected to have a compounded annual growth rate of 64 percent from 2015 to 2017. So fintech companies like Ant Financial have the advantage of economies of scale to further enhance their profits by taking advantage of economies of scope from other additional services, beyond being a trusted payment agent between buyers and sellers on Alibaba. Similar dynamics are seen in other Chinese fintech companies.

Chinese fintech companies saw exponential growth in 2013 and 2014 (see figure 8.1). Even with subscriptions to digital finance products being more tightly regulated and restrictions placed on payment transfers, the projections through 2020 are still in the double digits. This shows the potential of

---

5   See Qudian's Form F-1, as filed with the Securities and Exchange Commission in 2017 (https://www.sec.gov/Archives/edgar/data/1692705/000119312517287443/d282719df1. htm). According to the company's IPO prospectus, Qudian's total revenues increased from ¥24.1 million in 2014 to ¥235.0 million in 2015. Total revenues jumped 514 percent to ¥1.4 billion in 2016 and further surged 393.3 percent from ¥371.6 million in the six months ending June 30, 2016, to ¥1.8 billion in the same period in 2017. Qudian's net losses were ¥233.2 million in 2015. It turned profitable in 2016 with a net income of ¥576.7 million, while in the first half of 2018 alone it recorded a net income of ¥973.7 million (E. Lee 2017).

the sector, driven by innovation within and outside China. Many of these internet finance companies are planning to "step out of China," with listings on foreign exchanges, and have based their operations in countries such as the United States, Hong Kong, and Singapore.

FIGURE 8.1   Chinese fintech industry revenue, 2013–20

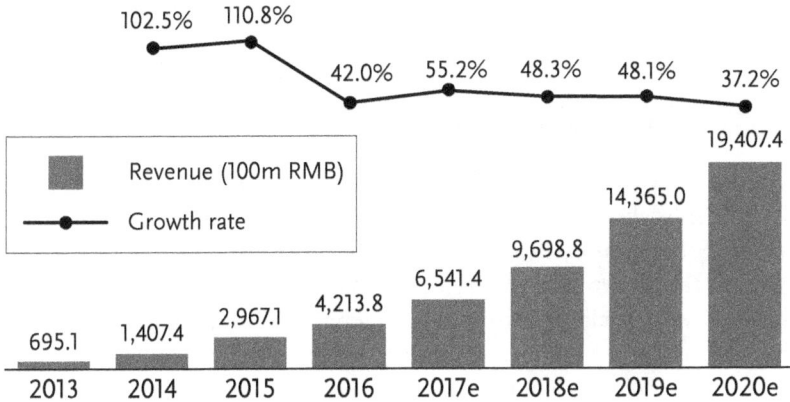

SOURCE: iResearch and Statista, 2018.
NOTE: "e" = estimates.

In summary, under weak governance capabilities that act to resemble a decentralized policy governance model, gradual and disruptive innovations in China have produced many top global companies in a very short period due to a sense of mission and Chinese business acumen.

The Singapore Case: Holistic Policy Response

The export-led model has helped Asian economies to grow their gross domestic product for the last 40 years. With the influx of multinationals, attracted by free land and worker subsidies, unemployment has come down from as high as 30 percent to below 2 percent for some countries such as Singapore. Tax incentives, ease of business setup, regulatory arbitrage, and other incentives have worked well for many Asian countries. Except for the 1997 Asian financial crisis, Asia's economies have been growing at a rapid pace, a phenomenon known as the East Asian Miracle. But if we look at the growth rates of some of the more advanced ASEAN countries in table 8.3, we can see that the export-led or catch-up development model is facing headwinds in countries like Singapore and Thailand.

TABLE 8.3 GDP growth at constant prices for six ASEAN countries, 2013–17 (%)

	2013	2014	2015	2016	2017
Indonesia	5.6	5.0	4.9	5.0	5.1
Malaysia	4.7	6.0	5.0	4.4	5.7
Philippines	7.1	6.1	6.1	6.9	6.7
Singapore	5.1	3.9	2.2	3.0	3.7
Thailand	2.9	1.1	3.7	3.6	4.2
Vietnam	5.4	6.0	6.7	6.2	6.8

SOURCE: ASEAN Statistical Yearbook 2019, ASEAN Secretariat.
NOTE: ASEAN = Association of Southeast Asian Nations.

Singapore is different from China in many aspects, but in particular, has fallen considerably behind in digital financial innovation. The Monetary Authority of Singapore (MAS) outlined its vision of a Smart Finance Centre as part of the Smart Nation initiative (MAS n.d.[b]). It envisages that technology is not just about increasing efficiency, creating opportunities, and allowing for better management of risks, but also devising new financial services and products to improve lives. There is a distinct value proposition that embodies developing a vibrant ecosystem, promoting open banking platforms, providing safe spaces to experiment in sandboxes, instituting financial sector technology and innovation schemes, building Singapore's tech start-up ecosystem, promoting accelerators and incubators, and building strong talent capabilities. There are some grants and schemes available to support these efforts through Spring Singapore (merged with International Enterprise to become Enterprise Singapore in 2018), the Infocomm Media Development Authority (IMDA), and the MAS (MAS n.d.[d], n.d.[f]; StartupSG Network n.d.; IMDA n.d.).

These schemes cover the setting up of accelerators, co-investment in start-ups, co-investment via mentors, granting special permits for foreign start-up founders, facilitating internships and initiatives to attract Singaporean talent, investing in new technology concepts, financing to assist SMEs in building capabilities, and providing support for the creation of a vibrant innovation ecosystem.

It is interesting that application programming interfaces (APIs) have caught the interest of Singapore's central bank.[6] The MAS understands that APIs are crucial for harnessing the benefits of fintech's global nature in a timely and efficient manner. The MAS, together with the Association of Banks, has developed a financial industry API playbook that identifies

6   An API is a set of formalized commands that allow software applications to seamlessly communicate. APIs make it possible for innovative applications to leverage on foundation services to create better customer-centric services.

common and useful APIs for industry and cross-sector stakeholders. This playbook also sets out the standards and governance models for all fintech players (MAS n.d.[a]). However, a top-down approach may be very different from a bottom-up decentralized community approach that takes ownership of its own efforts. It is only through crowdsourced talents and wisdom that incumbents can leverage and tap emerging and innovative fintech. Execution is always tricky, as most incumbents are comfortable with their board directions focusing on short-term profitability. Most of the growth, both in employment and investment, is not coming from the top-down bank tech but the open community bottom-up decentralized fintech community. In terms of fundraising, the growth of funds and employment are from the decentralized blockchain community. The self-regulated, leave-you-alone but direction-guiding approach of the MAS seems to have worked well so far, just as we have seen in earlier times in the Chinese internet finance market.

Centralized Governance with a Decentralized System

The most promising project in Singapore's digital transformation is Project Ubin, which creates central money using DLT (MAS n.d.[e]). If this project, which explores DLT for the clearing and settlement of payments and securities, is adopted, then the scalability of Singapore's financial system will be phenomenal. The entire ASEAN payments and securities market can then be integrated to reduce friction and increase trade in a collaborative P2P manner rather than on a government-to-government level, something that ASEAN has been trying to achieve, but so far has not succeeded in doing. Phase one of creating domestic interbank payments using a central-bank-issued Singapore-dollar equivalent has been completed; phase two of going regional into ASEAN and with applications that allow real-time settlement versus delivery of digital assets such as tokenized securities will be interesting to watch (MAS n.d.[e]). The MAS states no intention to create a cryptocurrency; if it adopts a cryptocurrency resembling Zcash[7] with a nontransparent ledger, this will be a bridge to the crypto-token economy with a zero marginal cost global payment and settlement system.

The fintech regulatory sandbox has attracted global attention as policy-makers are struggling to regulate fintech innovations. The sandbox allows fintech players to experiment with innovative financial products or services within a well-defined space and duration. It safeguards the consequences of failure and maintains the overall safety and soundness of the financial system. With Singapore trying to maintain its position as the center of financial

7 Zcash uses a privacy-proof construction called zero-knowledge succinct non-interactive argument of knowledge (zk-SNARK).

innovation, there are many uncertainties regarding whether innovations meet regulatory requirements. Initial coin offerings have become high-profile cases, as some are imposing a layer of blockchain technology over existing securities that are governed by the Security Industry Act. The position of the MAS is that it would be "undesirable" for innovations to be "stifled" when there is a lack of regulatory clarity regarding new financial products; thus, the MAS aims to encourage experimentation "within a well-defined space and duration" in the regulatory sandbox, where safeguards can "maintain the overall safety and soundness of the financial system" (MAS n.d.[c]).

Not unlike China in the earlier years, the MAS philosophy is to prevent regulation from prematurely derailing the adoption of useful technology. While it seeks to keep pace and run alongside innovation, the MAS will none-theless issue warnings and introduce new regulations whenever appropriate, especially where there are clear violations of existing rules or overspecula-tion in the market (MAS 2018). The other yardstick is the materiality and proportionality test, which means regulation will come in only when risk crosses a threshold. Even then, the regulation should be weighted carefully and in proportion to the risk posed. Finally, and perhaps most difficult, the MAS seeks to incentivize mitigating existing risks and restraining new risks that come with innovation. Some concrete initiatives include activity-based regulation to keep pace with payment innovations, specific guidelines to promote secure cloud computing, the enabling of digital financial advice and insurance, a regulatory sandbox to test innovative ideas, and the strength-ening of cybersecurity.

Using the Regulatory Sandbox to Enhance Capabilities

The sandbox, started in June 2016, is the most interesting of these initia-tives, as it leverages a range of technologies, including distributed ledgers, machine learning, and big data analytics. Given that Singapore has the high-est ratio of trade to gross domestic product (averaging 400 percent) in the world, trade and supply chain financing are two fascinating areas in which Singapore Customs has taken a keen interest. It is building the Networked Trade Platform (NTP)[8] as a trade and logistics IT ecosystem connecting businesses, community systems and platforms, and government systems. Singapore Customs and the Government Technology Agency have devel-oped the Multi-Banks Trade Finance Application Portal (TFAP) and Trade Finance Compliance (TFC) on the NTP (Singapore Customs n.d.). The NTP is

8   The National Trade Platform was renamed the Networked Trade Platform in September 2018 to emphasize the role of Singapore as a node in international trade, which is essen-tially decentralized.

a foundation on which Singapore can develop as the world's leading trade supply chain and trade financing hub. DLT will again be a very interesting application given that trade is inherently decentralized, cross-border, and requires the collaboration of parties that lack mutual trust.

Singapore's government, in recognition of the ingredients necessary for innovation, is striving to focus and enhance three areas in order to keep or gain competitive advantages.

The first area of focus is on the *critical complements to innovation investment* that are necessary to realize high potential returns. The policies described above demonstrate Singapore's commitment to innovation investment. The two Singapore sovereign wealth funds (GIC and Temasek), the Economic Development Board's investment arm (EDBI), IMDA's investment arm (SGInnovate), and Temasek-linked companies are at the forefront of investing in technology companies. Recent investment in P2P lender Dianrong by GIC, the investment of Vertex (Temasek's venture capital arm) in the cryptocurrency exchange Binance, EDBI's investment in the mining equipment manufacturer Bitmain, and SGInnovate's investment in AidTech signal high interest in blockchains, cryptocurrencies, and inclusive fintech. While their amount is small as compared to the entire portfolio, these investments demonstrate Singapore's willingness to invest in nascent and deep technology—and, in the process, to acquire knowledge about emerging technology. Capabilities that focus on financial inclusion are being built into some corporations (e.g., Fullerton Financial Holdings). However, most investments still focus on the top of the pyramid. Private-sector investments are much broader, with foreign investments being the primary driver. Many technology companies such as PayPal, Lufax, CreditEase, Ant Financial, and others have set up offices in Singapore. In particular, many ICO projects set up their foundations and headquarters in Singapore, taking advantage of its professional workforce, branding, clarity in regulation, advanced infrastructure, desirable lifestyle, and inclusive culture. These include ICO pioneers TenX, OmiseGo, and Qtum, which collectively have gained access to more than US$120 million in token sales. Many financial-inclusion-based ICOs, such as PolicyPal and Sentinel Chain, are making waves in ASEAN. Sentinel Chain has gained international fame, with the World Economic Forum and others regularly citing it as an exemplar of serving the underserved. It is one of the best examples of blockchains being used to promote financial and technological inclusion, as it uses high-quality private, consortium, and open blockchains to serve those excluded from economic systems. Many others have used Singapore as a base to reach out to the international market. A 2017 government announcement of the relaxation of venture capital license conditions is another sign that the island nation recognizes the importance of innovation investment (MAS 2017). A vibrant and liquid capital market for innovation has been successfully created for the token economy and start-ups (Singapore Business Review 2018).

The second area of focus is the *range of firm capabilities* necessary to undertake innovation and take it to market. Although many institutions of higher education offer training schemes and courses geared toward these efforts, the ability of SMEs to transform remains weak. These schemes may eventually bear fruit, but it takes time to change mindsets.

Though deep-technology skills are still missing in many industries, the many global start-ups and technology giants that are relocating to Singapore are driving a change. The benefit of a small, open economy is that it welcomes all to partake in its transformative efforts. Results are beginning to show with many of the best in blockchain, artificial intelligence (AI), and big data relocating to Singapore. Many of the top Chinese fintech and blockchain firms are also relocating to Singapore and transferring their deep skills to those based there. The Singapore University of Social Sciences has revamped courses to focus on financial and technical innovation with short- and long-term high-skill courses in fintech, blockchain, AI, smart contracts, and big data for midcareer and part- and full-time students in Singapore and China. Ngee Ann Polytechnic, SGInnovate, and other universities have also refocused on training students for many technology-based careers including in biotech, bank tech, and fintech. Many biotech, BankTech, and fintech and blockchain incubators have started operation in Singapore, with notable ones located in the Science Park, 80RR, Block 71, and Block 79. The training arms of the National Trade Union Congress, Singapore FinTech Association, and ACCESS are all conducting regular deep-skill courses and seminars for the community and enterprises.

Finally, while certain government capabilities are clearly required to be able to implement effective innovation policies, just as critical is the ability of those departments and programs to *collaborate* with one another. The MAS set up the FinTech & Innovation Group (FTIG) with sandbox regulation and SGInnovate with a focus on deep skills; the IMDA encourages innovation and investing in start-ups; and JTC, Ascendas-Singbridge, and others provide start-ups with office space. The FTIG group has been implementing Project Ubin to use DLT to create a payment system that allows untrusted parties to collaborate. A Hinternet is defined as an e-platform with a large number of sticky customers that empowers cross-border selling of low-margin value-added products and services. By building a Hinternet (Lee 2016), just as Ant Financial has done, Singapore is ready to take advantage of the One Belt, One Net strategy, as opposed to the Belt and Road Initiative (previously known as the One Belt, One Road Initiative), which focuses on hardware.[9] Collaboration among different departments is now more prominent than previously observed, and the Smart Nation initiative is taking shape. The success of these efforts will depend on collaborative efficiency. Reorganization of various units, ministries, and departments is underway.

Unlike Singapore, most ASEAN member countries, despite investment in innovation, face problems as they fail to import the appropriate technology, engage trained workers and professionals, and draw on new organizational techniques, all of which contribute to their low investment returns in innovation. On the contrary, Singapore is well aware of the high cost of doing business in the country, and focuses on having an open trade regime, a competitiveness framework, capital markets development, intellectual property (IP) protection, and on avoiding market failures that disincentivize the accumulation of knowledge. Singapore sets up supporting institutions and takes care of all the complementary factors needed for innovation by subsidizing costs, promoting free trade, ensuring fair competition, developing capital markets for start-ups, initiating IP protection, digitizing data, and enhancing knowledge. Singapore emphasizes learning and raising firms' capabilities in innovation and has moved away from clustering or focusing on specific sectors. A hands-off decentralized bottom-up open community approach, with authorities minimizing unnecessary interference and even diminishing themselves in the eyes of participants from neighboring countries with open-source software and hardware, while providing support in stealth mode, is a break from Singapore's previous approach. This decentralized system approach empowers and invites participation.

Regulatory Rent-Seeking and Innovation

These policy initiatives ensure Singapore and its firms are not lagging in capabilities necessary to catch up with China's digital economy. But unlike China, Singapore's firms lack the capacity to respond to disruption and to identify new technological opportunities (as most SMEs are intermediaries), let alone to develop a plan to explore these and to cultivate the necessary future skills for innovation. The government is focusing on solving structural unemployment issues and leaving the identification of future skills to private enterprises. However, if private enterprises are clueless on how to counter the disruption or refuse to change their mindset, there will be a market failure in future skill training, and specifically a nationally funded

---

9   In 2015, China initiated a digital silk road national strategy to ensure digital connectivity abroad.

effort to provide Singaporeans with the opportunities to develop their fullest potential throughout life. While two universities[10] have been chosen to assist in the transition, it remains to be seen how the human resources will be retrained in the face of incumbents' resistance. Incumbents protected by regulation will tend to promote business as usual, with no incentives to train for the disruption. There is evidence to suggest that the incumbents do not understand the threat of new technology, and if they do, have demonstrated their unwillingness to be part of the transformation due to short-term profit motives. These are all consistent with observations from recent research that managerial capabilities are driven by good managers but failures to innovate are a result of (1) enabling the most inefficient or regulation-protected firms to survive, (2) failing to provide adequate incentives for firms to upgrade, and (3) failing to recognize that firms with diffused ownership tend to be among the best, whereas government- and family-owned companies are weaker.

Recent examples in Singapore's transportation sectors, including Uber and Grab's successful breaking of the monopolistic market, sent a crucial message to incumbents in the financial sector. Monopolistic regulation instills a false sense of comfort to incumbents in a well-organized society. However, such mindsets, which have hindered behavior change, may slow innovation, and a country like Singapore may face challenges that other ASEAN economies can leapfrog.

The successful examples of financial innovation in China and Singapore—a large domestic market versus a small one—have in common the approach of using regulation or its lack as a way to influence firms' behaviors. Both countries have used incentives to attract foreign multinational companies but have not been successful in changing the behavior of incumbent multinational companies in the new disruptive economy. There are challenges in changing the mindset and behavior of large organizations. These two countries have been successful in empowering the disruptors through investment but have not been successful in changing the incumbents' behavior. Singapore has changed its strategy by attracting technology giants such as Dyson, Facebook, and Google to set up in Singapore.

Culture, besides regulation or the lack of it, plays an important role in China. In Singapore, innovative policymaking that takes advantage of regulatory arbitrage almost always bears fruit in the financial sector, as evident in hedge fund management, private banking, and real estate investment trusts. Up until 2012, a license was not required to set up a fund management firm in Singapore. That changed with the repeal of the chapter 298 Securities and Futures Act Section 41, 1(e). But by then, thousands of fund management

10   Singapore University of Social Sciences and Singapore University of Technology and Design.

firms had already been set up, benefitting the economy. Something similar happened in private banking and among advisory firms that serve ultra-high-net-worth investors, and real estate investment trusts, with many foreign participants setting up in Singapore. Can Singapore continue to transform itself by attracting new entrepreneurs or by creating and encouraging its own to flourish under a new set of policies? The city-state has grown by being internally inclusive of businesses set up within Singapore, but can it be externally inclusive as start-ups and businesses venture outside the country without the advantage of regulatory arbitrage? Decentralized inclusive tech, where both offline governance and systems are decentralized, may be a way forward.

What Can Decentralization Achieve?

Cirera and Maloney's (2017) most important thesis is that the observed low level of technological adoption in developing countries is a rational response of firms to a range of adverse conditions they face: barriers to accumulating physical and human capital, low firm capabilities, and weak government capacity. We are suggesting here that decentralized technology may be one of the solutions and may result in accelerating catch-up via inclusive fintech technology. A lack of technology, mobile human resources, and access to capital are major pain points for low-income economies endeavoring to catch up. The more freedom a network has, the faster its innovation (Aidis, Estrin, and Mickiewicz 2012).

Lack of adoption is made worse by many physical barriers, a lack of transparency, and regulations that institute control, encourage opaque capital flows, and on the whole, perpetuate monopolistic power. Ease of entrepreneurial entry is inversely related to the size of the government, and more weakly to the extent of corruption. Unlocking the enormous growth potential of countries moving closer to the technological frontier is not so simple if countries and businesses have no access to global talent and capital and are facing incumbents' conflicting interests. General policy prescriptions have been made from the centralized policymaking perspective, for example, to provide additional research and development incentives. But moving countries closer to the frontier will require far-reaching policy changes that tackle multiple constraints to technological adoption. Technology, if decentralized, may induce more technological adoption if the country or business has access to open-source software, a benevolent economic incentive structure that embodies the interests of most, and a global market reach.

Decentralization, especially with blockchain and ICOs, has brought about the diminishing role of jurisdictions and become borderless on the internet;

it has solved the pain point of access to global capital, it has addressed the issue of the global reach of developing countries, and it has allowed for fractional ownership with a 10^{-8} denomination of digital assets, using technology like blockchain. Thus, it has addressed all the pain points of the catch-up hypothesis. The International Monetary Fund has recently called on banks to be mindful of the rise of cryptocurrency and its power of disruption (Lagarde 2017). In particular, national cryptocurrency or central bank cryptocurrency can be created with weak linkages to the money supply. Central banks and large licensed financial institutions may benefit from the disruption of a crypto-fiat. China is in the process of creating its national cryptocurrency, and JP Morgan recently planned a JPMCoin to reduce cross-border in-house settlement time and costs. Successful banks may have to revise their idea of "too big to collaborate" in a decentralized world, and embrace decentralization for a more inclusive, innovative world.

Both the International Monetary Fund and MAS, while acknowledging that decentralized technologies can be susceptible to new methods of money laundering and illicit activities, have urged that the potential of the token economy be harnessed. Decentralized and distributed technologies should be leveraged for public and social good, provided that international efforts be taken to prevent them from being used as havens for illegal activity or from becoming sources of financial vulnerability.[11] However, few policymakers have speculated what the benefits could be, beyond saying that it is a new form of an immutable distributed ledger, a new trust machine for untrusted parties to work together, and a decentralized network that allows for useful applications such as smart contracts and exchange of value.

Conclusion

China and Singapore can teach us much about development economics and innovation. We have seen how, for example, the use of Yu'E Bao in an imperfect money market, under a decentralized governance environment, acted as a catalyst to trigger the growth of China's entire internet finance industry. We have seen how China has stoked fear in comfortable incumbents like Singapore and Japan; both are now seeing challengers arise from leapfrog economies. Forward-looking regulators such as Singapore and Japan[12] are

---

11   Such dangers are addressed in Lagarde (2018) and Menon (2018).

12   On May 25, 2016, Japan's Payment Services Act (PSA) was amended to regulate virtual currencies. The main changes to the PSA were as follows: (1) definition of virtual currency (Article 2-5); (2) registration of virtual currency exchanges (Article 63-2); (3) regulation of virtual currency exchanges' operations (Article 63); and (4) supervision of

taking considerable calculated risks to allow for regulatory arbitrage for DLT so that innovation can take place. We have also discussed how a decentralized system and technology with digital transparency/privacy, such as blockchain, can be a real game changer in addressing the limitations of the catch-up hypothesis and the innovation paradox. It can circumvent real bottlenecks, like barriers that are set up to retain monopolistic power and regulations to ward off challengers.

However, the paradox is that a decentralized system's success factor will lead to its failure. Given the speed of the innovation, especially if it is driven by financial innovation, both financial and technical literacy will never be able to catch up. It is precisely the speed of the diffusion of information on innovation investment opportunities that will lead to scams, bubbles, and speculation, taking advantage of the financial and technically illiterate. Overvaluation of investment and overspeculation by the masses will introduce systematic risk to the financial system. While education and consumer protection are essential for stability when the euphoria rises too high, a good balance between innovation and regulation is essential for the catch-up hypothesis to become a reality. An environment where regulation is at the fore and innovation lags is unlikely to be conducive to sustainable innovation. For sustainable and rapid growth in developed economies, it is important to ensure that regulation is more or less in step with innovation. Innovation in the fourth industrial revolution requires technical literacy at the board and governance level, and that is the challenge for many governments and corporates.

A decentralized structure, with coded governance that bypasses monopolistic regulation and inefficient governance, may be a systematic way to allow for faster diffusion of innovation. Emerging decentralized technology will likely spawn new organizational forms.[13] The innovation investment that is happening is perhaps very different from the time when foreign land had to be bought, factories had to be built, workers had to be trained, raw materials had to be imported, and hard transport and utility infrastructure had to be built. With high rates of digital handphone penetration and other new technologies, the existing agriculture, livestock, basic housing, basic utility, digital assets, and digital goods and services are all low-hanging fruits for the tokenization of nonsecuritized assets such as livestock and airtime, among others. With tokenization comes value transfer and trading, and thus the ability to leapfrog with almost no hindrance from incumbents,

---

virtual currency exchanges (Article 63).

13   Smart contracts or decentralized autonomous organizations may be future innovation drivers. They have the potential to disrupt centralized organizations such as exchanges, with buyers and sellers searching for each other through the internet.

regulations, or legacy issues. A decentralized autonomous organization (DAO), under certain circumstances, may be economically more efficient than governmental and business organizations. More important, if the DAO is structured correctly, with coded governance and coded execution via smart contracts, it may improve production relationships and avoid the tragedy of the commons, thus leading to a more efficient outcome of lower consumption and administrative costs (Ostrom 1990).[14]

Developing economies run into pain points as they attempt to catch up. Decentralization may eventually help to avoid some of these. Decentralization has great potential to level the playing field for economies and actors that are small, less endowed, and with a weaker degree of access. Infrastructure building or technology transfer can be via the provision of open-source, decentralized software such as Project Ubin I and II, and even open-source hardware, to developing economies. Borderless bottom-up communities may be formed to complement the top-down approach of governmental and business organizations and achieve higher economic efficiency. Among ASEAN countries, 73 percent, or 483 million people, are unbanked. However, in six developing ASEAN countries, handphone penetration is over 100 percent. Sustainable businesses and growth without leverage may be the right decentralized inclusive tech approach to leapfrogging. Even more interesting is that these countries rely on agriculture; sparsely populated areas without debt can be cost efficiently connected through the use of drones, drones with balloon Wi-Fi, mesh networks, solar energy, virtual and augmented reality, and other inclusive technologies. Connectivity inclusion has never been so cheap, as it is no longer necessary to build roads, lay cables, or link to satellites to have the same impact. Even the cost of a satellite uplink is rapidly decreasing. All these will allow the user innovation model to gain momentum via digital devices with sustainable business models. There are already numerous blockchain projects—such as Sentinel Chain, AidTech, and SmartMesh—in operation in developing economies.

Earlier literature has argued that decentralized governance will lead to worse inequality geographically, especially if governments lose the power to reallocate resources from richer to poorer communities. However, decentralization with technology creates a borderless, transparent, virtual world with a network that embodies the interest of all in the community. With new decentralized technologies such as smart contracts, different communities can be linked to a larger ecosystem. It is this borderless concept that addresses

---

14   The tragedy of the commons is a social-science term that describes a situation in a shared-resource system where individual users, acting independently according to their own self-interest, behave contrary to the common good of all users by depleting or spoiling a resource through their collective action.

the pain points of the catch-up hypothesis and allows for leapfrogging.

However, confusion and misinformation about the capabilities and promise of decentralized technology, systems, and governance continue to influence mindsets. It may not be surprising to many of us that the biggest hindrance to catching up or leapfrogging may simply be our stubborn mindsets. In particular, many governments are still hesitant to adopt an open attitude toward open innovation. Some recent words from Ravi Menon, MAS managing director, regarding the token economy (shunned by most financial centers), are appropriate here:

> Gresham's Law . . . is loosely interpreted as "bad money drives out good." We must work together—regulators and the crypto industry—to make sure that bad money does not take hold. And that a new generation of crypto tokens emerges, that harnesses the potential of blockchain technology for social good while mitigating the risks today's tokens pose. (Menon 2018)

Although decentralization technology offers a new perspective, the implications of decentralization with regards to the catch-up hypothesis and innovation still need to be further studied. Nonetheless, it seems clear that the decentralization of offline policy governance and distributed innovation offer policy options for governments of developing countries to achieve economic growth and perhaps leapfrog developed economies.

References

Abramovitz, Moses. 1986. "Catching Up, Forging Ahead, and Falling Behind." *Journal of Economic History* 46, no. 2: 385–406.

Acheson, Noelle. 2017. "China's Ban: Understandable, Reasonable and (Probably) Temporary." Coindesk, September 12. https://www.coindesk.com/chinas-ico-ban-understandable-reasonable-probably-temporary/.

Aidis, Ruta, Saul Estrin, and Tomasz Marek Mickiewicz. 2012. "Size Matters: Entrepreneurial Entry and Government." *Small Business Economics* 39, no. 1: 119–39.

Bekey, George A. 2005. *Autonomous Robots: From Biological Inspiration to Implementation and Control.* Cambridge, MA: MIT Press.

Center for International Earth Science Information Network (CIESIN). N.d. "What Is Decentralization?" In *The Online Sourcebook on Decentralization and Local Development.* Accessed September 16, 2019. http://www.ciesin.org/decentralization/English/General/Different_forms.html.

Chesbrough, Henry William. 2003. *Open Innovation: The New Imperative for Creating and Profiting from Technology.* Boston, MA: Harvard Business School Press.

———. 2006. *Open Business Models: How to Thrive in the New Innovation Landscape.* Cambridge, MA: Harvard Business School Press.

Cirera, Xavier, and William F. Maloney. 2017. *The Innovation Paradox: Developing-Country Capabilities and the Unrealized Promise of Technological Catch-Up.* Washington, DC: World Bank.

Food and Agriculture Organization of the United Nations (FAO). 2002. *Environment in Decentralized Development—Economic and Institutional Issues.* Training Materials for Agricultural Planning 44. Rome: United Nations.

Fudenberg, Drew, Richard J. Gilbert, Joseph Stiglitz, and Jean Tirole. 1983. "Preemption, Leapfrogging, and Competition in Patent Races." *European Economic Review* 22, no. 1: 3–31.

Gabison, Garry, and Annarosa Pesole. 2014. *An Overview of Models of Distributed Innovation: Open Innovation, User Innovation and Social Innovation.* JRC Science and Policy Report JRC93533, Joint Research Centre. Luxembourg: Publications Office of the European Union. http://publications.jrc.ec.europa.eu/repository/bitstream/JRC93533/jrc93533_ap.pdf.

Greene, Robert, and David Lee Kuo Chuen. 2019. "Singapore's Open
    Digital Token Offering Embrace: Context & Consequences." *Journal
    of British Blockchain Association* 2, no. 2: 39–50.
Infocomm Media Development Authority (IMDA). N.d. "Capabilities
    Development Grant—Technology Innovation (CDG-TI)." Accessed
    2018. https://cdggrantprogram.com/.
Lagarde, Christine. 2017. "Central Banking and Fintech—A Brave New
    World?" International Monetary Fund, September 29. https://www.
    imf.org/en/News/Articles/2017/09/28/sp092917-central-banking-and
    -fintech-a-brave-new-world.
———. 2018. "Addressing the Dark Side of the Crypto World." IMFBlog,
    March 13. https://blogs.imf.org/2018/03/13/addressing-the-dark-side-of
    -the-crypto-world.
Lederman, Daniel, and William F. Maloney. 2012. *Does What You Export
    Matter? In Search of Empirical Guidance for Industrial Policies.*
    Washington, DC: World Bank.
Lee, David Kuo Chuen. 2016. "The FinTech Promise." *The European
    Financial Review*, June 23. http://www.europeanfinancialreview
    .com/?p=6093.
———. 2017. "Decentralization and Distributed Innovation: FinTech,
    Bitcoin and ICOs." Presentation at the Stanford Asia-Pacific
    Innovation Conference, October 26. https://www.slideshare.net
    /DavidLee215/decentralisation-and-distributed-innovation-fintech
    -bitcoina-and-icos.
Lee, David Kuo Chuen, and Gin Swee Teo (Jinrui Zhang). 2015.
    "Emergence of FinTech and the LASIC Principles." *Journal of
    Financial Perspectives* 3, no. 3: 1–26.
Lee, David Kuo Chuen, and Linda Low. 2018. *Inclusive FinTech:
    Blockchain, Cryptocurrency and ICO.* Singapore: World Scientific.
Lee, David Kuo Chuen, and Robert Deng. 2017. *Handbook of
    Blockchain, Digital Finance, and Inclusion.* San Diego: Academic
    Press.
Lee, Emma. 2017. "Chinese Micro Lender Qudian under Fire after
    Splashy US IPO." Technode, October 23. https://technode.com
    /2017/10/23/chinese-micro-lender-qudian-under-fire-after-splashy-us
    -ipo/.
Maloney, William F. 2017. "Revisiting the National Innovation System
    in Developing Countries." Policy Research Working Paper WPS 8219,
    World Bank, Washington, DC.

Maloney, William F., and Felipe Valencia Caicedo. 2017. "Engineering Growth: Innovative Capacity and Development in the Americas." CESifo Working Paper Series 6339, Center for Economic Studies and Ifo Institute, Munich.

Monetary Authority of Singapore (MAS). 2017. "MAS Simplifies Rules for Managers of Venture Capital Funds to Facilitate Start-Ups' Access to Capital." Media release, October 20. Accessed 2018. https://www .mas.gov.sg/news/media-releases/2017/mas-simplifies-rules-for -managers-of-venture-capital-funds.

———. 2018. "MAS Warns Digital Token Exchanges and ICO Issuer." Media release May 24. Accessed 2018. https://www.mas.gov.sg/news /media-releases/2018/mas-warns-digital-token-exchanges-and-ico -issuer#:~:text=The%20Monetary%20Authority%20of%20Singa pore,its%20digital%20tokens%20in%20Singapore.

———. N.d.(a). "Application Programming Interfaces (API)." Accessed 2018. https://www.mas.gov.sg/development/fintech/technologies---apis.

———. N.d.(b). "Fintech and Innovation." Accessed 2015. https://www .mas.gov.sg/development/fintech.

———. N.d.(c). "FinTech Regulatory Sandbox." Accessed 2018. http:// www.mas.gov.sg/Singapore-Financial-Centre/Smart-Financial-Centre /FinTech-Regulatory-Sandbox.aspx.

———. N.d.(d). "FSTI Proof-of-Concept Scheme." Accessed 2018. http:// www.mas.gov.sg/Singapore-Financial-Centre/Smart-Financial-Centre /FSTI-Proof-Of-Concept-Scheme.aspx.

———. N.d.(e). "Project Ubin: Central Bank Digital Money Using Distributed Ledger Technology." Accessed 2018. http://www.mas.gov .sg/Singapore-Financial-Centre/Smart-Financial-Centre/Project-Ubin .aspx.

———. N.d.(f). "Setting up Your FinTech Business in Singapore." Accessed 2015. http://www.mas.gov.sg/Singapore-Financial-Centre /Smart-Financial-Centre/Setting-up-your-Business.aspx.

Menon, Ravi. 2018. "Crypto Tokens: The Good, the Bad, and the Ugly." Speech at Money20/20, Singapore, BIS, March 15. https://www.bis.org /review/r180321c.htm.

Murray, Fiona, and Siobhán O'Mahony. 2007. "Exploring the Foundations of Cumulative Innovation: Implications for Organization Science." *Organization Science* 18, no. 6: 1006–21.

Nakamoto, Satoshi. 2008. "Bitcoin: A Peer-to-Peer Electronic Cash System." http://bitcoin.org/bitcoin.pdf.

Ostrom, Elinor. 1990. *Governing the Commons: The Evolution of Institutions for Collective Action*. New York: Cambridge University Press.

Pace Project. N.d. "Decentralization." Accessed September 2019. http://isr.uci.edu/projects/pace/decentralization.html.

People's Bank of China. 2017. "Public Notice of the PBC, CAC, MIIT, SAIC, CBRC, CSRC and CIRC on Preventing Risks of Fundraising through Coin Offering." The People's Bank of China, September 8. http://www.pbc.gov.cn/english/130721/3377816/index.html.

Prud'homme, Remy. 1994. "On the Dangers of Decentralization." Policy Research Working Paper WPS 1252, World Bank, Washington, DC. http://documents.worldbank.org/curated/en/218141468739288067/On-the-dangers-of-decentralization.

Rogers, Everett. 2003. *Diffusion of Innovations*. 5th Edition. New York: Free Press.

Schumpeter, Joseph. 1942. *Capitalism, Socialism and Democracy*. New York: Harper Collins.

Scotchmer, Suzanne. 2004. *Innovation and Incentives*. Cambridge, MA: MIT Press.

Singapore Business Review. 2018. "Are Singapore VCs Losing Out to ICOs?" February 18. https://sbr.com.sg/financial-services/in-focus/are-singapore-vcs-losing-out-icos.

Singapore Customs. N.d. "Networked Trade Platform." Accessed 2018. https://www.customs.gov.sg/about-us/national-single-window/networked-trade-platform.

StartupSG Network. N.d. "Enhancing Capabilities of Accelerators and Incubators." Accessed 2018. http://www.startupsg.net.

Tirole, Jean. 1988. *The Theory of Industrial Organization*. Cambridge: MA: MIT Press.

von Hippel, Eric . 2005. *Democratizing Innovation*. Cambridge, MA: MIT Press.

West, Joel, and Scott Gallagher. 2006. "Challenges of Open Innovation: The Paradox of Firm Investment in Open-Source Software." *R and D Management* 36, no. 3: 319–31.

CHAPTER 9

A Comparative Study of East Asian Economies
Business Structure and Innovation Strategy

Hwy-Chang Moon and Yeon W. Lee

overnment policies aimed at promoting the growth of small- and
medium-sized enterprises (SMEs), alongside measures designed to bolster social cohesion, are increasing throughout the world as demands
for fair distribution and shared growth increase. For example, South Korea's
current government has initiated a series of economic measures aimed at
boosting start-ups and SMEs while regulating the nation's large enterprises
(LEs), particularly the *chaebol*. Key agenda items put forth by the Moon
Jae-in government have included income-led growth, employment, a fair
economy, and innovative growth to facilitate a recovery in consumption and
the market. A closer examination of efforts toward these four policy aims
reveals that most have focused on fostering the growth of SMEs, grounded
in the belief that South Korea's prolonged unemployment problem can be
solved by the active creation of start-ups and SMEs. Efforts toward a fair economy are directed at increasing the monitoring and regulation of *chaebol*, to
reduce the unbalanced power game between LEs and their suppliers. A call
for growth in innovation seems timely, as the global economy and businesses
transition toward the fourth industrial revolution, yet related efforts have
been short-sighted; the government is merely encouraging attention-grabbing
start-ups modeled on Uber and Airbnb. Taken together with the economic

democracy programs left over from the Park Geun-hye administration, the budget spent on SMEs has been steadily increasing, reaching ₩16.5 trillion in 2017, reflecting the level of hype surrounding SMEs and start-ups (Jung 2017).

South Korea is not the only economy making increasing efforts to bolster and produce SMEs and start-ups. With Silicon Valley producing one success story after another, the start-up boom has clearly gone global (Singh, Garg, and Deshmukh 2008). In 2015, Japan's prime minister, Shinzo Abe, visited Stanford University to get a glimpse of the Valley's successful start-ups and SMEs. The irony, however, is that the successful Silicon Valley firms are no longer SMEs, a critical fact of which SME advocates should be aware. Contrary to popular belief and perhaps hope, the global economy is still dominated by conglomerates, giant firms that are not downsizing but instead scaling up by integrating or linking with different industries (*The Economist* 2016). Firms such as Hewlett-Packard, Apple, Microsoft, Google, Facebook, Airbnb, and Uber may have once been start-ups, but they have successfully grown into innovative LEs that represent the aspirations of many entrepreneurs. In fact, most of the global indices for innovative companies place LEs such as Apple, Google, Tesla Motors, Samsung, and Amazon at the top of their rankings.

Historically, demand for public support of SMEs has portrayed them as a countervailing force to the evils of monopoly, one that can diversify product commercialization so as to cater to consumers' individual tastes (Rothwell and Zegveld 1982). SMEs have been seen as entities that increase consumer value and utility, whereas LEs were regarded more as price setters that distort free competition and true value. That said, there have been various views and government approaches. Until the 1960s, European governments favored LEs and gave birth to national flagship companies in key sectors such as computers, while the United States pursued the opposite policy direction, as seen in the creation of the Small Business Act of 1953. However, since the 1970s, European governments have shifted in favor of SMEs, encouraging them as more efficient employment creators than LEs (Birch 1979). And small high-tech firms of the 1980s, originating mainly from Silicon Valley and Route 128, stimulated the creation and growth of new technology-based firms in both Europe and the United States (Rothwell 1989).

Even up until recently, start-ups and SMEs were touted as the new hope to resolve increasing economic disparity and a decades-long economic slowdown. However, there are also some sobering stories, including a growing number of media reports about start-up booms fizzling out (e.g., Solon 2017). Some reports suggest start-ups are running out of money and investors are becoming more cautious and selective because of decreasing confidence in investment returns. Some signs even point toward something like the 1990s dotcom crash, further stoking investors' concerns. It turns out that large government expenditures have had little effect on either employment rates or the success rate of start-ups. Lu and Beamish (2001) observed the failure rates of new businesses in Australia, the United Kingdom, Japan, Taiwan, and Hong Kong to be around 25 percent within two years of creation and 63 percent within six years. In terms of value creation, the productivity of average labor tends to decrease as the firm size decreases, thereby significantly lowering the competitiveness of firms (Moon 2016). These problems call for a more accurate analysis of the relationship between the size of firms (SME vs. LE), innovation, and business performance.

In considering the dynamics among these three factors, this final chapter compares six Asian economies: Hong Kong, Singapore, Taiwan, Korea, Japan, and China. After a review of research findings on the influence of firm size on innovation and growth, we will compare and contrast the growth trajectories of businesses in these six economies. It is hoped that this analysis will have useful implications for innovation strategies and policies in this current era of rapid transition. In the end, innovativeness and competitiveness are not directly related to firm size (O'Regan, Ghobadian, and Sims 2006), but rather to how firms engage or coordinate through clusters and global value chains (GVCs). By briefly examining the business and political economy of these six economies, we conclude that they have sustained their differentiated positions through the proper utilization of clusters and GVCs, which, regardless of firm size, can further enhance innovation and entrepreneurship.

Literature Review:
The Link between Firm Size and Innovation

In order to analyze how the strategies and strengths of SMEs and LEs differ in terms of innovative capacity, this literature review will examine the investigations of earlier studies into firm size. Academic debate on how firm size relates to technological change and economic growth has been ongoing since the late 1950s. Notable economists such as Galbraith (1957) addressed the importance of large size and monopoly power, while Schumacher (1973) strongly advocated that "small is beautiful."

Innovation has long been recognized as a critical factor in a firm's competitive advantage (Brown and Eisenhardt 1995; Motwani et al. 1999; Cooper 2000; Zimmerer and Scarborough 2002; Stock, Greis, and Fischer 2002). In addition, innovation cannot be discussed without mentioning Schumpeter (1942), who suggested that exceptional and creative independent entrepreneurs undertake risky innovative developments that ultimately lead to the launching of radical new products and industries. However, Schumpeter, in his later research, focused on the importance of endogenous science and technology, mainly through the dominant roles played by the research and development (R&D) of LEs. He emphasized that there will be an increasingly substitutive and complementary role played by LEs that replace the exogenous inventor's role with an endogenous one.

Winter (1984) also proposed that SMEs' innovative activities (or innovative entrants) respond to a different technological and economic environment, meaning the supply of innovation at a particular time is determined to be successful by the *joint occurrences of innovative ideas* that are relevant to the industry. On the whole, the earlier studies suggest that the relative role of SMEs and LEs in technological change and industrial production will significantly vary over the industry cycle. Most studies confirm that innovation is not clearly associated with the size of firms (Rothwell 1989). However, studies that investigated successful manufacturing SMEs (e.g., Damanpour 1992; Terziovski 2010) pointed out that the key drivers of growth in these firms were innovation strategies and formal structures that mirrored LEs.

SME innovations are usually related to entrepreneurial dynamism, internal flexibility, and responsiveness to changing circumstances. This means that the advantages possessed by SMEs tend to be more behavioral in nature. On the other hand, LEs have advantages because of their relatively larger collection of financial, human, and technological resources, which are material-based resource advantages (Rothwell and Dodgson 1991; Wagner and Hansen 2005; Spithoven, Vanhaverbeke, and Roijakkers 2013). However, LEs tend to create a bureaucracy that is unfavorable to creativity, and so may be less flexible (Kamien and Schwartz 1975; Cohen and Klepper 1996; Hudson, Smart, and Bourne 2001). In this respect, the disadvantages of either group may be overcome and enhanced by combining both resource and behavioral advantages because each side has its own, separate advantages that can be complemented when joined together.

One of the common approaches to studying innovation is to measure R&D expenditure. However, as PricewaterhouseCoopers' Global Innovation 1000 ranking reports, many firms that are recognized as highly innovative often rank relatively low in terms of their R&D spending. For instance, Apple spent only 2.6 percent of its sales ($4.5 billion) on R&D and ranked thirty-second on the list, while Samsung ranked second by spending $13.4 billion on R&D. This result shows that there is no clear relationship between the two. Regarding firms' efforts in R&D and innovation, academic studies reveal similar conclusions. For example, Acs and Audretsch (1988) showed that the association among R&D expenditures, patented inventions, and innovation is not consistent.

Cohen and Klepper (1996) analyze the role of R&D in innovation by drawing comparisons between process and product innovation among SMEs and LEs. Although they find that LEs have an advantage in process innovation because of the larger output over which they can spread the costs of their R&D, they conclude that LEs do not necessarily have a higher level of efficiency in process innovation than do SMEs. Other studies (e.g., Wagner and Hansen 2005) that try to delineate process and product innovation adopt Porter's (1996) framework on sources of competitive advantage by arguing that operational effectiveness (process innovation) is less important than strategic positioning (product innovation). This view has developed into the idea that LEs incur more inefficiency and produce fewer innovations over time, which highlights the importance of product differentiation by SMEs. As these studies show, there is no clear and consistent linkage between firm size and innovation, particularly when measured in terms of firms' R&D inputs.

The focus of academic research and government policies has gradually shifted toward identifying which firms have the highest growth potential, referred to as high-growth firms (HGFs). An increasing number of academic studies question the effectiveness of blindly supporting start-ups and instead suggest policies that focus on small HGFs in the economy. For example, Nicolaou and Shane (2009) question supporting start-ups that may have limited growth ambitions, capabilities, or chances of survival. Hölzl and Friesenbichler (2010) examine the relationship between SMEs and entrepreneurship policy and argue in favor of supporting entrepreneurs of HGFs who have greater growth ambitions. This trend has been increasingly adopted by governments and international organizations. For instance, the European Commission drew the distinction of supporting high-growth SMEs as a political objective in its Europe 2020 strategy, and the Organisation for Economic Co-operation and Development (OECD) similarly evaluates how governments promote HGFs (Coad et al. 2014).

However, most of these earlier studies examine the governance, operation, and strategy of Western firms. There are only a few comparative studies on innovation in SMEs and LEs in the East Asian context. A notable exception is by Lin and Chen (2007), who explore the innovation practices of SMEs in Taiwan and find that administrative innovations, not technological ones, are the crucial factors in sales and performance. Xu, Lin, and Lin (2008) investigate the relationship between the network structures of SMEs in Guangdong, China, and their innovative capabilities. Chen (2006) examines Chinese SMEs that were created after the three periods of government political initiatives—1978–92 for the quantitative growth of SMEs, 1992–2002 for the growth of state-owned SMEs, and the period after 2002 for implementing laws promoting SMEs—and concludes that fundamental market systems, such as resource allocation and self-operation status,[1] were essential to the growth of SMEs. An important implication of this study is that the creation of a fair competitive environment is likewise crucial for SMEs.

Despite these efforts, fundamental research into links between the structure and size of Asian firms and their performance has been relatively neglected; lacking in particular is comparative analysis of LEs and SMEs. Therefore, we next examine the key business characteristics of firms in East Asian economies, from their creation through their growth.

The Creation and Growth of Firms in Six Asian Economies

The six Asian economies we consider—Hong Kong, Singapore, Taiwan, South Korea, Japan, and China—may appear relatively homogeneous compared with those of the West. However, starting from their historical beginnings, there are many more relevant differences than similarities. Table 9.1 summarizes these economies' key characteristics in an effort to describe their political economy and how these factors influenced their economic development.

We can categorize these six into three types based on population size. Hong Kong and Singapore, with populations smaller than eight million, are more like city-states; they serve as centers of regions beyond their borders—*de facto* capitals for industry, finance, commerce, information, education, and culture (Vogel 1991). Although Taiwan is half the size of Korea, both are categorized as medium-sized economies, while Japan and China are considered large economies (Cho and Moon 2013).[2] The demographics are important because they determine current and potential market size, and reflect the structure of the economy as well as the potential reach and impact of government policies.

The next category looks at historical influences: Singapore and Hong Kong were shaped by Western, namely British, colonialism, whereas Taiwan and Korea were mainly influenced by Japanese governance. Japan, as the first adopter of Western industrialization, as far back as 1854, has been the most differentiated economy. Conversely, China was the latest adopter after first attempting to benchmark the Soviet Union's system, only to experience shortfalls. Of the six, Hong Kong and Singapore were the first to adopt British/Western culture and language, an important tool for facilitating

---

1   In other words, the capability of an SME to regulate itself, instead of being subject to government control.

2   This study categorized sixty-two major developed and developing countries in the world into three groups—small, medium, and large economies—in terms of land size and population.

TABLE 9.1 Growth trajectories of six Asian economies

	Small		Medium		Large	
	Hong Kong	Singapore	Taiwan	South Korea	Japan	China
Population (millions)	7.4	5.7	23	51	127	1,400
History (influence)	British colony (Western)		Japanese colony (Eastern)		Early industrialization (West + α)	Communism (Soviet + α)
Openness	High	Highest (immigration)		Medium → high		Low → medium
Economic system	Free market		Planned capitalism → free market			Socialist market
Growth strategy	Mixed		Balanced	Unbalanced → balanced		Mixed
Firm type	Network (to China)	Network (ASEAN and the world)	SMEs	Chaebol	Zaibatsu/ Keiretsu	SOEs and SMEs
Differentiation	Finance hub (finance, trade)	Global cluster (finance, trade, manufacturing)	Part of GVC (e.g., parts, components)	Tight coordination of GVC	Tighter coordination of GVC	SMEs: Part of GVC

SOURCE: Authors.

NOTE: ASEAN = Association of Southeast Asian Nations; GVC = global value chain; SME = small- and medium-sized enterprise; SOE = state-owned enterprise.

international business transactions. More importantly, both carried out active open-door policies to invigorate commerce and industry on account of their small domestic markets.

Taiwan and Korea are their opposites. With their history as Japanese colonies, they still retain remnants of Japanese administrative, educational, and commercial systems. The two also faced a communist military threat, although the situation was much more serious in Korea than in Taiwan. Compared to Taiwan, Korea started with a smaller industrial base; Korea's gross domestic product was ten years behind that of Taiwan when war broke out on the Korean Peninsula in 1950. In terms of trade policy, the governments of both Taiwan and Korea strove to protect fledgling firms through trade measures in the form of tariffs and legal restrictions on the entry of foreign firms.

The Japanese government carried out a similar degree of protection in trade and inward foreign direct investment until the 1960s, actively involving itself in industry building and trading in sectors, including steel, semiconductors, computers, and electronics (U.S. Congress 1991; Bebenroth 2015). While Japan adopted the Western market system, its industrial structure was unique: the big four *zaibatsu* (Mitsui, Sumitomo, Mitsubishi, and Yasuda) controlled more than half of all major Japanese industries, including mining, steel, trade, and banking, prior to Japan's defeat in World War II (Bebenroth 2015).

In the war's aftermath, Western occupational forces dissembled the *zaibatsu* structure by dividing them into separate firms, in order to prevent the reemergence of strong Japanese war industries. For example, the biggest *zaibatsu*, Mitsui, was split into more than one hundred independent firms (Westney 2009). This change resulted in the creation of industrial groups, or *keiretsu*, which are closely linked through a mutual shareholding mechanism. Korea's *chaebol* followed a similar pattern, although corporate banking was prohibited from the late 1960s by President Park Jung-hee, in the pursuit of tighter government control over capital allocation.

Despite some evident similarities among these economies, there are significant differences in the way their governments fostered growth through industrial policies. The postindependence leaders of Singapore were closely linked to British socialism during a time when socialist governments and the nationalization of key European industries were at their peak. Therefore, Prime Minister Lee Kuan-yew and his government continued to believe in the desirability of government-led enterprises, along with other common socialist features such as government responsibility for social security, housing, and medical care. One interesting fact is that Singapore's government-run businesses created a close link between business and politics, where leading business entrepreneurs were also allowed to serve as government bureaucrats.

Hong Kong's economic model developed in striking contrast to Singapore's. Hong Kong, which by 1990 achieved the average per capita income of its colonial motherland, Great Britain, is often referred to as the best example of free-market capitalism (Vogel 1991). However, its success was aided by the government, whose civil servants greatly facilitated industrial planning and the development of local industries. These government officials used public funds to develop areas as industrial estates and then made the land available to manufacturing firms, at below-market prices. There were also policies that promoted exports and local textile firms. Yet, despite the government's shadow role, Hong Kong's entrepreneurs were at the forefront, stimulating businesses and industries.

Taiwan's growth policy can be characterized as a balanced one that promoted general SME expansion as a growth engine. Unlike in other developing economies, the government of Taiwan put great emphasis on family-oriented small businesses. Since there was a great division between the Kuomintang mainlanders and the locals, the Kuomintang government strove to maintain order through balanced growth. This is the political backdrop that allowed SMEs to flourish in Taiwan, unlike in Korea, where an unbalanced, *chaebol*-led growth took place.

Among the six economies, China's growth trajectory is the most different. It was only after Deng Xiaoping's open-door policies in 1978 that the country began to join the open market system. Although China still embraces a communist political regime, the competition-based market mechanism serves as the backbone of the economy's dynamic and fast growth in recent years. Another distinguishing feature of China's business and economy is that most of its large firms are state owned. The central government controls these large firms, in particular massive banks and oil and utility companies, through the State-Owned Assets Supervision and Administration Commission of the ruling State Council, which appoints chief executive officers and makes decisions on large investments (Cendrowski 2015).

Differentiated Growth and Innovation Strategy

As summarized in table 9.1 above, these different growth trajectories have evolved to create differentiated business systems and structures, ultimately allowing each economy to assume unique strategies for continuous innovation and growth. For instance, Hong Kong is now a part of mainland China, and its firms are enjoying the network advantage with a gateway to China's abundant pool of resources for both production and consumption. In addition, since mainland China has greater competitiveness in manufacturing, most of Hong Kong's businesses are concentrated on financing and trading. Therefore, while Hong Kong's infrastructure for manufacturing is thinning, the economy is transitioning to build up more competencies in services. On the other hand, Singapore, by targeting the neighboring countries of the Association of Southeast Asian Nations and the world in general, has a more network-oriented business ecosystem. Nowadays Singapore benefits from its role as a gateway into Asia, particularly into Southeast Asia.

Taiwan, Korea, and Japan have evolved to be capable of producing global-standard-quality products and components for sophisticated technologies, and as a result these economies now take up an important share of the GVC.[3] As explained by Hsieh in chapter 5, Taiwan's competent parts and components industrial bases have succeeded in developing Taiwan's SMEs. On the other hand, Korea's and Japan's conglomerates are closely coordinating their activities with the GVC. Korean and Japanese firms are distributing their manufacturing activities by establishing their foreign affiliates in the most efficient production sites and maintaining global market competitiveness. Therefore, although these two countries continue to maintain the strong role of conglomerates, there is an increasing number of competent SMEs that have grown to support such a massive scale of operations. Studies show that suppliers to the conglomerates have higher competitiveness and growth rates than nonlinked SMEs (SERI 2014).

As a result of their histories and growth trajectories, Hong Kong has become a financial hub and Singapore has become a center for global firms by building a global cluster (see Wong, chapter 4); Taiwan has been efficiently taking part in the GVC, whereas Korea and Japan tightly coordinate with the GVC. Chinese firms currently participate in the GVC, mainly in assembling and manufacturing, so these Chinese firms have much to learn and will need to embrace differentiation and innovation strategies once the government adopts a more market-based approach with free competition.

Despite these differences among the East Asian economies summarized so far, these economies can nonetheless share common strategic directions while maintaining their uniqueness. We suggest two strategic directions for the sustainable development of these economies. First, on a macro level, the unit of analysis should change from a national to a regional level. The proper model, then, is the cluster's ecosystem (e.g., Silicon Valley, Singapore, Hong

---

3   The six economies are all included in the world's top 25 exporting economies, and the GVC participation rate of all these economies exceeds 50 percent through either upstream or downstream linkages (UNCTAD 2013). Upstream linkages refer to the foreign value added that is used in a country's exports. Downstream linkages refer to the value added to other countries' exports (UNCTAD 2013).

Kong).[4] We will first show the analysis of Silicon Valley's competitiveness as a benchmarking case and suggest implications for the Asian economies, particularly Singapore and Hong Kong. Second, on a micro level, the firm-level analysis should change from a single firm to the GVC system. This perspective is important to derive useful implications for facilitating global collaboration among multinational firms and parts suppliers.

Macrolevel Strategy: From Nation to Regional Cluster

Increasingly, interfirm activities are blurring traditional boundaries like geopolitical borders and business types. This change calls for government strategies to shift their focus from the national level to the level of regional cluster building. Innovation arises from simultaneous interactions among firms—including large and small firms and start-ups—and regional clusters are the best method for enabling this interaction. Silicon Valley is a good example, and if examined in detail, Silicon Valley's competitiveness can be explained in terms of agility, benchmarking, convergence, and dedication (ABCD).[5]

Silicon Valley is one of the most dynamic places in the business world. There is a fast process of idea generation and operation, followed by entrepreneurship that prizes commercialization and business innovation. The region, which boasts the highest concentration of high-tech workers with the highest average salaries in the United States, has a high-tech workforce that is 57 percent foreign born, reflecting a high degree of diversified experiences and expertise (SVCIP 2017). The number of firms that are newly created or move in is offset by the number of firms that close or move out by a ratio of six to five. The region is clearly very dynamic and its market system functions efficiently.

---

4   Singapore and Hong Kong are two independent economies; however, due to their small size, their entire economies can in fact be regarded as business ecosystems, thereby being comparable to Silicon Valley.

5   The analysis of Silicon Valley's competitiveness using the ABCD model is abstracted and extended from Moon (2017). The ABCD model was developed in order to better explain the success factors of Korea and its firms, such as Samsung, POSCO, and Hyundai. This model comprehensively and systematically identified four critical factors and eight subfactors: agility (speed, precision), benchmarking (learning, best practice), convergence (mixing, synergy creation), and dedication (diligence, goal orientation). These factors were derived from the rigorous examination of earlier studies on national development and strategic management. The ABCD model has been further applied to various studies, including non-Korean firms such as Tata Group as well as first movers such as Apple. The model was also useful in providing solutions for national agendas such as Korea's policies on emergency and relief, medical industry, and aging society. For more details, see Moon (2016).

There is a continuous churning of companies and jobs where the regional dynamics are created by the region's vast facilitation of start-ups as well as by failures that lead to exchanges of knowledge among a wide range of people. The region has developed a relatively secure safety net, including a social and talent safety net, where firms and individuals are supported even after their failures (*The Economist* 2015; Joffe 2017). When people can find jobs even after failure, not only is a culture created where failure is acceptable and normal, but also a very efficient system of knowledge and skill transfer is generated, whether intentionally or not.

The third factor is convergence, or the synchronization of diverse fields and actors that allows for a full-scale business and living environment—the ecosystem. The ecosystem then divides into two layers: the industrial ecosystem and the living ecosystem. The industrial ecosystem is the coming together of industries such as computers, social media, biotechnology, energy, and business services, including financial and legal firms, which have been mentioned in the earlier chapters in this book (refer to chapters 5 and 6). Silicon Valley's infrastructure for supporting its regional dynamics is mature and easily accessible. The region possesses the basics for starting and running a company, from good research institutions like Stanford and UC Berkeley that will work side by side with entrepreneurs, to financing and accounting firms. Furthermore, the region is also connected to diverse business fields that are eager to adopt innovative technologies. The living ecosystem includes a quality environment for families, with good schools, markets, access to leisure and cultural facilities, and a pleasant climate. Although the region is suffering from growth pains that have made home ownership close to impossible for the average worker and commuting painful for many, it nonetheless still holds a huge attraction for tech workers and their families.

The final factor that sets Silicon Valley apart from other regions may be the most important but least tangible: its motivational spirit. Despite concerns related to the high cost of living, this region is growing and rapidly expanding by including multiple cities and local governments, including San Francisco and other Bay Area cities. There are approximately four to six million people that make up today's Silicon Valley. The region's extreme income disparity, increasingly noted by critics and civic leaders, may ironically be an important factor in its popularity, because the region also boasts the highest economic mobility in the United States. It is a place where it is relatively easy to improve the economic status of individuals, with the rate of moving from the bottom 20 percent to the top 20 percent income group as high as 12.5 percent, meaning that one out of eight people can change their economic status from poor to rich. This mobility raises the motivation to work harder and realize the new American dream (SVCIP 2015).

These four factors have been essential to Silicon Valley's evolution into the promised land for innovative firms. This region is not characterized by the dominance of SMEs or LEs, but by a good blend of the two, reflecting that size is not the key factor for innovation or growth. The proper orchestration and synchronization of firms, large or small, is what fosters dynamics and promotes a healthy business environment.

The Japanese government's cluster policy, discussed by Okubo in chapter 6, led to low productivity and innovativeness due to the lack of focus on network synergy. Similarly, the eighteen Korean innovation clusters created by the government since 2014, dispersed across seventeen regions, have low productivity and a lack of synergy among themselves. In contrast to the Silicon Valley model, the cluster policies of the Korean and Japanese governments have shown that designing clusters that are too narrowly focused and overly influenced by government is unlikely to yield success. In this regard, the Silicon Valley case provides meaningful implications for how resources can be spent for the efficient establishment of a regional cluster that may propel true innovation.

Silicon Valley can be used as a good benchmarking case for East Asia, which still lacks efficient and innovative regional clusters. Kim and Lee's comparative study in chapter 7 on Korea's Daedok Innopolis and Germany's Silicon Saxony shows that efficiency is greater when innovation is initiated by firms rather than by government research institutions, which tend to have a more constrained system and networks. This evidence shows that policy restrictions by the government should be minimal, while policy mechanisms should be directed at rewarding capable and competitive innovators. Rather than supporting young entrepreneurs simply for trying, policies should encourage true competitive innovation. This is in fact how Korea's *chaebol* were created. A common misconception is that the *chaebol* survived and grew through close government relationships, but the truth was in some respects the reverse: the *chaebol* demonstrated efficiency and good export performance, thus winning government support and enabling their growth (Moon 2016). The *chaebol* surviving today, out of the many in competition since the 1960s, are the ones that succeeded in meeting government targets and thereby reaped the incentive rewards. The business-government networks were not born out of personal ties or nepotism.

The Silicon Valley spirit of risk taking is praised by and resonates with many young entrepreneurs. But governments cannot blindly encourage innovation and risk taking without providing a proper safety net and social system. Also, successful entrepreneurs take risks, but those decisions are based on careful assessment and analysis, not simply on recklessness or a thirst for challenge. Governments need to encourage and reward agile mindsets while learning to create synergy among old and new resources and capabilities.

In fact, the innovation strategy requires an accurate interpretation of goal setting and diligence, as successfully implemented by Deng Xiaoping beginning in 1978 (see chapter 2 and Moon 2016). Also, as examined in chapters 2 and 4, innovation that enhances competitiveness in the market should be perceived as a commercial innovation, not a scientific discovery or just a technological breakthrough (also see Moon 2017). Having a correct perception regarding innovation and competitiveness is the basis of strategic thinking, which leads to increased value creation. A proper understanding of the business environment and a healthy ecosystem also lead to a new perspective on the relationship between LEs and SMEs, as will be discussed in the following section.

Microlevel: From Single Firm to Global Value Chain

If a well-functioning ecosystem is the new macro approach to a nation's growth, the GVC is the new microlevel approach to how governments and businesses should develop strategy. Today's business segments are more intertwined than ever. Digitalization and the integration of information technologies into nearly the entire spectrum of industry characteristics are causing volatile market conditions, requiring more cooperation and partnership as technology changes quickly and frequently. When firms can no longer efficiently and profitably handle their entire business operations alone, the GVC serves as the most viable and logical strategy for creating and sustaining competitiveness. Firms can execute two types of GVC strategy: insourcing and outsourcing.

Samsung Electronics, which was built on its strong manufacturing capabilities, is a good example of an insourcing strategy. Beginning in 2009, Samsung gradually began shifting its production facilities to Vietnam as its global manufacturing hub as part of its GVC strategy. Starting with its mobile phone division, the company spent a total of US$6.7 billion to set up production in Bac Ninh (mobile phones), Thai Nguyen (mobile phones and chips), and Ho Chi Minh (home appliances). The sudden growth in Samsung's mobile division demanded a huge production volume and a larger labor force. Vietnam, with a labor cost one-sixth of that of South Korea's Gumi plant, and a vast labor pool, offered an attractive solution to their production problem (Vu and Nguyen 2014).

Another approach to the GVC is Apple's strategy. Unlike Samsung, Apple outsources its manufacturing and assembling operations to other firms, like Foxconn. In fact, Apple outsources most of its manufacturing jobs to China and other countries. The strategy is not simply based on cost, but also aimed toward greater agility.[6] Other critical parts of Apple products—LCD (liquid-crystal display) panels, chipsets, batteries, DRAM (dynamic random-access memory), and flash memory—are supplied by Korean and Taiwanese firms such as LG, Samsung, SK Hynix, and TSMC. Although Samsung and Apple are clearly rivals in the (end-product) smartphone market, the two are in fact partners in other sections of the GVC.

In this respect, the GVC approach is important, as it allows us to capture the cooperative aspects beyond the perspective of simple competition among firms. This is particularly relevant to understanding the relationships among SMEs and LEs where they simultaneously engage in mutual dependence in creating the final product. This is because, as noted by Hsieh in chapter 5, the lead firms, usually LEs, orchestrate innovation activities and rent capturing. This means that the relationship among firms extends beyond the rivalry of individual firms. Also, this brings up the importance of the perspective of the ecosystem. While Samsung's business ecosystem is in competition with Apple's, there is also room for cooperation. Through the GVC, firms can truly benefit from integrating several different sources of capabilities and resources. For example, the technology prowess of parts makers (SMEs) can contribute to technological change, thereby decentralizing the production process. Whether the GVC is established through outsourcing or insourcing, the engaged parties can strengthen their own competencies while efficiently and strategically utilizing other available competencies through networking. In the GVC, synergy creation is maximized for value creation to all participating stakeholders.

Engagement with the GVC and the ecosystem suggests important lessons and strategic directions for the six Asian economies. Hong Kong and Singapore are already good forerunners since they have managed to network with other firms and nations through effective clustering. Taiwan has grown through strong and competitive SMEs that produce competent technology-related components; these firms need large multinational corporations that can sell the end products to consumers, so Taiwanese firms can participate in the GVC as strong suppliers and affiliates. South Korean firms such as Samsung and Hyundai represent the opposite case: they coordinate their individual value chain activities across several locations. As GVC coordinators, these firms have to actively and strategically find the most efficient location

---

6   The agility and speed aspects of Apple's strategy are illustrated by a well-known anecdote. Only a few weeks before the launch of the first iPhone, Steve Jobs grew dissatisfied with the plastic screen and insisted on glass. The material would be U.S. supplied, but Apple needed a factory and labor to actually cut all the glass. Foxconn built the factory even before a contract was signed, and when the glass arrived there at midnight, they woke up the dormitory-housed workers and immediately began production.

for their activities in order to remain competitive. Flexible coordination through outsourcing or insourcing becomes a key strategy for these firms.

Japanese firms are similar to the Korean case; firms such as Toyota are in the position of coordinating and controlling activities within the GVC. However, Japanese firms tend to have tighter controls and coordination, which must be relaxed to optimize their activities. Perhaps through forming more outside partnerships with other firms and global regions, Japanese multinational firms may find a route to better strategies that allow them to remain competitive. Lastly, China stands out as the country with most opportunity for change. As China is less developed than other major players in Asia, Chinese firms mainly participate in the GVC by assembling final products or manufacturing cheap goods. Thus, Chinese firms need to move up the GVC to more value-added activities. The different strategies noted here for these six economies reiterate our argument that it is not firm size but clusters and GVC that are increasingly critical for future sustainability.

Ultimately, the truths about entrepreneurship and innovation reveal four important lessons to success, which can be encapsulated in terms of the ABCD model. The first lesson pertains to agility. The trend of valuing start-ups and SMEs must be sufficiently backed up by speedy processes and transparent rules for easy business transactions. Governments should first focus on building infrastructure and social safety nets to allow entrepreneurs to easily turn their business ideas into commercial products. Singapore is a good example where new companies can be set up in hours and intellectual property is well respected (Anthony 2015).

The second is to practice benchmarking, for which policymakers must correctly understand the limits and advantages of smaller firms. Germany's *Mittelstand* firms, or the midsized manufacturers, have been used as popular benchmarking cases by many; however, even these firms now adopt best practices from the global community. *The Economist* (2014) reported that these firms are linking more with foreign labor and systems in order to stay competitive. This is another important lesson for governments that try to protect SMEs and start-ups from global competition. There needs to be a proper degree of global exposure for sustainability, if smaller firms and start-ups want to remain competitive. This is because global exposure allows firms to learn from other market leaders as well as consumers and related industries.

The third lesson is convergence. Evidence shows that innovation-led "smart" growth mainly occurs under conditions where medium-to-large firms spin off SMEs. These firms are often created from LEs or even from universities, or from a network including both. This finding suggests that the key element of competitiveness stems from an ecosystem that links different elements and sources of knowledge and competitiveness (Mazzucato 2015). This is highly relevant to how efficient integration of different elements through the ecosystem or the GVC may offer more than simply focusing on the creation of a single firm.

Lastly, fostering dedication, equipped with a clear and value-creating goal, coupled with hard work, is the most foundational element behind a successful innovation strategy. This is true for all firms regardless of size and age. Many studies have shown that giving too many incentives to SMEs has discouraged these firms from growing and scaling up. This is evident across various development stages. An OECD report on Japanese SMEs emphasized that there is little evidence that the Japanese government's financial support improved the performance, growth, and employment of SMEs (OECD 2015). In fact, this tendency has been humorously dubbed Peter Pan syndrome, whereby firms or entrepreneurs become complacent and stop pursuing growth.

Conclusion

Innovation and entrepreneurship have never been hotter buzzwords than they are today, and yet these two concepts still lack adequate definitions and well-considered approaches to fostering their growth. Governments and the media have blindly used these concepts to criticize the growth of LEs, without demonstrating solid evidence for their economic role. As the studies on SMEs and LEs reveal, there is little relationship between firm size and growth of the national economy. A close examination of the literature on SMEs reveals that increasing the number of SMEs has little relevance to raising the employment rate as well.

Our analysis of six Asian economies has provided a similar answer to how governments and businesses should approach SMEs and LEs. These economies all joined the market system at a relatively late stage; however, they succeeded in producing differentiated yet effective results. Although this chapter has not dealt with the Indian case, the Indian government could also take lessons from these regional-level cluster strategies and firm-level GVC strategies to enhance the Indian manufacturing sector (see chapter 3). All the chapters in this book discuss the role of government policies and firm strategies that can be cross-benchmarked.

SMEs and LEs generate different advantages for the economy, which means there are greater opportunities if they collaborate. Therefore, implementing one-sided policy tracks in favor of SMEs should be reexamined. The answer to the problem of conflicting perspectives on firm size is that size itself is not the operative factor: it is the way that firms interact in effective clusters and how they function effectively in GVCs that is critical. As exemplified in the Silicon Valley case, along with Samsung and Apple's approaches to the coordination of activities, clusters and GVCs are viable solutions to many current and pending issues like employment, the fourth industrial revolution, innovation, entrepreneurship, and firm size.

This chapter showed how the six Asian economies have evolved over time despite similar, yet different, political economies and histories. The lesson these differences offer for future policymaking is that, despite the different strategies and approaches that influenced their business structures (i.e., firm size, governance, structure), the six economies have all succeeded in maintaining growth and competitiveness. There is no one perfect answer to innovation strategy, which means a rigorous, comprehensive, and systematic analysis over the entire time frame is necessary for understanding the business economics of firms.

Although each chapter of this book deals with different topics, the key messages are about the role of clusters and GVCs. In fact, these two concepts have been discussed in all the chapters, although they are expressed in different words, such as *platform, network, collaboration,* or *interaction.* Chapter 2 discussed how disruptive innovation can be initiated through platforms that link different economic agents in China. In fact, the GVC serves as the platform for diverse economic and noneconomic agents, thereby creating clusters. Chapter 3 showed, by comparing success stories and failures from India's software and hardware industry, that the government alone is not effective at creating a successful industry or cluster of firms. Chapter 4 introduced the government-linked clusters of Singapore and demonstrated the importance of the complementary roles of research, government, and businesses. Chapters 5 and 8 explored the role of the network economy in the context of SMEs, highlighting the increasing effect of collaborative learning in Taiwan (chapter 5) and the fintech industry (chapter 8). Chapter 6 also highlighted the importance of networking and indirect government support for the Japanese clusters, while chapter 7 discussed the role of loose, unconstrained interactions among firms, research institutions, and government from the perspective of social capital theory by comparing Korea and Germany's clusters. Finally, chapter 9 identified the importance of both macro and micro approaches to innovation by examining the role of clusters and GVCs in the development history of six Asian economies.

These Asian economies represent unique growth trajectories; they can learn from one another and take on board the way government policies for clusters and business strategies for GVCs are becoming the central issues for sustainability and competitiveness. The studies in this book, which assessed individual economies through a comprehensive analysis integrating political economy and strategy, can be both broadened and deepened in further research.

References

Acs, Zoltan J., and David B. Audretsch. 1988. "Innovation in Large and Small Firms: An Empirical Analysis." *The American Economic Review* 78, no. 4: 678–90.

Anthony, Scott D. 2015. "How Singapore Became an Entrepreneurial Hub." *Harvard Business Review*, February 25. https://hbr.org/2015/02/how-singapore-became-an-entrepreneurial-hub.

Bebenroth, Ralf. 2015. *International Business Mergers and Acquisitions in Japan*. New York: Springer.

Birch, David L. 1979. *The Job Generation Process*. Cambridge, MA: MIT Centre for Policy Alternatives.

Brown, Shona L., and Kathleen M. Eisenhardt. 1995. "Product Development: Past Research, Present Findings, and Future Directions." *Academy of Management Review* 20, no. 2: 343–78.

Cendrowski, Scott. 2015. "China's Global 500 Companies Are Bigger Than Ever—and Mostly State-Owned." *Fortune*, July 22. http://fortune.com/2015/07/22/china-global-500-government-owned/.

Chen, Jia. 2006. "Development of Chinese Small and Medium-Sized Enterprises." *Journal of Small Business and Enterprise Development* 13, no. 2: 140–47.

Cho, Dong-Sung, and Hwy-Chang Moon. 2013. *International Review of National Competitiveness: A Detailed Analysis of Sources and Rankings*. Cheltenham, UK: Edward Elgar.

Coad, Alex, Sven-Olov Daunfeldt, Werner Hölzl, Dan Johansson, and Paul Nightingale. 2014. "High-Growth Firms: Introduction to the Special Section." *Industrial and Corporate Change* 23, no. 1: 91–112.

Cohen, Wesley M., and Steven Klepper. 1996. "Firm Size and the Nature of Innovation within Industries: The Case of Process and Product R&D." *Review of Economics and Statistics* 78, no. 2: 232–43.

Cooper, Robert G. 2000. "Product Innovation and Technology Strategy." *Research-Technology Management* 43, no. 1: 38–41.

Damanpour, Fariborz. 1992. "Organizational Size and Innovation." *Organization Studies* 13, no. 3: 375–402.

Galbraith, John Kenneth. 1957. "Market Structure and Stabilization Policy." *Review of Economics and Statistics* 39, no. 2: 124–33.

Hölzl, Werner, and Klaus Friesenbichler. 2010. "High-Growth Firms, Innovation and the Distance to the Frontier." *Economics Bulletin* 30, no. 2: 1016–24.

Hudson Smith, Mel, Andy Smart, and Mike Bourne. 2001. "Theory and Practice in SME Performance Measurement Systems." *International*

Journal of Operations & Production Management 21, no. 8: 1096–115.

Joffe, Benjamin. 2017. "The Untold Secret of Silicon Valley: The Talent Safety Net." Medium.com, September 10. https://medium.com/sosv -accelerator-vc/the-untold-secret-of-silicon-valley-the-talent-safety -net-a6ab29e16b47.

Jung, Suk-yee. 2017. "Small Business Promotion: More than 16 Trillion Won to Be Spent on Supporting SMEs in Korea This Year." *Business Korea*, May 23. Accessed October 5, 2017. http://www.businesskorea .co.kr/english/news/smestartups/18151-small-business-promotion-more -16-trillion-won-be-spent-supporting-smes-korea.

Kamien, Morton I., and Nancy L. Schwartz. 1975. "Market Structure and Innovation: A Survey." *Journal of Economic Literature* 13, no. 1: 1–37.

Lin, Carol Yeh-Yun, and Mavis Yi-Ching Chen. 2007. "Does Innovation Lead to Performance? An Empirical Study of SMEs in Taiwan." *Management Research News* 30, no. 2: 115–32.

Lu, Jane W., and Paul W. Beamish. 2001. "The Internationalization and Performance of SMEs." *Strategic Management Journal* 22, nos. 6–7: 565–86.

Mazzucato, Mariana. 2015. *The Entrepreneurial State: Debunking Public vs. Private Sector Myths*. Hachette, UK: Anthem Press.

Moon, Hwy-Chang. 2016. *The Strategy for Korea's Economic Success*. New York: Oxford University Press.

———. 2017. "The Strategy for Korea's Economic Success: Innovative Growth and Lessons from Silicon Valley." [In Korean.] *Review of International and Area Studies* 26, no. 3: 1–33.

Motwani, Jaideep, Thomas Dandridge, James Jiang, and Klas Soderquist. 1999. "Managing Innovation in French Small and Medium-Sized Enterprises." *Journal of Small Business Management* 37, no. 2: 106.

Nicolaou, Nicos, and Scott Shane. 2009. "Born Entrepreneurs? The Genetic Foundations of Entrepreneurship." *Journal of Business Venturing* 23, no. 1: 1–22.

O'Regan, Nicholas, Abby Ghobadian, and Martin Sims. 2006. "Fast Tracking Innovation in Manufacturing SMEs." *Technovation* 26, no. 2: 251–61.

Organisation for Economic Co-operation and Development (OECD). 2015. *OECD Economic Surveys: Japan*. Paris: OECD Publishing.

Porter, Michael E. 1996. "What Is Strategy?" *Harvard Business Review* 74, no. 6: 61–78.

Rothwell, Roy. 1989. "Small Firms, Innovation and Industrial Change." *Small Business Economics* 1, no. 1: 51–64.

Rothwell, Roy, and Mark Dodgson. 1991. "External Linkages and Innovation in Small and Medium-Sized Enterprises." *R&D Management* 21, no. 2: 125–38.

Rothwell, Roy, and Walter Zegveld. 1982. *Innovation and the Small and Medium Sized Firm.* London: Francis Pinter.

Samsung Electronic Research Institute (SERI). 2014. *The Global Competitiveness of Korean Large Firms and the Strategy of Job Creation.* [In Korean.] Consulting report. Seoul: SERI.

Schumacher, E. F. 1973. *Small Is Beautiful: A Study of Economics as if People Mattered.* New York: Harper & Row.

Schumpeter, Joseph A. 1942. "Capitalism, Socialism, and Democracy." University of Illinois at Urbana-Champaign's Academy for Entrepreneurial Leadership Historical Research Reference in Entrepreneurship. https://ssrn.com/abstract=1496200.

Singh, Rajesh Kumar, Suresh K. Garg, and S. G. Deshmukh. 2008. "Strategy Development by SMEs for Competitiveness: A Review." *Benchmarking: An International Journal* 15, no. 5: 525–47.

Solon, Olivia. 2017. "Has the Tech Bubble Peaked? Signs That the Startup Boom May Be Fizzling." *The Guardian*, March 17. https://www.theguardian.com/business/2017/mar/17/startup-boom-fizzle-san-francisco-housing-investment.

Spithoven, André, Wim Vanhaverbeke, and Nadine Roijakkers. 2013. "Open Innovation Practices in SMEs and Large Enterprises." *Small Business Economics* 41, no. 3: 537–62.

Stock, Gregory N., Noel Greis, and William A. Fischer. 2002. "Firm Size and Dynamic Technological Innovation." *Technovation* 22, no. 9: 537–49.

SVCIP. 2015. "Silicon Valley Competitiveness and Innovation Project—2015." Silicon Valley Leadership Group and Silicon Valley Community Foundation. Accessed July 28, 2017. https://svcip.com/files/SVCIP_2015.pdf.

———. 2017. "Silicon Valley Competitiveness and Innovation Project—2017." Silicon Valley Leadership Group and Silicon Valley Community Foundation. Accessed October 8, 2017. https://svcip.com/files/SVCIP_2017.pdf.

Terziovski, Milé. 2010. "Innovation Practice and Its Performance Implications in Small and Medium Enterprises (SMEs) in the Manufacturing Sector: A Resource-Based View." *Strategic Management Journal* 31, no. 8: 892–902.

The Economist. 2014. "German Lessons." July 12. Accessed September 29, 2017. https://www.economist.com/news/business/21606834-many

-countries-want-mittelstand-germanys-it-not-so-easy-copy-german
-lessons.

———. 2015. "Silicon Valley: To Fly, to Fall, to Fly Again." July 25.
http://www.economist.com/news/briefing/21659722-tech-boom-may
-get-bumpy-it-will-not-end-repeat-dotcom-crash-fly.

———. 2016. "The Rise of the Superstars." September 17. Accessed
September 29, 2017. https://www.economist.com/news/special-report
/21707048-small-group-giant-companiessome-old-some-neware-once
-again-dominating-global.

United Nations Conference on Trade and Development (UNCTAD).
2013. *World Investment Report 2013*. New York and Geneva:
UNCTAD.

U.S. Congress. 1991. *Competing Economies: America, Europe, and
the Pacific Rim* (OTA-ITE-498). Washington, DC: U.S. Government
Printing Office.

Vogel, Ezra F. 1991. *The Four Little Dragons: The Spread of
Industrialization in East Asia*. Edwin O. Reischauer Lectures vol. 3.
Cambridge, MA: Harvard University Press.

Vu, Trong Kahn, and Nguyen Anh Thu. 2014. "Samsung Considers
$1Billion Investment in Vietnam." *Wall Street Journal*, June 9. https://
www.wsj.com/articles/samsung-considers-1-billion-investment-in-viet
nam-1402312208.

Wagner, Ernesto, and Eric N. Hansen. 2005. "Innovation in Large Versus
Small Companies: Insights from the US Wood Products Industry."
Management Decision 43, no. 6: 837–50.

Westney, D. Eleanor. 2009. "The Multinational Firm as an Evolutionary
System." In *Images of the Multinational Firm*, edited by Simon
Collinson and Glenn Morgan, 117–44. New York: Wiley.

Winter, Sidney G. 1984. "Schumpeterian Competition in Alternative
Technological Regimes." *Journal of Economic Behavior &
Organization* 5, nos. 3–4: 287–320.

Xu, Zongling, Jiali Lin, and Danming Lin. 2008. "Networking and
Innovation in SMEs: Evidence from Guangdong Province, China."
Journal of Small Business and Enterprise Development 15, no. 4:
788–801.

Zimmerer, Thomas W., and Norman M. Scarborough. 2002. *Essentials
of Entrepreneurship and Small Business Management*. New Jersey:
Prentice Hall.

Index

The authorized representative in the EU for product safety and compliance is:
Mare Nostrum Group
B.V Doelen 72
4831 GR Breda
The Netherlands

www.ingramcontent.com/pod-product-compliance
Lightning Source LLC
Chambersburg PA
CBHW030646270326
41929CB00007B/228